THE FUTURE ARRIVED YESTERDAY

THE RISE OF THE PROTEAN CORPORATION AND WHAT IT MEANS FOR YOU

THE FUTURE ARRIVED YESTERDAY

MICHAEL S. MALONE

CROWN
BUSINESS
NEW YORK

Published in the United States by Crown Business, an imprint of the
Crown Publishing Group, a division of Random House, Inc., New York.
www.crownpublishing.com

CROWN BUSINESS is a trademark and CROWN and the Rising Sun colophon
are registered trademarks of Random House, Inc.

Library of Congress Cataloging-in-Publication Data

Malone, Michael S. (Michael Shawn), 1954–
  The future arrived yesterday / Michael Malone.—1st ed.
      p. cm.
  1. Technological innovations—Management.   2. Organizational change.
I. Title.

  HD45.M313 2009
  658.4—dc22

                                                          2008050638

ISBN 978-0-307-40690-3

Printed in the United States of America

Design by Maria Elias

1   3   5   7   9   10   8   6   4   2

First Edition

CONTENTS

ACKNOWLEDGMENTS

Having, at this point in my career, written a number of books on a wide range of subjects and in a number of different styles, I've come to appreciate that every book is the product of the collaboration of many people, both recognized and anonymous—from the author to the typesetter to the line editor to the clerk at the local bookstore. Some of these participants are always celebrated, others never. But everyone contributes to the enterprise in some vital way—indeed, that is the subtext of this very book.

So I would like to use these acknowledgments to thank every one of the people involved in the creation, production, and distribution of this book. That said, there are certain individuals who have played such a key role in making this book possible—indeed, it would not exist without them—that I'd like to identify them by name: my agent, Jim Levine, who took an idea that had been buzzing in my brain for a decade and showed that its time had finally come; my editor, John Mahaney, who brought the old-fashioned hands-on editing to this book that I had assumed was sadly long gone; fellow ex-HPer, Chuck House, who convinced me to speak about the Protean Corporation at his Stanford University Media X conference and thus forced me to organize my thinking on the subject; and my assistant, Leslie Johnson, who spent the long hours in Web searches for which I didn't have the time or the patience.

I would also like to thank those individuals who, during the course of my career, made me think about entrepreneurship, about how different personalities see the nature of work, and about how organizations really operate: Al Bruno, Bill Davidow, Tom Peters, and Tom Hayes. With each of them I've been, at various times, a student, partner, and editor . . . and have learned from them every step of the way.

Finally, as always, I'd like to thank my family for their superhuman patience in living with a professional writer, who only meets one deadline to work under the shadow of the next.

O Heaven, were man
But constant, he were perfect: that one error
Fills him with faults; makes him run through all sins
Inconstancy falls off, ere it begins.

—Proteus, in Shakespeare's *The Two Gentlemen of Verona*

INTRODUCTION

Catching the Future, Again

In 1992, not even twenty years ago, venture capitalist Bill Davidow and I predicted the rise of a new organizational form, what we called—in a book of the same name—the *virtual corporation*. It would be an adaptive organization, driven by technology, global in reach. It would be the form required of more and more organizations—if they are to compete effectively, if they are to survive.

When first proposed, our ideas seemed far out, their implementation something for a future generation. Yet today "virtual corporation" is a commonplace term, and most of us work in one. The revolutionary notions of 1992—telecommuting, global work teams, technology-based marketing and sales, and inverted organization charts—are now standard features of daily working life in much of the world.

The Virtual Corporation was written in anticipation of, but before the arrival of, the Internet Age. Davidow and I could already see that modern corporations faced a serious challenge, even a threat, if they did not recognize the profound *social* and *cultural* implications of the emerging new technologies on the way they organized themselves, related to their customers, communicated internally and externally, and even designed their products. We also argued that the organizations that intelligently embraced this change would end up the winners of the new economic era, and time has proven us correct.

A lot has happened in the last two decades. We now live in the age of Web 2.0, global wireless, intelligent cell phones, and the pending arrival of a billion new consumers. And the revolution we predicted in corporate organization is now largely complete, at least in the developed world.

But technology, and society around it, move on and at an ever faster pace. To anyone looking closely, it is obvious that the advances of the intervening years now pose a threat, and an opportunity, to modern organizations—not just corporations, but government institutions and non-profits—that will be even greater than that which created the virtual corporation. As I will show in this book, the situation is now even more perilous than most of us realize:

Every trend in the corporate world—technological, managerial, financial, and cultural—is pushing companies toward ever-greater virtualization, the dismantling of every traditional organizational structure, and their replacement with networks of free agents. At the same time, mounting evidence is warning us that this model *doesn't work*.

Perhaps it's because change has been occurring so quickly that it's been hard to do anything but react. Or perhaps we've been waiting for a new generation of entrepreneurs and thinkers, men and women who grew up in the Internet Age, to come up with new solutions. Or perhaps it's just been a failure of imagination.

But one thing is certain: while the institutions have, philosophically at least, stood still, the world around them, and the people within them, have been transformed in some very important ways. And the fit between company and people, the employer and the employed, management and labor—never very good even in the best of times—is becoming less secure with each year. Whenever this has occurred, it has led to friction, strife, even violence.

We need bold, new ideas. We need new ways of thinking about organizations that reflect the changing reality of the people who are part of them. And we need those ideas *now*.

Thus, the Protean Corporation.

AS WE WILL SEE in the pages that follow, the best companies of the future will use the latest information processing, communications, and social networking technologies to become *shape-shifters*, constantly restructuring themselves to adapt to changing circumstances and new opportunities. They will become *protean*.

Just as the notion of a "virtual" corporation seemed radical right up to the very moment it became everyday, the notion of a "protean" corporation is both hard to imagine . . . and just around the corner.

A number of these early stage "protean corporations" and organizations already exist:

<> **Google** has become one of the most successful new companies in the world by having not one corporate culture, but many under one roof, each designed for the maximum comfort and productivity of its people. This in turn has required a radically new kind of management: the boss as quick-change artist.

<> **Wikipedia,** a loose confederation of thousands of contributors that has all but replaced encyclopedias, is one of the most venerable of publishing industries.

<> **Pajamas Media** and the **Huffington Post,** aggregations of independent bloggers, is establishing a powerful model of the online newspaper of the future.

<> **Approtech,** an "appropriate technology" company that has transformed the economies of Kenya and Tanzania with foot-powered water pumps, operates successfully in the gray area between being a for-profit and non-profit company.

<> Blogosphere legend Evan Williams, founder of **Blogger.com,** bought back his podcast company Odeo from its investors, and transformed it into a successful new company incubator. Its first spin-off, **Twitter,** is one of the hottest new companies on the Web.

<> Giant corporations, from **Hewlett-Packard** to **Intel** to **IBM,** are becoming such loose confederations of empowered employees that as many as one-third of their professionals have never met their own bosses.

<> The **U.S. Army,** after its experiences in Iraq and Afghanistan, is hurriedly restructuring itself to be able to change its shape

to meet any threat in the world with an appropriate combat force that adapts on the ground to an ever-shifting battlefield reality.

And there are hundreds more, most of them in the emerging world of so-called Web 2.0. This shift to protean organizations will have a profound effect not only on the corporate world, but on society itself. The transformation has already begun in the United States where, little noticed by the media, the very personalities that work best in protean organizations are now being honored, rewarded, and cultivated.

For example, almost every MBA program in the United States (and most of the rest of the world) now offers a program in entrepreneurship—something that was unheard of in their curricula just a decade ago—meaning that this generation of B-school grads is as likely to be trained as independent operators as corporate infighters. What Fortune 500 business executive has enjoyed more favorable media coverage than any other in recent years? Undoubtedly it is Steve Jobs of Apple, who has led his company through three radical transformations (computers, consumer electronics, telecom) in a single decade. And the most celebrated new CEOs of Gen-Y? The founders of social networks, such as twenty-three-year-old Mark Zuckerberg of Facebook, who have built companies composed of small core teams serving tens of millions of users/co-creators.

Protean organizations, by their very mutability, will also soon begin to erase the traditionally rigid lines between for-profit and non-profit organizations, as well as between start-up companies and mature enterprises. These boundary lines are so entrenched that distinct cultures have arisen on opposite sides of these walls, and as those walls crumble, there are likely to be dislocation and frustration as both sides struggle to adapt, when non-profits find they have to become more competitive (and their financials more carefully scrutinized than ever before) and established companies find themselves (sometimes to their horror) with wild-eyed mavericks and renegades in their ranks.

———

THE MODERN CORPORATION has undergone radical changes in the last two decades. But you haven't seen anything yet.

Powerful forces—major economic cycles, generational shifts, technology revolution, and a historic cultural transformation—are converging. Before they are done they will rewrite the definition of what it means to be a company. These "Protean Corporations"—not just companies, but non-profits and government agencies—will behave like perpetual entrepreneurial start-ups, continuously changing their form, direction, even their identity. They will be true corporate "shape-shifters."

Protean Corporations will be so attuned to the times, so competitive, and so fast-moving that they will sweep all before them. By the middle of next decade, this new corporate form will dominate the marketplace.

And that's just the beginning: By the time this revolution is complete, America itself will be profoundly changed. It will finally become what it has been moving toward for two centuries: *the world's first truly entrepreneurial society*. That is to say, the first nation (as opposed to a region or city-state) where the dominant ethos is innovative, risk-taking, amnesiac, opportunistic, and thoroughly independent and individualistic.

Why "protean" corporations? Because the forces at play demand it, including:

TECHNOLOGY

Current semiconductor research and Moore's Law (the hugely influential prediction, first made in 1964 and supported by evidence ever since, that the complexity and power of the computer chip will double every eighteen to twenty-four months) both suggest that by 2010 we will see the arrival of low-cost terahertz—1 *trillion* calculations per second—microprocessors. By the same token, memory technology will place as much as 100 terabytes of storage on a single handheld computer disk. Meanwhile, the capacity to most private homes in the United States (and most of Europe) of fiber optic cable, i.e., the third generation of the Internet, will approach one gigabit per second.

Together, this represents a technological leap of almost unimaginable proportions, the equivalent of putting all of the world's computing power in 1990 into a single Apple iPhone. Equivalent technological leaps will occur in wireless, nanotechnology, at the interface between silicon and biotech, micromachines, displays, software, and interfaces. Large computer networks will exhibit extraordinary powers of decision making, modeling and simulation, speech recognition, and even cognition.

As the decade progresses, the experience of using a digital device will become transparent, ubiquitous, and increasingly indistinguishable from real life. Because it will be multimedia, rich in content, and supported by vast data resources, in some applications (such as product design) digital interaction may, for the first time, be *better* than face-to-face contact, at least in the sense that what is lost in physical immediacy will be more than offset by the flood of supporting data. This will be the case particularly when the distances are long, the travel costs are high, and the time zones many. Moreover, thanks to powerful global wireless networks, stunning new handheld devices, and universal GPS, these experiences will be accessible from almost anywhere on the planet.

Inevitably, this will atomize the already edgeless modern corporation, as well as other sophisticated institutions. Dealing with that, holding together a diverse population of employees scattered around the globe, will require powerful new management tools that are already in development—virtual workstations, broadband intranets, online corporate gatherings, new forms of team-building.

ORGANIZATIONAL

With implementation, these organizational tools will begin to change the way companies structure themselves. The current trend toward decentralization, de-massification, and the destruction of hierarchies will not only continue, but accelerate. So will telecommuting, global workteams, and real-time enterprise networking.

Even more important, the rate at which companies *reorganize* themselves will also accelerate. Instead of shifting from one form to another (i.e., product divisions to market sector groups to integrated operations)

over the course of generations, companies will increasingly restructure for greater competitiveness in just months, even weeks. Thus, these new companies will become corporate shape-shifters, forever transforming themselves to meet a rapidly changing world.

This fluidity of form, this impermanence of structure, will have the ironic effect of making the best of these companies *more* permanent and enduring. That's because protean companies will be less likely to succumb to structural weaknesses than traditional companies. They will be more likely to focus on capabilities over products.

This new kind of organization will reinforce the primacy of strong corporate mythologies, philosophies, and traditions—the key component of companies "built to last"—to be the glue that holds their disparate parts together.

However, the durability of these organizations will not be matched by their predictability. The company that employs you for the next twenty years may radically change a dozen times, and you will have to find your place in each of those reincarnations.

HISTORICAL

The history of American business is the story of long periods, a decade or more, spent consolidating the current and received business model, punctuated with the sudden appearance of a new, replacement model. These rapid transformations typically occur in the aftermath of wars or economic downturns, at the arrival of a new generation, or after profound technological change. The middle years of the next decade are likely to feature the rare conjunction of all three.

From the Industrial Revolution forward, the trend in business organization has been toward increasing independence of employees, ever greater flexibility of operations, and more pervasive implementation of technology. The "virtual" corporation was an outgrowth of the rise of the Internet, the laptop computer, the cellular phone, and teleconferencing, as well as the mass customization made possible by the IT revolution. It also lent itself neatly to the antitraditional attitudes of Generation X.

·Those changes have been assimilated. Now a host of new forces presents itself. First are the major technological advances in chips, memory, and bandwidth, whose effects will be amplified by powerful new software tools in real-time corporate information, multimedia work-sharing, and employee/customer/supplier relationship management. There are also the as yet unknown implications of 9/11 and the rise of international terrorism, including the greater need for the decentralization of facilities and a greater dependence on secure networks and the distribution of records, decision making, and staff.

Just as important is the ongoing shift away from distinct products and models to aggregations of capabilities, "smart" products and services, and true mass customization. The fact that these products and services will be increasingly Web-enabled will only speed this development.

GENERATIONAL

Finally, there is the rise of a new generation, an event that is often the catalyst for radical change. The emerging "Gen-Ys" are distinctly different from the generations that came before. Not only is it the first generation to be born in the computer age (today's grad students were born the year of the Macintosh introduction), it also combines deep tech literacy with a skeptical pragmatism about its uses. This is the "fix-it" generation, the roboteers, who want most of all to make current technology work right. It is also extremely entrepreneurial.

This cohort, many with parents who have always worked at home, has little interest in *ever* taking an office job, or working for a business that doesn't change, They will expect their jobs to change as rapidly as the rest of their lives.

As the following pages will show, the process of combining all of these will be volatile, and the resulting explosion will force change upon all of our cultural institutions, starting with the world of business.

So why haven't you heard about this? Because the emergence of each of these forces has happened in isolation. In the last few years there have been a number of stories about the next generation of workers, the broadband

Internet, real-time operations, intellectual capital, and global virtual work teams. But no thinker or book has ever put them together to see their combined impact, a serious omission, because I believe the overall impact of the Protean Corporation will be greater than the sum of its parts.

The *Wall Street Journal* has estimated that there are more than 40 million self-employed workers in America, up 30 percent from 1998. Add that to the existing small-business owners and start-up entrepreneurs in America, plus the Gen-Xers anxiously awaiting the chance to bail out of their last-resort corporate jobs, plus the millions of Gen-Ys who, thanks to their freelancing parents, have little experience or comprehension of corporate or bureaucratic life, and by 2013, perhaps two-thirds of all adult Americans will be classified as entrepreneurial.

That number suggests that this transformation is inevitable. What that means is that our economy is likely to be even more innovative than it is today. Twentieth-century America may have been the most inventive country ever, but we may look back at it as a mere prelude to the twenty-first. Innovation is likely to spread across society, not just as products and inventions, but as new ways of living, new types of organizations, and new cultural breakthroughs.

Yet entrepreneurial America will also be much more volatile and competitive. In the continuous fervor to create new institutions, it will become increasingly difficult to sustain old ones. New political parties, new social groupings, thousands of new manias and movements, and millions of new companies will pop up over the next few decades. While the rest of the world will still be building global Goliath enterprises, America will be creating, to user blogger Glenn Reynolds's phrase, "an army of Davids" to sweep around and over them. And if today's large U.S. corporations don't figure out how to somehow combine permanence with perpetual change, they will be swept away as well: *right now, those corporations lack the model to do this.*

This higher level of anarchy will be exciting, and often rewarding, but it will also sometimes be painful. Economic swings will be more frequent but of shorter duration. Entire industries will die almost overnight, laying off thousands, while others will just as suddenly appear, hungry for employees. Continuity and predictability, in almost everything, will become the rarest of commodities. And if the entrepreneurial personality honors smart failures, by the same token it has little pity for weakness. That fraction of Americans, 10 percent or 20 percent, who still dream of the gold watch or the thirty-year pin, will suffer the most, and unless their needs too are somehow met, they will remain as a perpetually open wound in our society.

The Protean Corporations will be at the heart of that new world because they alone both offer a model for corporations to survive in this new environment and recognize not only the needs but vital importance of those left behind.

A PROTEAN CORPORATION will be a very dynamic place. Companies will complete the move further away from hierarchies and toward a model of highly interconnected craft guilds. With a workforce scattered around the planet, linked virtually, the last obstacles to inclusiveness will also fall, meaning virtual job shops, temporary talent hired off the Web, more permanent part-time workers, and the hiring (in unusual new relationships) of the retired, the young, and the unlikely (illiterates, for example).

Management of a Protean Corporation will be both complex and demanding. The leadership of Google Inc. offers a clue: there, CEO Eric Schmidt must deal with a half-dozen different company subcultures— buttoned-downed accountants, slick salespeople, seat-of-the-pants server farm mechanics, and eccentric code writers, among others. All are held together by common history, purpose, and a chameleon-like top management.

Reconciling these diverse constituencies will be an immense task for HR and corporate communications. They will accomplish this with a wide portfolio of tools—virtual all-hands meetings, daily online newspapers, e-mail, and no doubt many techniques yet to be invented.

Protean Corporations will be an unlikely combination of volatile and stable. They will be loose confederacies of cultures, but with venerable and sturdy hearts. Among current institutions the closest comparisons are with movie studios, international relief agencies, and traveling arena shows (circuses, ice capades, rock bands). In each case, a group of talented professionals quickly aggregates around an idea or a business opportunity, forms a workable internal structure, expends the necessary time—weeks, months—to create and deliver their products and services, then distributes the subsequent rewards and goes their separate ways.

This type of behavior is now beginning to show up in progressive corporations to often extraordinary effect. Most famous, Apple quickly formed design teams and then product groups around two radically new (and unrelated to the company's core business) products, and one revolutionary new service—the iPod, iPhone, and iTunes, respectively—and ended up with some of the most successful new businesses of the decade. Amazon did the same thing with its Kindle electronic book, Nintendo with the Wii. And at Google, employees are *expected* to devote as much as a quarter of their time to pursuing new business ideas and forming project teams around them.

Like the entrepreneurs that people them, Protean Corporations will appear to be risk-takers with their constant shifts and turns; but they will, in fact, be risk-aversive, changing their form and direction to minimize risk.

Being extremely stable at their heart, Protean Corporations will also likely be more politically active (in support of their attitudes and values), an easier target for unions (if a new form of organized labor arises to meet their unique needs), and extremely innovative with regard to employee benefits, pay structures, services, and motivational tools. Like any entrepreneurial start-up, these firms also will be equity-driven, using not only stock options but wholly new forms of financial participation.

Protean Corporations and the institutions that mimic them will take the American economy to the next level of competitiveness, to a place where few other companies (or nations) will be able to follow.

I'VE ORGANIZED THIS BOOK into five parts.

The first part sets the ground rules for this book: the premises on which it is written, the forces at work in our society, the central paradox of modern business, and the deeper meanings of "protean." Finally, I establish a formal definition of the Protean Corporation.

Part two follows the three threads—historic, technological, and entrepreneurial. The goal in this section is to show not only how the Protean Corporation is the natural next step in these stories, but also—for important reasons—why it *isn't*.

The third and most critical part anatomizes the Protean Corporation, from the boardroom to the most distant sales office. This is not a simple task, given that there are no examples in the world of a fully mature Protean Corporation—yet. For that reason, in this section I am very careful to distinguish between what is based on existing examples and what is speculation.

Part four looks at how the Protean Corporation is likely to behave, especially as a competitor, as a financial enterprise, as participant in the global economy, and as a social force.

Part five will speculate on the impact of numerous Protean Corporations (embedded into an entrepreneurial society) on the American economy and culture. If my predictions are correct, the Protean Corporation, like the centuries-old institutional models before it, will ultimately transform society, ultimately turning it "Protean" as well.

IF NOTHING ELSE, I hope the reader will take away from this book the realization that despite the fact that our society has undergone enormous changes over the last twenty years, business—the place where we spend much of our adult lives, the source of our economic health, and the wellspring of the many products and services that improve our lives—has *not yet* caught up with those changes. Today's companies no longer reflect who we are now.

That gap creates enormous vulnerability, and danger. I believe the reader will finish this book not only understanding that we must address this problem immediately, but also better equipped with ideas for how to do so. I hope entrepreneurial readers come away from *The Protean Corporation* realizing that this gap also presents a historic opportunity and that they now have the tools to capitalize on that opportunity.

In the end, if this book does no more than provoke a discussion about new business strategies for a new world, it still will have done its job.

PART

I

THE NEW WORLD

A NEW BUSINESS MODEL FOR A NEW WORLD

IN THE AIR

THIS IS A RADICAL BOOK. It calls for fundamental changes in the organization of businesses and other institutions in the face of the equally revolutionary changes in society and commerce, all brought on by the ever-accelerating pace of technological change.

This is a reactionary book. It calls for the restoration to the center of our institutions of those structures that preserve and nurture the enduring attributes of human nature and culture.

If this seems a contradiction, then so be it. As this book makes clear, a basic contradiction will lie at the heart of the most successful corporations of the future.

This contradiction will create perpetual tension in these organizations, pulling them in one direction toward disintegration and the other toward ossification; to centralization and decentralization; to tradition and perpetual revolution; and to permanence and oblivion. This tension will need to be constantly monitored, managed, and maintained in equilibrium, and that will be an immense executive challenge.

But the companies that succeed will enjoy a success that is itself a kind of contradiction: they will be nimble but substantial, adaptive but established, long-lived but perpetually young. Most of all, these organizations will be able to adapt and change themselves at lightning speed—they will be shape-shifters, "Protean Companies"—yet they will retain at their core something enduring and unchanging. And it is precisely this last contradiction that will define them and make them formidable adversaries.

Protean Corporations will dominate large segments of the global economy by mid-century, not just because they will prove highly competitive against existing, traditional national and multinational companies, but also because they will be the best defense against the rapid change, the unexpected new competitors, and the economic chaos that will be unleashed by the next billion consumers emerging from the developing world.

In other words, Protean Corporations will define and lead the next great world economic era, not just because they will successfully compete with their traditional competitors, but because they will outsurvive them. Like better-adapted creatures facing a worldwide environmental catastrophe, Protean Corporations will survive when their counterparts cannot.

Needless to say, as the situation becomes more desperate, smart and increasingly anxious companies will rush to embrace the new scheme just as innovative and highly competitive new organizational models did in the past, such as in General Motors' divisional reorganization of the 1930s. Unfortunately for them, as history shows, each great new organizational model of the past century has not only been more difficult to implement, but that implementation must take place within an ever shorter window of opportunity.

Thus, while companies (including GM's direct competitor, Ford) had nearly two decades to learn from Alfred Sloan and reorganize their companies along divisional lines before they risked being overrun by the competition, by the 1990s those companies that didn't "virtualize" by reorganizing themselves around internal information networks, mass customization, and sales force automation tools were often left behind by their more progressive competitors in less than five years.

There is no reason to believe that this trend will change with the arrival of the Protean Corporation. In fact, it may actually accelerate. That's because, unlike the virtual corporation, the tools to bring about this "Protean" revolution are already readily available. That's good news, because it means that all that is really needed to be a Protean Corporation is the *will* to become one. But it's also bad news, because unlike the past few organizational revolutions, there is no obvious technological imperative forcing the change, at least not at the beginning. And after that it will probably be too late.

Strange as it may seem, thanks to the electronics revolution of the last half-century, we are now more likely to accept the historic inevitability of our latest inventions than we are to adopt four thousand years of meditation on human motives and desires. Almost every modern company has learned to incorporate Moore's Law of semiconductors (processing power doubles every eighteen to twenty-four months) and Metcalfe's Law of networks (the value of networks grows exponentially to the number of participants) into its business model, if only as a fundamental acceptance of continuous change and of the value of interconnection. Yet most firms still are regularly caught flat-footed by the changing needs of an aging workforce, the need for people to gather in social groups, and the human desire to both build up and tear down hierarchies—lessons that could have been learned from the ancient Egyptians, Greeks, and Sumerians.

That's why empirical management techniques—from Taylorism to

MIS systems to this week's newest CRM/ERM software—have never really worked as well as their proponents have claimed, and why management still isn't the "science" it was predicted to become. Great executives still are born, not made, in the sense that their most important talents are those life skills they gained from experiences in their youth, rather than learned at an MBA seminar.

That is what will make this particular turn in the trajectory of organizational theory different from those that came before: it will be a *humanistic* revolution as much as a technological one.

I use that term warily, as it tends toward the squishy, the self-righteous, and the correct. That is precisely what I *don't* mean by "humanistic." Thirty years as a journalist covering high tech entrepreneurship, as well as being part of the rise of "social" entrepreneurship, has taught me that enterprises that adopt enlightened management practices for their own sake—or worse, as the raison d'être of the enterprise itself—are almost always doomed to fail.

Rather, what I am talking about is the kind of tough-minded leadership that sees people-oriented management as a competitive advantage, one that increases productivity and innovation, reduces turnover, and makes the company less vulnerable to market shifts and to competitive shocks. This is management that fulfills the spiritual, emotional, and moral needs of subordinates not because it is inherently decent (though that is certainly the grounding for these actions), but because it makes the organization they inhabit *more effective.*

This is the kind of pragmatic leadership that historically has been found in the best managed and most admired organizations, from Hewlett-Packard and IBM a half-century ago to Grameen Bank and Google today. These firms are inevitably admired for their innovation, their employee policies and work environments, and their contributions to society, but what they should be celebrated for most is their recognition that the secret to building an unbeatable, world-class enterprise lies in understanding not just the heads, but the hearts, of their employees and customers.

But enlightenment means little if it isn't built on financial success. That was the mistake made by the legions of start-up companies during the dot-com boom. Having read all the right business books, the managers of these hot, young companies took great pains to do all the things expected of caring bosses: freely handing out stock options, buying ergonomic chairs, turning their offices into college dorms, paying for employee junkets, putting espresso machines in the lunchroom. . . . Unfortunately, they forgot to actually build businesses, create revenues, and, ultimately, convert that high employee morale into productivity, profits, and job security.

The story of high technology is filled with companies that offered their employees all kinds of perquisites, from par courses to day care centers, from massages to free automobiles. But because those perks were merely add-ons, untethered to the actual operations of the company, they were quickly taken away the moment the economy turned down.

Meanwhile, during those same downturns, other companies, many of them notorious for their lack of employee frills and their no-nonsense attitude toward the bottom line, were much more successful at staving off layoffs and saving their employees' jobs. Ultimately, which is better: an employee weight room or keeping your job during a recession?

Say what you will about the personalities of Bill Gates, Andy Grove, Steve Jobs, or Larry Ellison, they have over the last two decades given tens of thousands of people steady employment, and made more than a few of those workers very rich—and changed the world for the better in the process. Theirs may not be most enlightened management, but when you think of those thousands of families able to buy homes, raise children, and escape into early retirement, it would be hard not to call it humane.

Thus, we have two kinds of corporations likely to be the early adopters of the Protean model: the enlightened ones, which are wise enough to recognize the competitive power of inspiring their employees, and the pragmatic ones, which are shrewd enough to know a new competitive advantage when they see one, and are willing to do what it takes to obtain it.

These two groups are already beginning to recognize that existing organizational models are losing their effectiveness in the face of an emerging (wireless) global Web, a new generation of workers, changing cultural standards, and an unprecedented and explosive expansion of the global marketplace. They are also becoming acutely aware of their comparative sluggishness and of their growing vulnerability to fast-moving new competitors who may emerge at any moment from the most unexpected sources.

And they are getting scared.

It is from these two types of companies, one attuned to its people, the other focused on finding an edge, that the first Protean Companies will emerge. Not because they will embrace a clever new academic theory, but rather because it is the best path to future success. Most, searching for a new, long-term organizational strategy, will simply back into this model, realize that it works, and dive in. For the enlightened companies, the transition to becoming Protean Corporations will be easy because they will discover to their surprise that they are almost there anyway. And the pragmatic companies will get there quickly because their cultures are designed for fast, focused, and opportunistic transformations.

By the same token, at the other end of the business spectrum, new start-ups are, by their very nature—small, loyal teams surrounded by layers of contractors, part-timers, and simple hangers-on—already Protean. Becoming true Protean Corporations will require of them merely an adjustment in trajectory, not a fundamental reorganization. In fact, one can make the case that the Protean Corporation is, at least structurally, an entrepreneurial start-up writ large. Thus, for new companies, becoming Protean may simply mean keeping on doing what they are already doing.

By comparison, it is the vast majority, the millions of companies in the middle, that will have the most difficulty responding to the growing competitive threat created by the changing global marketplace and the emergence of the first Protean enterprises. For them there will seem to be every reason *not* to follow this path. After all, there is the precedent of past success, the dangers of organizational disruption, current profitability, comfort with the power arrangements of the status quo, nervous shareholders, a large existing capital investment, and most of all, a fear of abandoning a proven business to go chasing after opportunities that may prove to be phantasms.

Indeed, there are a million reasons not to change. And a million companies will likely do just that. They will stand pat right up to the moment when their entire business begins to evaporate. Just ask the newspaper industry. Or the video industry. Or the music industry . . .

SETTING THE STAGE

Before we go any further, we need some definitions.

The bane of modern business is the adoption of terms and buzzwords— *memes*, *Web 2.0*, *social networks*, and *viral networking*, for example—before their precise meanings are solidified. The result is a kind of amorphousness that ultimately encompasses just about everything and thus means almost nothing. This often happens because there are a lot of businesspeople out there (especially the ones looking for investors) who want to attach themselves to a hot new fad without actually having to do the work or take the risk to adopt it.

The worst case is when companies, trying to gain respect, stake their futures on these inchoate and unproven ideas. How many companies died between 1999 and 2001 because they believed that traditional notions such as "profit" were meaningless in cyberspace?

So let's set these definitions right now so that we are all on the same page.

First the premises:

‹ 1 ›

The pace of technological change will continue.

Sometime, perhaps around 2020, Moore's Law may finally hit some unbreachable wall put up by the natural world: quantum effects, electron channeling, and the sheer cost of fabricating nanometer chips. But in a world of twenty-four-month product generations, that is not our immediate concern. For now, the pace of tech, that metronome of the modern world, is going to continue along its same exponential path—a trajectory that is now nearly vertical and that will produce mind-boggling advances in the next decade.

‹ 2 ›

The number of new consumers in the world is about to triple, making the world economy structurally more volatile.

Between now and 2015, thanks to the Internet and cheap mobile phones, the number of consumers actively participating in the global economy will jump from one billion to three billion. As Silicon Valley marketing guru and blogger Tom Hayes has noted, it took twenty thousand years for the first billion consumers to populate the global economy, twenty years for the second billion, and probably just five years for the third.

The series of shock waves that will be produced by this consumer population explosion is hard to imagine: new products, companies, and fads appearing spontaneously from the most unexpected and exotic places; hundreds of millions of potential customers with little understanding of commercial transactions or business law; and huge new markets that are unlike any that exist today. Entire new industries will appear almost overnight, and disappear almost as quickly; companies will pursue customers in the most inaccessible places using the most unlikely marketing techniques (working through local chiefs, for example) and wealth will shift to those new entrepreneurs and companies that can adapt to this changed world.

In this world of the Third Billion, no market will be secure and no company, no matter how well run, will be safe.

‹ 3 ›

Industrialized nations, but especially the United States, are becoming more entrepreneurial.

Every survey of career plans taken everywhere in the developed world over the last twenty years has shown a growing percentage of the population abandoning the old dream of safe, life-long employment at a large company for the higher risk strategy of becoming a free agent, an entrepreneur, or the member of small, start-up company. So complete is this shift in the United States that (as we will discuss at the end of this book) this country may now be considered the first true entrepreneurial society in human history.

This shift in attitude brings with it a host of secondary effects, both good and bad. But one fact is indisputable: an entrepreneurial society, with its perpetually migrating armies of independent workers, is much more volatile than its corporate counterparts. And any company that wants to last long in the face of this change will have to develop strategies to either swim against the current or learn to navigate with it.

« 4 »

A new generation of young people, with different attitudes toward institutions and authority, is entering the workforce.

This goes hand-in-hand with an entrepreneurial society. The new cohort of young people just beginning to enter the workforce is already being called "The Entitlement Generation" for their independence, their scorn of hierarchies, their unwillingness to compromise, their lack of loyalty to anyone but themselves, and their sense of personal destiny.

Here's what author Jake Halpern writes in the *Boston Globe Magazine* about this "New Me Generation":

They are members of the so-called Entitlement Generation, the upstarts at the office who put their feet on their desks, voice their opinions frequently and loudly at meetings, and always volunteer—nay, expect—to take charge of the most interesting projects. They are smart, brash, even arrogant, and endowed with a commanding sense of entitlement.

. . . At the University of South Alabama, psychology professor Joshua Foster has done a great deal of research using a standardized test called the Narcissistic Personality Inventory (NPI). The NPI asks subjects to rate the accuracy of various narcissistic statements, such as "I can live my life any way I want to" and "If I ruled the world, it would be a better place." Foster has given this personality test to a range of demographic groups around the world, and no group has scored higher than the American teenager. Narcissism also appears to be reaching new highs, even within the Entitlement Generation, among American college students.

. . . All of this would seem to suggest that this generation, which is flooding into the workplace, will create chaotic, unpleasant, and utterly unproductive work environments that will drive many a good business directly into the ground...[1]

Managing this generation may not only be a nightmare, it may actually be impossible. It is quite likely that some sizable percentage of these new workers (and, being the so-called "echo" of the Baby Boom, their numbers are huge) will *never* work in a steady job on the payroll of a single employer. And an equally large segment may never know a career different from that of a "permanent part-timer," contractor, or consultant.

Yet you need these young people desperately because they are bright, (infinitely) confident, and entrepreneurial. As even Halpern admits: "It may be that this much-reviled generation will revitalize the economy and ensure the prosperity of America for years to come."[2]

Now, add to the Entitlement Generation a billion more young people, many of them immensely talented, entering the workforce from developing nations around the world—individuals with little education or training, and a rudimentary understanding of business etiquette and social customs, and living in isolated locations—and you have all of the ingredients for employment anarchy.

Where will all of those people come from? More important, how will they be constrained from destroying those companies from the inside?

‹ 5 ›

Companies, by their very nature, want to grow and endure.

Hayes has also predicted that the next quarter-century will see the first trillion-dollar valuation multinational companies. Incredibly, that actually now seems reasonable, particularly with the prospect of a global market with three times as many customers as there are today.

But that prediction also assumes that in this increasingly volatile global marketplace, characterized by dangerous competitive threats coming out of nowhere, and a restive employee population that resists large organizations, companies will stay alive long enough to reach that size, or that they will want to.

I think they will. Not to sound too anthropomorphic, but I believe that companies have a will to live, and a desire to grow and prosper, and that this arises from a natural human need to be part of something larger than ourselves that we can be proud of, that provides us with an identity and a sense of belonging, in whose success we can share, and that becomes a legacy we pass on to those who follow.

I further believe that in this new competitive landscape, smart enterprises will find a way to survive and thrive, and that they will learn new ways to fulfill this human desire to belong—even among their most independent and renegade employees. And they will conclude that the best way to do this is to become Protean Corporations.

‹ 6 ›
Human nature has not changed.

This is ultimately the most important premise of this book. For all of the changes wrought by technological innovation, and by the push and pull of fad and novelty, human beings have not fundamentally changed in thousands of years. They are still ambitious, charitable, egocentric, social, violent, and nurturing. And like all living things, people constantly strive to keep these impulses in equipoise; they work endlessly to create some kind of productive and healthy equilibrium.

But the world is always changing, not least the world of work. As new technological innovations—the PC, the Web, cell phones, online communities, smartphones, etc.—come at us at an ever faster rate, distorting traditions in one direction or another, first industry then society races to restore its lost equilibrium.

In this light, new organizational models such as the Protean Corporation can be seen both as a response to the arrival of the latest technologies and as a "fix" to the unanticipated distortions arising from the previous organizational schemes.

THOSE ARE THE PREMISES on which this book is based. If you do not agree with them, you should be highly skeptical of all that follows.

Now we'll look at the forces that affect these premises. They take two forms: *centrifugal forces*, which are pulling enterprises apart, and *centripetal forces*, which are drawing them together.

THE *CENTRIFUGAL FORCES* are technology, culture, and demographics.

In technology, the rise of the broadband World Wide Web, powerful personal and laptop computers, BlackBerrys, iPhones, and other intelligent, Web-enabled cellular phones, billions of embedded microprocessors, and ubiquitous Wi-Fi (and soon, WiMAX) coverage has had two effects. The first is to take already "wired" workers in the developed world and untether them from the need for a traditional office in a large building at some centralized location. This transformation to "telecommuting" began a decade ago and is now reaching a second generation; there are now hundreds of thousands of veteran employees who have *never* worked in a traditional office.

One can chart the progress of this social transformation by dropping in at any Starbucks late some morning and counting the number of professional people working at its tables. Suburban neighborhoods these days fairly hum with professionals, home for two or three workdays each week, filling the air with their wireless interconnects.

Meanwhile, on any given day, tens of thousands of virtual work teams, their members scattered in offices and laboratories in every time zone around the planet, meet online or via satellite video links and swap ideas, hold meetings, or hand off projects to their compatriots just starting their workdays. In the modern, virtual global corporation, work is almost continuous 24/7/365, offering a competitive advantage no local company can match.

But the role of technology as a centrifugal force doesn't stop with the industrialized world. In developing nations, such as India and China, talented knowledge workers are being pulled away from work at a local company (if there was any work) to work for companies based half a world away, empowered by the Internet. Thus, the growing number of R&D labs built by large U.S. corporations in countries as diverse as Israel (where Intel has had a lab for thirty years), Ireland (once the poorest nation in Western Europe, now the fastest-growing), Estonia (software engineers), China and India (more new engineering graduates each year than the rest of the world combined), and Indonesia.

Conversely, thanks to Moore's Law, each succeeding generation of cheaper and more powerful computers, servers, hubs, and routers means that a growing number of domestic companies in those nations can now grow and compete on the world stage, forcing their more veteran First World competitors to set up shop there and compete with them. (The classic example of this is Intel, which, faced with a devastating threat in consumer chips from Samsung, has moved a number of its assets and employees to South Korea.)

Meanwhile, throughout the developing world, in both the teeming cities and in the villages of the "bush," cheap cell phones, now numbering in the billions, are enabling budding entrepreneurs to use everything from eBay to illegal Nigerian "419" e-mail scams to reach out to the global marketplace for very little cost but with the potential for huge returns.

Put all of this together and almost everything in the global marketplace seems to be spinning apart. Established companies are extending themselves outward over time and geography; ambitious young careerists are (virtually) abandoning their homes for the world, regional companies are jumping to the international stage, and entrepreneurship is spreading like wildfire to the most remote territories.

In the face of this, no enterprise can compete unless it expands outward—through marketing, distribution, satellite sales and service offices, and remote research labs—almost boundlessly. And this need for nearly infinite extension is only going to get worse as the technology continues to advance.

And as we've already noted, technology isn't the only centrifugal force at work on companies today. Culture may be even more important.

In the United States we have one generation, the Baby Boomers, that pioneered the idea of entrepreneurship (or, at least, serial employment) and telecommuting as a lifestyle; a second, the X-Gen, that has largely lived it through most of its professional life, and a third, the Y-Gen (or Millennials or the Entitlement Generation) that was born after the tech revolution, is as at home in cyberspace as in the natural world, and assumes that it is normal for one or more parent to regularly work at home or take 5 A.M. phone calls from Kiev. The first of these generations is likely to stay employed as long as possible, the second is preparing to take over the reins of corporate power, and the third (as big as the first) is just now entering the workforce.

In other words, we will very soon have an employment base in the United States that defines work more as a fluid experience of moving from job to job, project to project, carrying your 401(k) along with you, operating out of cubicles, tables at coffee joints, and the den at home, than any traditional notion of a single job at a large company for thirty years followed by a gold watch and a pension. This may seem self-evident to the reader, but please note that it would not have seemed so as late as 1990, a measure of how sweeping this cultural transformation has been.

And it has only begun. We Boomers have an unequalled ability to take care of ourselves under the guise of universal benevolence, so we can be sure that the next few years will see all sorts of legislation to protect us from the growing cost of health insurance and our general lack of pensions and retirement savings accounts. The larger result will be to further free subsequent generations from the need to attach themselves to particular careers, companies, and communities. And this will spin them even further from traditional notions of job, employer, and loyalty.

Finally, there is the matter of demographics, the most centrifugal force of all.

The media is filled these days with Cassandra-like warnings about the declining birth rate in Japan, Western Europe, and just about every other industrialized nation. And even if some of the claims are overstated, there is still no question that the citizens of the industrialized nations are largely failing to meet their replacement birthrates and, immigration aside (its own crisis), they are likely in the next twenty-five years to possess populations that are both diminishing and growing elderly.

Leaving all other concerns aside, this is not a recipe for business growth. Once again, technology will likely ride to the rescue, with a continuous array of new products. But upgrading current customers will take you only so far; the real opportunity lies with capturing new customers and starting them up the curve.

If the industrialized nations don't have those new consumers—and it's likely they won't, at least not in sufficient numbers—then we *do* know where to look. It's those two billion brand-new consumers emerging in the developing world right now. Not only are they a sufficient replacement for what is being lost in the industrialized nations, but also this gigantic population may very well represent the greatest new business opportunity in human history.

That is, if we can get to them. And it won't be easy; everything from religion to topography will get in the way. And that's why—despite our linked, virtualized world—companies are still going to have to throw human bodies at the problem, sending employees to the far corners of the globe, stationing them in offices in the most obscure places. Furthermore, because the situation on the ground at these outlying locations will be so alien to anything experienced at headquarters, and because (thanks to the linked world) events will occur so quickly, those outlying employees and contractors will need to be empowered to make critical decisions based on their own judgment, and over time that will make them even less attached to the company with which they are, ostensibly, employed.

Those are the formidable forces pulling companies apart, atomizing their traditional operations, and challenging any sense in their employees of loyalty or identity with the organization.

THE *CENTRIPETAL FORCES* are the human needs for socialization, commitment to a larger purpose, continuity and constancy, and a sense of legacy.

You may have already noticed a certain symmetry here. The centrifugal forces are mostly external and anonymous, and deal with large, sweeping global trends. The centripetal forces, appropriately enough as they draw the members of the organization inward, are mostly personal, small, and local. And if the centrifugal forces are mostly the product of larger institutions and functions in society, the centripetal forces deal with human nature in its most intimate manifestations as personal identity, small groups, and family.

Organizational transformations, like military academies, tend to fight the last war and fail to anticipate the unique challenges of the next one; they solve one set of familiar problems while creating a new set of unexpected ones. The rise of virtual corporations over the last fifteen years has enabled companies to mass-customize their products and services, free their workers to largely escape the traditional office and the equally traditional organization chart—even as it empowered those workers to make more decisions—and made massive amounts of useful information available top-to-bottom throughout the company to improve decision making.

Those are pretty impressive accomplishments, and so sweeping and complete has been this transformation that it is hard, even for those veterans who were there, to remember a work environment run on a strict nine-to-five schedule, with an even stricter vertical reporting hierarchy, hard-copy interoffice memos and telephones as the sole source of company news, and fixed product catalogs with little room for customization or discounts.

But if the virtual corporation did much to cure the stultifying work environment of the Organization Man, and salved the unpredictability of Innovation companies that designed products for which there was no obvious market, it also quickly exposed its own flaws.

It wasn't long before the "progressive" companies that had quickly embraced the tenets of virtualization found themselves facing all sorts of wicked institutional problems for which they were wholly unprepared. Organizational psychologists soon discovered that employees who worked at home were less likely to be stuck with grunt work by their bosses, creating resentment in those who stayed at the office. But the other side of "out of sight, out of mind" was that these same telecommuters were also more forgotten when it came time for promotion and pay raises.

At the same time, many of these spun-off employees experienced a sense of isolation, of abandonment, and of being left out of the crucial events of the company in which they were ostensibly part. Some drifted back to the office, while others found succor in alternative groups, professional societies, even the camaraderie of fellow virtual employees.

Meanwhile, HR departments began to discover to their dismay that many of these telecommuters were spending more time in coffee shops or satellites working alongside competitors than they did at the office with their fellow employees. There was something of a crisis in many companies about whether they were slowly losing the loyalty of these employees.

Time has smoothed over many of these problems, but it hasn't really solved them. In many ways, the situation has only grown worse, and we have merely grown more inured to it. We now accept the fact that modern employees are typically less loyal to their employers than their predecessors. We accept that working at home or as a road warrior or as part of a global virtual work team entails a certain loneliness and detachment, and we assume that it is part of our daily work the same way our grandparents dealt with un-air-conditioned offices in the summertime, and our parents with being anonymous cogs in a great corporate machine. Many of us also know at least one person who is closer to her online community—or her fellow avatars on Second Life—than she is to her actual physical neighbors. And probably every person over forty reading this book has had the dispiriting experience of realizing that upon retirement, he or she will only be able to look back on a career spent hopping between companies that no longer exist, and asking themselves the devastating question: *What was it all for?*

Both industry and society continue to experiment with new ways to deal with this growing sense of estrangement, anomie, and pointlessness; industry does so in order to reduce turnover and increase productivity, society to reduce the general level of discontent. But ultimately, it is hard not to believe that this situation is anything but untenable, in the same way that the time-motion/Taylorized world of the first third of the twentieth century and the executive suite/organization man world of the second third finally had to crack under the weight of their own internal contradictions.

And if this situation is becoming acute for those workers for whom the notion of an entrepreneurial lifestyle is at least moderately appealing, it is becoming truly desperate for those folks for whom stability and commitment are the defining elements of their character.

Here, as with many things in corporate life, the 80:20 rule obtains. In every great organizational restructuring, the new architecture is inevitability designed to appeal to the needs of 80 percent of the participants, while the remaining 20 percent are left out. A century ago, the first modern corporations were designed for those four-fifths of employees who were looking for an efficient infrastructure, employment benefits, career-long stability, and a pension. The small minority of renegades, mavericks, and entrepreneurs who resisted that structure were typically fired, blackballed, or, if they were too talented, quarantined inside the organization where they couldn't do much damage.

Today, that same majority of people (or, more accurately, their great-grandchildren) who once wanted into the big, safe company now want *out*. And that is what companies over the last quarter-century have struggled to give them.

But, human nature being what it is, that 20 percent minority still remains, only now it is composed of the kind of people for whom entrepreneurship and maverick behavior is an anathema. What these people want is to get *in*—to lifelong jobs in stable companies.

It would be easy to dismiss this group as the inevitable minority in any population that just doesn't fit in, that yearns for a distant, long-gone past, and that just refuses to go along with the program. After all, the other 80 percent has more than enough talent, available and uncomplaining, to pick from.

But that would be repeating a foolish mistake made many times in the past. It's interesting to remember that this ratio is simply a flip-flop of the old 80:20 Rule, Pareto's Principle as it is formally called and named after an Italian economist. Whenever the 80:20 ratio appears, it is inevitably used to segregate the valuable and productive from the trivial and worthless. But Joseph Juran, the quality guru who named the Principle in the late 1940s, was very careful not to do so, but to give everyone their role and value in the organization. Juran carefully described this ratio as "the vital few and the useful many," which is a beautiful description of the Protean Corporation.[3]

And, indeed, there is within that 20 percent of nonentrepreneurial corporate types a bunch of people whose talents are absolutely vital to your company's future success. From those mavericks and malcontents of a century ago came most of the innovation, flexibility, and sheer energy that hierarchical corporations needed to grow, move into new markets, take risks, and thrive. And, by the same token—as modern virtual corporations are just now beginning to discover—within that current 20 percent of risk-averse, steady, corporate fuddy-duddies are most of the folks who maintain the corporate culture, serve as the institutional memory, and maintain structural cohesion and integrity, and are ultimately the key to organization's long-term survival.

To one degree or another, *every* company these days is virtual, horizontal, innovative, and adaptive. The new competitive differentiator, the one that will separate the winners and the losers in the volatile years to come, identifies which ones are *structurally consistent*. And to succeed at that will, once again, require the help of the marginalized—ironic but also exhibiting a wonderful symmetry and justice. Order needs chaos, and it seems that the reverse is also true.

THE SHAPE-SHIFTER

THE PARADOX OF PERMANENCE
AND CHANGE

A BUSINESS PARADOX

BUT OUR DEFINITION IS NOT YET COMPLETE. We now have our basic assumptions and the various forces, internal and external, at work on them. The final step is to come up with a vision of what this new organizational model for corporations should look like to meet the rapidly-changing, brutally competitive, and anarchistic global environment that is right now bearing down on us.

I have already spoken of the core business contradiction of the years ahead, a solution that is both radical and reactionary. The contradiction is:

Successful companies of the future must find a way to continuously and rapidly change almost every one of their attributes—products, services, finances, physical plant, markets, customers, and both tactical and strategic goals—yet at the same time retain a core of values, customs, legends, and philosophy that will be little affected by the continuous and explosive changes taking place just beyond its edges.

The challenge is not in building this solid core, nor in this ever-changing periphery; the last century of corporation organizational theories has taught us how to do both quite well. What we *don't* know how to do is to marry the two together and make them work in synchrony without ripping one apart or stultifying the other. That is the great challenge for corporations in this century.

In 1991, when Bill Davidow and I began writing *The Virtual Corporation*, we struggled for a term that would best capture what we saw as the growing impact of digital technology and communications on every aspect of corporate life. We chose the term "virtual" because it harkened back to a thirty-year-old technical term: "virtual computing," an early form of multiprocessing that enabled each of the numerous users of a computer to feel as though the entire computer were dedicated just to them. We believed that the new information technologies would enable customers and employees to feel that way about their companies.[1]

"Virtual Corporation" also resonated with a new term "virtual reality," the use of computing power and specialized interfaces to create a compelling simulacrum of the natural world, an experience that, thanks to Moore's Law, would only grow more realistic by the year. We felt the same was happening to the modern corporation: individual employees up and down the organization chart would be empowered by ever-greater quantities of useful information to make quick and important

decisions. They would thus be able to provide customers with more customized products and prices as well as more dedicated service.

Whatever else came out of the "virtual" revolution, almost every part
of this scenario came true. What began as a metaphor and an analogy
quickly became a reality.

Through watching the behavior of a number of large corporations in
recent years, I first began to have a notion of where organizations would
go next. For example, take IBM, that most venerable of computer companies. In the most extraordinary move in its history, it sold off its PC
operations in the span of just four years to China's Lenovo and transformed itself from a manufacturer to a consulting company—and thrived.
In the 1970s it had already morphed from a mainframe to a minicomputer
company, in the 1980s to a personal computer company, and in the 1990s
to an online retailer. These days, the world's greatest computer company
is no longer in the computer business.

Cisco Systems, badly battered by the dot-com bust and largely ignored thereafter, made a spectacular reentry three years later, not as the
router maker for which it was known, but as a world leader in networking and communications technologies, including to the home. Most famously, Apple Computer, under the returned Steve Jobs, had gone so far
from its core computer business into iPods and iPhones that it even
dropped the word "Computer" from its name.

How did this happen? Having been a business reporter for nearly
thirty years, I had long ago learned (from considerable evidence) that
for a company to abandon its core business—or worse, have it disappear
beneath you—was all but a death sentence. At best, you might survive
bankruptcy and reemerge as a shadow of your former self. But that hadn't
happened to any of these famous companies: they had barely seemed to
skip a beat.

The term that came to mind was *shape-shifter*. These companies managed to fundamentally change who they were—and not only to do it on
the fly, but while barely missing a step.

It struck me then that I was being given an early glimpse of the future,
an augury of what would be the shared fate of most companies in the
twenty-first century, large and small. With a global market so vast and

physically extended, with ongoing and profound technological changes, with new competitive challenges coming from every direction, and with a restive population of mavericks and entrepreneurs, it seemed pretty obvious that *every* company in the world of any size was going to be under continuous, deadly assault—and if they wanted to survive they would have to change their nature over and over again. Moreover, these reorganizations wouldn't come once per decade, as they had with these celebrated companies, but perhaps even at the pace of Moore's Law; that is, *every couple years.*

If that weren't enough, it also occurred to me that these transformations might well extend beyond markets, customers, products, and org charts. They could even extend into heretofore sacrosanct arenas. These new shape-shifting companies might actually swing back and forth between public and private . . . even profit and non-profit. They might also be all of these things at once: dividing, reorganizing, and recombining in a mind-boggling combinatorics that would not only be hard to imagine today but, according to current securities law, might actually be illegal.

For this kind of extraordinary behavior, the term "shape-shifter" seemed inadequate. What was required was a more elemental descriptor, some term that had the complexity and power of an archetype.

That's when *Protean* came to mind.

Strictly speaking, the word "protean" means something or someone that easily and regularly changes its appearance. In everyday language, the term, somewhat rare, usually describes an individual—often a polymath like Francis Bacon, Leonardo da Vinci, Winston Churchill, or Teddy Roosevelt—who exhibits many different skills in diverse fields, often with a certain energy and brio. It is someone who can jump back and forth between disciplines—music, politics, literature, diplomacy—and make an important contribution in each. Needless to say, such protean figures are among the most celebrated in human history. (But it can also have its sinister, sociopathic side as well: Shakespeare's Richard III describes himself as protean in his ability to change his manner to insinuate his way into the halls of power.)[2]

In popular use, the word "protean" has come to mean not just the abil-

ity to change shape, but also to adapt to change; to be flexible enough to meet any new challenge with the right skills, attitude, and goals.

It's a small step from there to the idea of Protean Corporations being able to change their form and their business models to meet rapidly evolving market challenges.

But the etymology of protean holds other surprises, and even some lessons.

"Protean" comes from Proteus, a comparatively minor figure of Greek mythology who nonetheless has maintained a hold on the imaginations of artists—Homer, Virgil, Milton, Shakespeare, Wordsworth, Joyce—ever since. It's hard to imagine a more "protean" figure than one who manages over the course of three thousand years to make cameo appearances in *The Odyssey, Paradise Lost, Richard III,* a famous Romantic sonnet, and *Ulysses.*

The origins of Proteus are very old (the name even means "first" or "earliest") and lost in prehistory, suggesting some fundamental human attraction to the idea of shape-shifting. He appears to have begun as a sort of sea god. Homer called him the "old man of the sea" (resonating in a modern literary connection) who evolved with the development of Greek mythology into one of the offspring of Poseidon or various other ocean deities. He was the guardian of Poseidon's sacred ocean seals and was regularly depicted in the form of a great bull seal surrounded by a harem of females. He lived on Pharos, the island in the harbor of Alexandria at the mouth of the Nile, and later home of the famed Lighthouse of Alexandria.[3]

But as interesting and useful as the notion of a shape-shifter is, for our purposes it is the second part of the Proteus myth that is the most compelling. It seems that beyond his ability to change shape at will, Proteus's greatest gift was for prophecy: he was able to foretell the future and answer any other question put to him. The only problem was that first you had to catch him; the theme of catching the shape-shifter is a common one in mythology the world over.

The most famous figure in antiquity to attempt this capture was King Menelaus. In one of the side stories in *The Odyssey,* Telemachus travels to Sparta to learn from the king the fate of his father, Odysseus. As Menelaus

recounts it, on the king's own journey home from Troy with his wayward queen Helen, his ship was blown off course to Egypt. There he learns from Proteus's own daughter of the special powers of the old sea god and what he must do to hear a prophecy.

Menelaus, a tough old soldier, attacks the great bull seal and hangs on as Proteus races through one form after another—a lion, a snake, a leopard, a pig, water, and finally a tree—to escape the king's grip. But Menelaus holds on, and finally an exhausted Proteus surrenders. He agrees to answer Menelaus's questions.

The king's first question is to ask what he has done to invoke the gods' wrath and cause them to create a storm to blow his ship off course; and more important, what offerings and sacrifices he needs to make to regain their favor.

The second question Menelaus poses to the old sea god is to inquire after the fate of his fellow heroes of the Trojan War. Have they all gotten home safely? This is when Proteus delivers the shocking news that Menelaus's brother Agamemnon returned home only to be murdered by his wife and her lover. He also tells Menelaus that, in the bit of news that Telemachus came to hear, Odysseus is trapped on an island under the spell of Circe.

The one piece of good news Proteus delivers is that despite all of his struggles and woes, past, present, and future, the king is destined for heaven, for Elysium.[4]

The genius of myths is that through them, universal human truths are presented as compelling and often unforgettable stories. Myths are unequalled in their ability to capture the essential contradictions and paradoxes of human existence.

The myth of Proteus is no different. Proteus is the most transient of creatures. Yet whatever form he takes, he still retains his *self*. There is something elemental beneath all the many shapes, some core identity that remains eternal and true to Proteus. And it is his core identity that enables Proteus to see the eternal and the true, and thus the future.

The lesson for us from the Proteus myth is the same as it was for Menelaus: if you want the future, you must learn to wrestle and control the rapidly changing, shape-shifting world around you. Only then will

the true identity of this challenge reveal itself. Deep beneath the shape-shifting surface of the emerging Protean Corporation lies a small, solid core that is unchanging, fundamental, and (at least on the scale of a human career) immortal. Find it and you will learn the truth—and perhaps even control your destiny.

BY ITS NATURE

First the myth, now the metaphor.

If the last few pages seemed a bit, well, *literary*, please bear with me. We'll get to recipes and road maps for creating Protean Corporations soon enough. Right now, the task is to set this new business organizational model into the imagination, to *feel* its resonances and creative implications.

The truth is that every new business scheme begins this way, as a vision emerging from the most unlikely sources, and for which we have only a few, albeit important, real-life examples to point the way. We are mostly left to test the validity of the idea against how we think the world works, what we have seen tested in the crucible of everyday life, and what ultimately seems correct to us, not just logically, but *subjectively*. When approaching a new idea, the gut is often as useful as the brain.

At any moment in history, humans have tended to view the physical world and to build institutions on the prevailing scientific (or before that, theological) and technological metaphors of the time.

Thus, it is no coincidence that medieval society, with its hierarchy from serf to king, bears an uncanny similarity to the Christian heaven, with God presiding over archangels, angels, on down to the souls of the saved. By the same token, it is well documented that the appearance of the first lifelike automatons in the Renaissance provoked doctors and anatomists to begin thinking of the human body and its organs as a kind of "machine."

In the eighteenth century, the first companies and corporations exhibited the same kind of order, certainty, and predictability in their clockwork-like organizations that one finds in the Newtonian universe, first described a few years earlier. And in the nineteenth century, the rise of the mass-production factory with its interchangeable components coincided with the birth of atomic theory, which saw the entire universe the same way. It's probably not surprising then that these days everything from DNA to the universe itself is seen as analogous to the information processing and computation of modern computers and the vast databases and networks of the Web.

The twentieth century saw the rise of one powerful scientific theory-turned-metaphor after another: relativity, quantum mechanics, uncertainty, genetics, cybernetics, and string theory. Each in turn has affected—often in the oddest ways—art, music, politics, literature, and, of most interest to us, business.

One could argue that the entire history of business organization and theory in the twentieth century was one long struggle between our ever-growing ability to capture and store information and our ever-diminishing ability to put that knowledge to use: to cull actual facts from that data, to determine how what we've learned can be applied, even who should be the recipient.

This growing indeterminacy has come to define the modern company. The digital revolution, from mainframe computers in the 1950s all the way through to the World Wide Web in the 1990s, offered to enterprises the prospect of escaping forever the limitations of time and space. After all, the monolithic company of a century before had evolved into the headquarters linked to satellite offices around the country, then the world. So why wouldn't the process continue indefinitely, until the company itself evaporated into thousands of equivalent nodes scattered across the landscape? Once networks were sufficiently robust, why not send everybody home, or to remote offices, and then just aggregate them as needed to deal with a particular project? Who needed a headquarters when decision making was supposed to migrate to the field anyway?

This was company as grid, web, or matrix—post-structural and in continuous reconfiguration. It sounded good in theory, and a number of young dot-com companies, anxious to be on the cutting edge not only of technology, but of enlightened personnel policies as well, tried to implement it.

And everyone who tried it failed.

As a journalist covering the dot-com era, I cheered the new business models as much as everyone else. After all, who wouldn't want to work for a company with no hierarchies, no bosses (or at least not one standing nearby), and the opportunity to work from any place you pleased?

But even then I had second thoughts. I'd already worked for more than a decade from home as a freelance writer, and I'd come to appreciate the isolation, the feeling of unconnectedness, and the need to belong to something bigger that came with working away from the office. And I was a born entrepreneur, an independent type. What about all of those other people I knew, even in Silicon Valley, who wanted to identify with a company, who wanted to be part of a larger crusade, and who prayed for some continuity in their lives? How would they fit into this brave new world?

I noticed something else as well: a company without a center created no gravity to draw its employees, partners, and customers toward it. With "no there there" (apologies to Gertrude Stein), employees had nothing to keep them from moving on to other, marginally better opportunities, managers weren't given the ego rewards that drew them to that work in the first place, and customers had no sense of a real entity in which to place their trust.

A lot of companies, big and small, flirted with the idea of virtualization in the late 1990s, especially when they were desperate to try anything to hang on to employees being lured away by the siren call of dot-com stock options. But the crash of 2000 was a wake-up call, and the survivors quickly reasserted some structure into their businesses. Most of this "remassification" was strictly ad hoc, a response to impending disaster, and without any real strategy beyond retreat to the safer structures of the past.

It's now nearly a decade later. The same forces of virtualization and decentralization are still at work on the modern corporation, and growing worse by the month as technology accelerates, millions of new consumers enter the marketplace, and new competitors are being founded around the world. And still, no model has yet emerged for dealing with all these pressures.

I believe that we *already* have that model, and like its predecessors, it derives from the natural world. We just haven't recognized it yet. I also believe that those radical implementers of perfectly virtual corporations weren't entirely wrong. Their insight enabled them to recognize and deal with the centrifugal forces at work on the modern company, and in response they built what might have become shape-shifting companies.

But their mistake was to focus on the scientific side of the organizational model, not the humanistic one. They failed to deal with—since most of them were young and inexperienced, they probably never even noticed—the centripetal forces at work in their own hearts and the hearts of their fellow employees.

In other words, they got the cloudlike nature of the future corporation right but they failed to appreciate that for such an enterprise to have any presence and attraction, it also needed to have a small, hard core around which that cloud swirled. That was the only way the future corporation could solve the essential paradox of being permanent but transient, amorphous but structured, a shape-shifter with an enduring identity.

The fact that almost every company in the industrial world, post-Bubble, reverted to a form that was an uneasy compromise between a traditional hierarchal organization and a collection of ad hoc rules about working at home, company intranets, road warriors, permanent part-time workers, permeable firewalls, etc.—into rudimentary Protean Corporations—only underscores that the centrifugal and centripetal forces were still at work and we simply didn't know how to manage them in any systematic way.

An amorphous, ever-changing cloud around a solid core—where have we seen that before? What is the model in the natural world, the image from scientific theory that serves as the template for our vision of the Protean Corporation?

The *atom* as described by quantum theory.

Interestingly, you can make the case that almost *every* organizational model of the past 150 years has had its analog in the increasingly sophisticated contemporary image of the atom. Thus the solid, monolithic manufacturing company of the nineteenth century was similar to the ball bearing–like image of the atom at the time: elemental, irreducible, capable of being stacked and organized into a larger, rational economy.

Then came the Rutherford atom of the early twentieth century: the classic solid nucleus surrounded by orbiting electrons, the corporate counterpart being the central headquarters supported by distant plants and sales offices. Segment that nucleus into protons and neutrons and you have the classic division architecture of the corporation at mid-century: the more headquarters divisions, the more there are satellite operations and vice versa.

Thanks to Planck, Heisenberg, and a whole squad of particle accelerators around the world, we now see that atom as a comparatively solid nucleus composed of a myriad of subatomic particles, surrounded by a probability "cloud" showing the likely locations of the orbiting electrons at any given moment. This cloud grows denser the closer one gets to the nucleus, as the inner "rings" of electrons are more tightly bound to the nucleus than the outer ones, where the electrons can be stripped away or shared in bonds with other atoms.

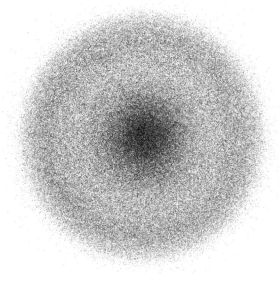

Look familiar?

Keep in mind that this is merely an image, a little memory theater from the natural world to help us better visualize the nature of the Protean Corporation and to set that image in our minds as we go forward through this narrative. I hasten to add that this is not a direct scientific correspondence—some higher orbit electron clouds resemble dumbbells and all sorts of other shapes—but the best visual fit to what I believe a Protean Corporation to be. I could just as easily have chosen (going up the size scale) a radiolarian, a dandelion, even certain elliptical nebulae. I chose the quantum atom because it looks the most like what to my mind a Protean Corporation would be like—and because it shows that this design not only is not rare, but is the single most common form in the entire universe.

IN FOCUS

We now have the context and the forces at play in creating the Protean Corporation, as well as the deeper emotional connections to archetypes in the natural world and within the human imagination. Thank you for your patience. Next let's consider a definition of the Protean Corporation:

A Protean Corporation is an enterprise that features: (1) an amorphous external form that uses technology to rapidly adapt to changing situations with regard to market, customers, competition, finance, and even ownership; and (2) a slowly evolving internal center that uses interpretive tools to maintain the identity and continuity of the enterprise over time.

The ever-changing external "Cloud" contains a majority of the individuals connected to the enterprise, including full-time and part-time employees, contractors and consultants, and other stakeholders. These stakeholders continuously migrate between greater or lesser attachment to the enterprise according to the level, duration, and intensity of their commitment to the enterprise. A majority of these individuals migrate across the surface of the company, provide their contracted serves, and move on. "Cloud" employees are mostly rewarded for their contribution.

At the center of the Protean Corporation is a solid "Core" that contains a comparatively small number of permanent employees, from all levels of the traditional organizational chart. These individuals bear the task of maintaining the Protean Corporation's core identity, philosophy, standards, stories, and legends, as well as relationships with strategic partners and investors, intellectual property, and public image. "Core" employees are mostly rewarded for their commitment.

The primary task of the "Cloud" of a Protean Corporation is to quickly and success-fully adapt to a changing world. The primary task of the "Core" is to maintain the enter-prise's core identity through these changes. The biggest challenge facing both is learning to work with the other.

As always, we need some secondary definitions to help explain our primary definition:

<> Note the term "enterprise" rather than "company" or "business." There are two reasons for this choice. First, as we have seen over the past few decades, organizational changes in the business world are increasingly finding applicability in other sorts of human institutions; not just commercial businesses and corporations (private and public), but also non-profits, governmental agencies, and, most recently, "social" enterprises. Second, and just as important, Protean Corporations, as they change their form, may *themselves* move through all of these types of enterprises. The word "business" may now be too narrow to encompass this next era of business.

<> By "amorphous," I don't mean that a Protean Corporation will have no shape, but rather that it will have no *fixed* shape, transforming itself to meet the changing marketplace.

<> By "interpretive" tools, I mean that the core operations of a Protean Corporation will focus upon *meaning*. That is, those things—from the institutional history and memory to patterns of behavior and company culture to the collection of intellectual and physical assets—that uniquely define the company. By comparison, the cloud operations of the company, freed from these concerns (but operating within them), will focus on reaching corporate goals and achieving measurable successes.

<> By the "fluid" nature of the Cloud operations, I don't simply mean the shape-shifting attributes of the Protean Corporation, but also the continuous up- and down-welling of employees and managers with different intensities of connection to the enterprise. This includes: (1) the streaming off of temporary employees and contractors whose relationship with the company is tenuous and

weak, and who continuously stream off as their work is done; (2) new employees, who may be joining the enterprises in temporary or semipermanent roles; (3) more committed employees and managers who are migrating down toward the center of the company, to what I will call the "Inner Ring," and perhaps even crossing over into the Core; and (4) other employees who, for career or personal reasons, are moving outward, loosening their connection to the enterprise, and who may ultimately move to a contractor or part-time role, or even leave the enterprise permanently.

<> When speaking of employees *from all levels* composing the Core, I mean just that. Odd as it may sound, it should be quite possible in a Protean Corporation for a hired gun CEO to inhabit the Cloud, while reporting (at least in some capacity) to his own veteran secretary within the Core.

In one respect, this is a radical departure from the traditional corporate organization chart, with its ever-upward solid and dotted lines of reporting and responsibility. On the other hand, it is also a realistic recognition of an age-old truth: that in every company, non-profit, or military unit, there is always that one secretary or engineer, fund-raiser or master sergeant, who has been around longer, understands the operations of the company better, and is more loyal to the organization than anyone else—including the people who ostensibly run the place.

These individuals are also usually the least entrepreneurial in temperament and the most stable in their careers, making them almost perfectly unsuited for the fast-moving modern corporation. Arguably, the biggest flaw of virtual corporations is that in their headlong pursuit of "agility," they are profligate with just this type of priceless talent. In the Protean Corporation, these individuals find their home in the Core—it is precisely for them that the Core was invented.

<> Finally, the biggest challenge facing the successful implementation of the Protean Corporation can be found in the last sentence of the definition—the endless task of making the Cloud and the Core of a Protean Corporation work together. One is a

changeling, the other a rock; one is forever looking outward, the other looking inward; one is there to tackle a project, make money, and move on, the other to nurture the company they love and stick around long enough for the gold watch.

I said the Protean Corporation is about contradictions, and nowhere will this be more visible than right at the *interface* between Core and Cloud, where those dedicated to careers at the Protean Corporation will meet their counterparts: employees who are making a comparable commitment to an entirely different set of goals. One is devoted to keeping the heart of the company the same, the other to making the rest of enterprise perpetually change.

HERE AND NOW

We have our definition, and the rest of this book will be devoted to elaborating on it and showing how it can be implemented.

But, before we begin, two final points:

First, there is a tendency in business books, because the technique attracts readers, to be either apocalyptic or utopian, and often both.

In hope of drawing readers and creating movements, authors typically call for a revolution in some part of the business world, warning ominously that if certain steps are not taken, catastrophe will result. That's the stick. The carrot is to present the postrevolutionary future as one in which all the problems of the present will be solved, and the newly metamorphosed company (or marketing department, sales force, executive row) will march into a shiny new world.

The fact is that business revolutions come along only rarely, perhaps once every couple of generations at most, and it is very likely, thanks to the Web, that we have already had ours. If there is to be another, it will most likely come from some technological invention that has yet to pop into the imagination of its creator.

Having survived the 2008 credit crunch and stock-market crash, it is also unlikely that we are about to have a massive economic meltdown. If there is an apocalypse in our future, it won't be coming from the business world.

For the foreseeable future, companies will continue to muddle along, with hundreds of thousands disappearing every year, and hundreds of thousands more being founded. There will be new superstar companies, and some currently celebrated companies will fade away. And when I speak about the rise of Protean Corporations, some companies will adopt the model early and be hugely successful, most will adopt the model late and incompletely but still manage to hang on and survive, and some percentage—a number that will be a function of the power of this new model combined with the number of early adopters in that particular industry—will succumb.

This is not to diminish the importance of the Protean Corporation, but rather to not oversell it. The Internet and the rise of virtual corporations have profoundly affected the modern business world, yet you can drive down to your local strip mall and find a half-dozen companies that still operate as if this business revolution never actually occurred. Are these firms world-beaters? No. Are they hugely successful? Probably not. But they endure, and each provides a living for its owners and perhaps a handful of employees

Do they need to worry about the rise of Protean Corporations? Maybe not, because any new threat created by this economic transformation is probably less a danger than a change in local zoning, a new landlord, or an up-tick in the neighborhood crime rate.

That isn't to say that they won't be affected by this change, if only marginally, just as they were by the Internet revolution. These days even your local dentist probably has a website, an in-office computer-controlled grinding machine, and ships his or her custom work via computer to a distant laboratory. Those operations haven't fundamentally transformed the business, but they have changed it in important ways. So too have the larger cultural shifts that have followed as we have moved toward a Web-empowered society. One merely has to look at that dentist's appointment book to see how many adult patients, working at home, now schedule their visits during the traditional workday.

The same thing is likely to happen as the business world becomes Protean. It too will affect even the smallest businesses in subtle but ultimately profound ways. Relationships with vendors will change, as will the pool of potential employees. The technology too will change, driven as always by the pace of technological change, but also by the changing nature of the companies manufacturing them. And then, as Protean Corporations begin to create a more Protean Society, small businesses, often unknowingly, will adapt to these changes as well. How these changes will manifest is what we will investigate later in this book.

Those are the small fry, in their legions. But when we look at larger enterprises, and by that I mean companies of fifty employees all of the way up the Fortune 500 (several million companies in total), the changes wrought by the rise of the Protean Corporation will be profound, so much so that these enterprises, now transformed, will drive massive changes in the societies around them.

It is among these firms that not only the adoption, but the *speed* of that adoption may prove the difference between success and failure.

How fast must this adoption be for a company to be safe? Let me use an anecdote to offer a clue: When Bill Davidow and I were writing *The Virtual Corporation*, we hesitated even to use that adjective because it was so little known that we were afraid that we'd be misunderstood. Both our agent and our publisher asked, "What exactly do you mean by 'virtual'? That it isn't real?"

Furthermore, as we were writing the book, even though it was apparent to us that in certain industries—from semiconductor chips to garage doors to customized clothing—clever companies were harnessing the power of computers and networks to create "mass customized" (another new term) products and services and steal market share from their slower-witted and more traditional competitors, there were as yet no complete virtual companies. Only by using these admittedly fragmentary examples and the well-established rate of technological change, were we able to extrapolate forward to the creation of fully "virtualized" corporations.

But how long would this revolution take? Our guess was about a decade, long enough for even the most retrograde company to catch on, even though we warned that in most markets, the first company to go "virtual" would likely dominate, the second in would assume a minor role, and all of the rest of the players would end up also-rans.

Why did we think it would take so long? The main reason was that the current technological infrastructures—especially information networks—of most corporations simply weren't robust enough to handle the job and would likely take years to do so.

Then came the Internet, and that changed everything. Within three years, our ten-year scenario came true, and more. Even Andy Grove, who scoffed at the concept of a virtual corporation in the pages of *Business Week*, was within a matter of months turning Intel into one.

By 1995, just three years after *The Virtual Corporation* was published, any large company that wasn't racing towards e-commerce, employee intranets, and Web-based customer communications was heading for disaster. What we had thought was an early warning proved to be a last-minute alert, and "virtual," the word that had been too obscure in 1992, had become a cliché three years later.

So, as you might imagine, I'm hesitant to make any prediction about how long it will take the world's corporations to adopt a Protean architecture.

What we do know is the forces that will drive companies to become Protean are already in place and well underway, and given that they are demographic, cultural, and anthropological, there is very little chance that they will suddenly disappear. Even more important, *the Protean Corporation doesn't need any more advances, much less revolutions, in technology to occur.*

That is the second and final point I want to make in this opening section. For the transformation of modern business from the virtual to the Protean model, we don't need another ten years of technological evolution or, conversely, just three years after the sudden arrival of some mind-boggling new commercial/consumer communications technology (i.e., super-broadband, universal WiMAX or G4, "3rd Screen" smart phones, etc.). Everything we need to go Protean is here *right now*.

Most companies today, were they to make an audit of their intellectual capital assets, would discover that they already have all of the tools to transform themselves nearly overnight into Protean Corporations. Many will discover they are already, unconsciously, well along the path.

But whether they will have the institutional courage to make the final leap is another matter. The story of the newspaper industry in recent years offers a useful warning: even after the evidence was clear that the industry had to make massive structural changes—from abandoning newsprint to changing its revenue model—few papers had the nerve to do so. Instead, most chose to pursue the traditional response—lay off or retire skilled reporters even when it became obvious that this was *exactly* the wrong thing to do. And by the time the newspaper companies realized their mistake, they had lost the key talent they needed to make the change. They were now trapped in a vicious downward spiral.

We will likely see this same kind of mistake made again and again in the years to come, as enterprises hesitate to abandon the known, no matter how troubled, for the unknown, no matter how promising.

Bizarre as it sounds, transforming an information-based company of today into a Protean Corporation of tomorrow will cost almost nothing. But it will demand something far more costly: a change in attitude.

How long will that take? For some risk-taking readers, it may happen before they reach the end of this book. For others—I will argue, to their deep regret—it may take forever. My hunch is that young companies are more likely to make the jump before the old, smaller before the larger, the entrepreneurial before the bureaucratic.

Most of all, it will be the courageous before the timid.

PART
II

REINVENTING THEMSELVES:
HOW CORPORATIONS EVOLVE

CHAPTER

‹ **3** ›

THE RISE OF THE CORPORATION

TO UNDERSTAND WHY MODERN ENTERPRISES find themselves in this current predicament, with its threat of impending crisis, we need to appreciate how we got here.

To do that, we will follow three threads through time: *organization theory*, *information/communications technology*, and *demographics*. I know this sounds self-evident, and you've probably read most of it a thousand times before. Stay with me—even in the areas you've visited before, I propose to take a whole new trail; and in everything else, I have a few surprises.

THE RISE OF THE CORPORATION

Let's begin with the history of business organizations. This is not an in-depth recounting of the story of corporations, but rather a look at certain key themes—the continuous expansion of employee empowerment, the impact (often dangerously preceding cultural assimilation) of new tools and technologies, and the changing role of management.

Please keep those three themes in mind as we quickly traverse a half-millennium of corporate life.

THE NOTION of a "commercial enterprise," of a true *company*, begins about four hundred years ago. Incredibly, there still exist a handful of companies today—gun-maker Beretta (1492) being the most famous—that actually predate this milestone by a century or more. But even these enterprises were, strictly speaking, confederations of artisans or trading groups for the many years leading up until their transformation into companies.

What we think of as the modern corporation appears at the beginning of the seventeenth century at the confluence of:

<> **Craft guilds,** which pulled together groups of individuals with common skills and set professional standards of work and behavior

<> **Market shops,** which grew from their beginnings as temporary stalls at medieval public markets to become permanent operations catering year-round to a loyal clientele

<> **Trading companies,** which combined high risk and a large upfront investment (often from the monarchy) with the potential for huge

returns, established the venture capital, modern banking, and insurance industries as well as established the first stock markets

<> **Modern cities,** which, having reached a threshold of both population and infrastructure, could now not only support a wide range of specialized skills and services, but also provide sufficient manpower to fill large enterprises

<> **Civil service,** dating back to Rome and the Qin Dynasty of China, which set the model for large organizational structures and hierarchies, were built on (at least in theory) rational decisions based on empirical data, and promoted via merit rather than social connections

The first true company was probably the Dutch East India Company (Vereenigde Oostindische Compagnie), which was founded in 1602 when the government of the Netherlands granted it a twenty-one-year monopoly on trade in the Far East.[1] Before, trading "companies" were mostly brief confederations of investors, who put their money behind a single trading voyage and dissolved the enterprise as soon as the ships returned (or were lost). With the Dutch East India Company, these confederacies were pulled together into a single operation, chartered to continue through voyage after voyage.

Being the pioneer, the Dutch East India Company is credited with many firsts in business history. For example, it was the first company to issues shares of common stock to its investors. It was the first multinational company. And, in copying the Chinese model and establishing a civil service in India, it set the pattern not only for the governments of Europe (especially England) to follow, but the enterprises of those countries as well.[2]

But for all its accomplishments and forward thinking, the Dutch East India Company as an institution was still very much a construct of its era, the Age of Kings. The company minted its own money, engaged in sea battles with competitors, enslaved entire populations to serve as workers, occupied cities—in many other ways, it behaved more like an aggressive, colonial monarchy than a commercial enterprise. At its peak, around 1670, the Dutch East India Company was the wealthiest commercial enterprise the world had ever seen, employing the equivalent of more than 1 million people today, with a fleet, including warships, larger than most maritime nations even now.

But at its worst, the Dutch East India Company was rapacious, brutal, rigid in its enforcement of power and hierarchy, and financially suspect. And, unfortunately, it was this dark side that would be imitated by other investor-driven "companies" over the next century, notably England's utterly despicable South Sea Company, which managed to combine slave trading with a financial pyramid scheme that, when the bubble it created burst, nearly bankrupted Britain.

But other forces were already at work to mitigate these darker forces and to create what we consider to be the modern corporation.

First and foremost was the rule of law. By the mid-eighteenth century and the Enlightenment, the divine right of kings was being increasingly superseded by the growing power of legislatures—first in England, then America, and by the end of the century, in France. The power of kings and queens to arbitrarily give away vast tracts of land and market monopolies to anyone who struck their fancy was severely constrained. And after disasters like the South Sea Bubble, legislatures too became wary of awarding monopolies.

This shift toward the rule of law was given an added impetus by the writings of Adam Smith and economic philosophers who recognized the positive power of unfettered market capitalism. After Smith's *The Wealth of Nations*, it became obvious to any thoughtful ruler that the surest path to economic health was to create a competitive environment that maximized fair competition and legally punished those who attempted to subvert it. While all of this was going on, other factors were at work as well. Most famous, of course, was the Industrial Revolution, which began in England in 1760, reached the United States by 1790, and spread across Europe during the first decades of the new century. It is still just now reaching many of the most impoverished corners of the world.

The causes for the Industrial Revolution were numerous and continue to be much debated. But certain factors rise above the rest:

<> *A combination of external forces,* including the collapse of feudalism, improved medicine, more efficient agriculture, and a rising standard of living creating a bigger, healthier, and more mobile population

<> *A more systematic application of the scientific method,* resulting in breakthroughs in applied science and engineering (especially iron and steel production)

<> *New energy sources,* notably water wheels and Watt's steam engine, being used to power machinery, such as the Jacquard loom

<> *More trustworthy systems and institutions* for managing both financial and intellectual capital (most notably, patent law)

All of this took a while to get underway, but once it did, the results were astonishing, as sweeping in their influence as anything since the agricultural revolution five thousand years earlier. Life expectancies, which hadn't changed much since the Roman Empire, suddenly jumped, and have continued to climb ever since, thanks to improved medicine, sanitation, and lower infant mortality rates. Per capita wealth, which had also been largely unchanged for millennia, suddenly skyrocketed ten-fold, even hundred-fold in those countries that had become industrialized. Meanwhile, no preindustrialized nation would ever again win another war on the battle-field, so complete was the transformation of armies and weapons.

During the next century, a majority of populations of these industrialized countries, all of whom had worked on farms since time immemorial, packed up and moved into cities and towns in pursuit of work, and were met by factory owners searching for just such pools of talent. Not only did this transform the nature of work itself—from the seasonality and high risk of farming to the predictability and wages of the factory—but it also brought considerable pressure to bear on such ancient institutions as the church and the family. In the case of the family, the move to the city brought pressure upon the extended multigenerational clan, which all but disappeared, but at the same time, thanks to predictable hours, local resources, and the simple fact that most children now lived to adulthood—it also reinforced the centrality of the nuclear family.

The Industrial Revolution, because it essentially threw out all of the rules, opened the door for a reappraisal of man's relationship to God, to nature, and to other human beings. It's not surprising that this same era saw the rise of "people's" revolutions (usually accompanied by the end of the monarchy) in America, France, Japan, Italy, and later, as they became industrialized, China and Russia. It also saw the rise of a new aesthetics, Romanticism, which stressed the individual's encounter with nature.

But the greatest change brought by the Industrial Revolution was on scientific enquiry and application. What had been, since the Middle Ages, a largely academic and idiosyncratic endeavor now became organized into societies and laboratories, tackled by teams of scientists, and disseminated through journals. The result was a systematic and empirical attack on the great unknowns of the natural world, and that produced the greatest explosion of new discoveries and inventions in human history.

THE GREAT REVOLUTION—*THE ENGLISH SYSTEM*

In 1988, Harvard Business School professor Ramchadran Jaikumar wrote a celebrated paper centered around the story of Beretta, which he rightly recognized as one of the few companies in the world that had been around long enough to have evolved through *every* stage of manufacturing, from craftsman's guild to computer-aided design and assembly.[3]

Jaikumar's most important insight was that what counted in the story of Beretta (and by extension, every other successful manufacturer) was not how the tools had changed, but how the people using them had.

Jaikumar divided the Beretta story into six epochs of change. The first, not surprisingly, was the Industrial Revolution, which arrived late (about 1800) after three centuries of craft work.[4]

For Jaikumar, those three centuries of production at Beretta were centered on the *product*, the guns themselves. The master craftsmen at Beretta used all sorts of jigs and files and other traditional tools to build the single type of gun that was their specialty. They built to an ideal of that gun, and they brought every bit of skill they had to making that gun perfect, the components custom-fitted to each other, the rifle custom-fitted to the owner. And a craftsman would spend a lifetime perfecting that skill at making that particular type of weapon.

The Industrial Revolution, what Jaikumar called *"The English System,"* changed all that.[5] The press of giant armies forming all over Europe in the face of the threat from Napoleon created a gigantic demand for arms that could not be answered by slow, carefully made, one-off guns.

The British factory system offered the answer to large-scale production. What is important for our purposes is to recognize, as Jaikumar did, that this was not simply a matter of buying the new tooling, water wheels, power belts, and gears, but a fundamental change in *attitude*.

In the English System, all activity centered around the *tools*: lathes, grinders, borers, drills, etc. Workers were no longer expected to learn a "craft," but a "skill"—such as operating a lathe—and expected to be able to regularly apply that skill to a new task.

The English System changed the world forever, making Britain, militarily and economically, the most powerful nation the world had seen since the Roman Empire.

But the English System brought with it its own set of internal contradictions that ultimately would require its replacement by a new organizational scheme that answered those questions, a pattern that we will see again and again. In the case of the English System, the new emphasis upon tools, radical as it was (indeed, it set the ground for the invention of mass production), also began the process of specialization of work . . . something for which late eighteenth-century society was ill-prepared.

Structurally, England and the other countries adopting its manufacturing scheme were still essentially feudal societies. Though the serfs were now free members of the working class, and a sizable middle class had formed, this was still very much a socially stratified world, with a rich and powerful aristocracy, a handful of entrepreneurs in the middle bucking the ingrained anticapitalist culture, and a vast body of workers, many of them slaves with little education and increasingly obsolete skills.

The obvious solution was to put these workers into large factories, make them subordinate to the tools they served, and then apply the only real management system anybody knew: the feudal estate, with its large population of laborers, watched by the factory equivalent of the old traditional farm overseer, with the owner largely detached from the process. Moreover, despite the existence of a robust stock exchange system, most of these enterprises were privately owned by one rich individual or a small consortium.

Thanks to writers like Charles Dickens, we have a vivid, if exaggerated, idea of the result. One should be wary of taking the contemporary descriptions of workhouses and exploitative and dangerous factories too literally; those millions who migrated from the countryside to the cities and mill towns certainly thought this work an improvement over the grinding poverty and hopelessness of farm life. Still, there is more than enough evidence that many of these horror stories were true (and it should be noted, the resulting prosperity allowed for the mobilization of individuals to fight these social ills). By making the machinery the centerpiece of the English System, it placed everything else, including people, in a subordinate role to those tools.

Worse—and this is what Karl Marx identified—it created a vast gulf between those who owned the machines and those who served them.

O BRAVE NEW WORLD—*THE AMERICAN SYSTEM*

What Marx missed was that a new organizational system was already replacing the English System and it was taking place in the United States.

For all its commonalities with the mother country, the United States was still a very different country. Compared to England, it was long on resources and short on population. It was also less socially stratified, with no monarch and no nobility. A nation built by shopkeepers, it was far more welcoming to both capitalism and entrepreneurs. And though it had its own underclass problems—a large population of slaves—that "peculiar institution" was localized to the South, which as a result would lag in industrialization for nearly a century. By comparison, the North-east was ready to (illegally) copy the British and build its factories and mills, using the vast West to supply it with raw materials.

All these factors, combined with a culture of risk-taking, all but unmatched anywhere else on earth, propelled the United States toward not only adopting the English System, but moving beyond it, toward a radically new organizational scheme of its own. Jaikumar called it the *American System*.[6] And, interesting, it was already being born just as England was perfecting its predecessor (We shall see that kind of overlapping corporate eras again.)

As befit a society with a seemingly infinite supply of resources, a shortage of labor, and "borrowed" tools of proven effectiveness, the American System placed greater emphasis (and thus respect) on its workers, and in the process shifted focus away from tools to *process* and, in particular, what combination of design, materials, tooling, and labor produces the most efficient and profitable result.

Appropriately, the first person to tackle this problem was the great American inventor/entrepreneur Eli Whitney (whose cotton gin would ironically make farming with slaves so profitable that the South would have little interest in adopting his system). In 1798, Whitney was given a huge contract to produce rifles for the U.S. Army. Wanting to increase his efficiencies, and thus his profits, Whitney took the English System as his starting point and then began to modify it for his unique needs.

In particular, Whitney made two important decisions. The first was to reduce the number of actual models being manufactured from essentially infinite (craft manufacturing) or dozens (the English System) to just three. By doing that, Whitney could now focus upon the actual manufacturing process, the combination of materials, tools, and labor to produce those designs. By recasting the problem in this way, Whitney could see that the best solution was to standardize the individual parts of those rifles. Thus the tools (and the workers) now became subordinate to the *interchangeability* of the components of the finished product.

What must have seemed like a subtle shift in perspective at the time (as the Protean Corporation does now) had an extraordinary impact on the century that followed. By creating a scheme by which components could be standardized, those components could now be manufactured almost anywhere to spec, without the need to be nearby and custom-fitted into the final product. Thus, where the English System had been a centralizing program, bringing people in from the countryside to work at a single, central factory or mill, the American System began a process of decentralization that has continued in business organization ever since.

This decentralization was further supported by the growing transportation network—railroads, canals, and roads—that was built between the major cities of the United States and out to reach the settlers opening up the West. By the mid-nineteenth century, this infrastructure was sufficiently advanced to allow component- and finished-manufacturing to take place almost anywhere in America, including California, and still reach consumers almost anywhere else at a competitive price. This opened the door for clever consumer products companies—the most famous being Sears, Roebuck—to begin offering their goods through surrogate "stores" such as flyers and catalogs and in the process, inventing modern marketing.

Another key attribute of the American System was *scalability*. "Interchangeable" meant that, in theory and often in practice, you could geographically disperse component production, contract it out to manufacturers to focus on your core competencies, and use multiple locations for final assembly. And this, in turn, meant you could grow fast and grow bigger than any manufacturing company of the past. The two crucial ingredients were capital (now available through a new financial infrastructure) and people (which, combined with the vast open spaces in the West, was the reason America absorbed most of the world's immigrants for the next century).

Not surprisingly, the impact of this new business model ultimately transformed society as well. The English System made its beneficiaries more prosperous, more urban, and more healthy. The American System filled their world with inexpensive goods, from housewares to clothing to medicine to food (this is the point at which hunger begins to disappear in the industrializing world). The members of Jane Austen's middle-class family, the Bennets, wear inexpensive, high-quality cotton and wool clothing (instead of homespun) and live in a house filled with furniture (instead of a single expensive piece).

A quarter-century later, thanks to the general adoption of the American System, not only had these goods become so cheap they could be bought in abundance by everyday working folks, but the growing precision of the mass production work, combined with the need for greater communication within a decentralized economy, had led to a recognition of the need for higher levels of literacy and universal, compulsory education. Thus, even in the small Mississippi River town of Hannibal, Missouri, Tom Sawyer is made to attend school by his Aunt Polly.

By mid-century, the American System had not only spread throughout the United States, but to Europe—and especially back to England. The principles of interchangeable-part mass production were now being adopted in almost every place they were implemented. And nowhere was the American System more powerfully used than in the business where it started: munitions.

At the start of the Civil War, the South had better generals, better soldiers, and the natural advantage of defense. But the North had the factories, and because of them, the population (largely immigrants) and the transportation infrastructure. And though Lee and his generals won almost every battle, they were eventually overwhelmed by a system that could produce, in the matter of three years, millions of rifles and cartridges, uniforms, cannons, blankets, tents, and food rations, and could transport them hundreds of miles in a matter of days.

BIG IRON—*THE INDUSTRIAL ERA*

If the American Civil War was the high point of the American System, it was also the beginning of its end.

The era after the war, which coincided with high Victorianism in England, the coalescence of modern Germany under Bismarck, the Meiji Restoration in Japan, and the Second Empire in France, was a time of great prosperity and commercial growth. Each of these nations, to one degree or another, had adopted the American System, and they now had the workforce, the capital, and the technology to make the next great organizational leap.

Jaikamur, because he focused solely on manufacturing, didn't give this era a name; but taking our cue from cultural historians, we can call this the *Industrial Era*. This was the age of great factories, giant machinery, and an explosion of new inventions that exceeded even the Renaissance. And thanks to photography and engravings in publications like *Harper's Weekly*, it also created the archetypal images of Work, Labor, and Capitalism that survive to this day.

The kick-off event of the Industrial Era was, it is generally agreed, the Crystal Palace Exhibition in London in 1851. Tens of thousands of British visitors, including Queen Victoria herself, walked through the spectacular glass and steel main Exhibition Hall and gawked at the latest ceramics, tools, housewares, farm machinery, hydraulic presses, diving suits, and every other magical creation of the new world of mass production and applied technology.

The idea of Progress, that philosophy of continuous change and improvement into the indefinite future that defines our own time, first took hold during this era. This new expectation—created by the Industrial Revolution—now turned around and profoundly affected the business world. From now on, almost every company would have to perpetually innovate or die.

Three factors created the Industrial Era:

1 > An **expectation** of markets for an endless stream of products that were ever-cheaper, ever-improved, and ever-available

2 > The **systemization** of the research laboratory and the acceleration of the application of new technologies

3 > An ever more **sophisticated** infrastructure that now included steamships, telegraphs, and transcontinental railroads

Put together, these factors enabled business owners to contemplate leaps in production literally in orders of magnitude. Where before they had looked at production in the thousands of units for regional markets, they now contemplated millions of units to be sold around the world.

The zenith of this new era—the single most emblematic industrial event of the nineteenth century—was the Philadelphia Centennial Exhibition of 1876.[7]

Its official name, International Exhibition of Arts, Manufactures and Products of the Soil and Mine, was a clue to the wonders visitors met inside. More than two hundred buildings, surrounded by a three-mile fence, offered the best of not only American, but also international industry, agriculture, science, and design. Each state had its own hall, as did most of the world's nations. The centerpiece was the Machinery Hall, with its two thirty-foot-tall Corliss Steam Engines powering the rest of the Exhibition, vivid emblems of the new power of industry. Fittingly, under those great machines, Alexander Graham Bell would demonstrate the telephone, and Remington the first typewriter—two vital new tools that would once again transform the business world.

The heart of the Industrial Age was *control*: control of markets in the form of monopolies, control of production through verticalization from raw materials to finished goods, and control of operations, especially of labor. All of this served the driving force of *consistency*. The jump from thousands to millions of units, from hundreds to thousands of employees, and from millions to billions in capitalization, demanded the creation of organizations that were as scalable as the mass-production manufacturing operations they supported.

Quality had always been a competitive factor in manufacturing, but now it took on much greater importance. To produce at the rate required by the new marketplace, there could not be breakdowns or bottlenecks in the process. And that meant that the manufacturing process itself had to be studied, streamlined, and improved. By the same token, other operations in the organization—finance, legal, sales, research—had to be expanded and increasingly filled with specialists. The result was the rise of the *administration* of large corporations, a job until then mostly handled by bookkeepers and clerks.

What is often lost in the histories of this era is the fact that Industrial Era companies now began the crucial task of *systematizing* every aspect of their operations, in their obsessive pursuit of the consistency they needed in order to make the huge leap in quality and performance being demanded by consumers. Farmers, from the Great Plains to the Yorkshire Dales to the Pampas to the Ukraine, saw improvements in their quality of life because demand was now more predictable, payment more assured. Skilled workers and professionals such as attorneys and accountants now had a portable portfolio of skills that could be taken from employer to employer and sold to the highest bidder. Workers had precise records of their work schedules and steady paychecks.

When that systematization, combined with strong patent laws and a hungry market, reached the research laboratory, the result was an efflorescence of practical new inventions—from Bell's telephone to Edison's incandescent lightbulb to the Daimler Brothers' automobile. Goods were now being produced in such abundance and at such low prices, and new inventions were being mainstreamed so fast and furiously, that companies were now perpetually challenged to find new markets and to reeducate the ones they had—driving the new professions of sales (traveling salesmen) and marketing (billboards and catalogs).

But there was a dark side to all of this, and once again the seeds of a new organizational era were already being planted. The biggest problem was the stratification of society, a holdover from the feudal age. The serf no longer toiled for the nobleman, the slave for the master, but that ancient division between the worker and the overseer, and the laborer and owner, was still largely in effect.

The difference in the Industrial Era was one of degree: the good news was that the successful entrepreneur and businessperson had all but replaced the landed gentry; not only was there greater turnover among the wealthy from generation to generation, but more important, there was now a chance, albeit minuscule, for almost *anyone* to become successful, powerful, and rich in the course of a single lifetime.

The bad news was that the division between rich and poor, owner and worker—or to use Marx's powerful terminology, Capital and Labor—was stronger than ever, and reinforced by the educational system, inheritance laws, the lack of income tax, and even science in the form of Social Darwinism. Workers were workers; they had no stake in the enterprise for which they labored, but only drew wages for their efforts.

In other words, society was once again trailing innovation in business and technology, and the generation-long gap began to create considerable unrest. In Europe it led to mass movements, labor strife and strikes, and even revolution. Socialists, communists, anarchists, and members of other mass movements took to the streets, mobilizing workers, demanding workplace improvements, and manifesting an absolutism, itself a product of the age, that plotted to tear down existing governments and replace them with more "scientific" solutions.

In the United States, the defining moment of this backlash was the Homestead Steel Strike of 1892.[8]

Though there had been other major strikes in U.S. history, notably the Great Railroad Strike of 1877, none had ever been this organized—showing a growing self-awareness of workers of their changing position in society and their role inside the modern corporation. The Homestead strike was also notable for its violence: as many as a dozen men were killed. It would take eight thousand armed state militia members to finally quell the violence.

The Homestead strike was a turning point in labor/management relations in the United States. For workers it became a rallying cry, a powerful tool for labor organizers, and the very embodiment of the worst image of cold, manipulative bosses and tycoons.

Homestead had immense implications. Though the strike failed to organize the mill, it succeeded in galvanizing the labor movement in the United States and, ultimately, through union leaders and radical activists such as Emma Goldman, in Europe and Russia as well. The message of Homestead was not just that workers were not disposable; that had been the message of a century filled with labor strikes. Rather, the lesson of Homestead was that workers were now active participants in the operations of the company, that for the first time, they were *stakeholders*, capable of organizing themselves without bosses and overseers to fight the owners and actually defeat them.

Homestead's owners, Henry Clay Frick and Andrew Carnegie, were not evil, but they made the deadly mistake of not keeping up with the changing zeitgeist. They were men of their time, but the times were changing, and they became forever the symbols of that change.

The business leaders of the Industrial Age were now on notice that they would have to learn to understand, manage, and ultimately make the most effective use of this new generation of better educated, more prosperous, and more empowered workers.

What was needed now was the application of the same empirical tools to the management of people, not just equipment; and what was required was a new process to take advantage of the intellectual capital of workers, not just their muscle power.

A PERFECT WORLD–*SCIENTIFIC MANAGEMENT*

The watershed event in the United States of this new *Era of Scientific Management* was, once again, a World's Fair, this time the 1904 Louisiana Purchase Exposition, better known as the St. Louis World's Fair.[9]

Unlike the Philadelphia fair, the heart of the St. Louis fair wasn't industrial might and emerging technologies, but the greatest concentration of new consumer products ever gathered, including (just in food) the hamburger, hot dog, ice cream cone, ice cream sundae, corn dog, Dr Pepper, peanut butter, iced tea, and cotton candy. All were either introduced or first popularized at the Fair. The idyllic modern life presented at the Fair was so enticing that the Fair itself would become for future generations a symbol for American life at its best.

That image of the genteel life, so different from the rough, dangerous reality of the frontier or the greedy factory world of the Gilded Age, had enormous appeal to the vast new middle class—literate, enjoying more leisure time, and with more disposable income—that had emerged as beneficiaries of the Industrial Era. Combined with mass advertising, catalog purchasing, and improved distribution systems (that were about to take yet another quantum leap with the arrival of the automobile, airplane, and radio), this new desire created the modern consumer economy.

The Homestead strike of a dozen years earlier had been a warning that the old model was obsolete. Now, to that stick had been added the carrot of huge new consumer markets created in large part by educating, empowering, and rewarding workers for their different individual efforts.

The best known industrialist of this era was Henry Ford, who applied the lessons of interchangeable-part mass production to previously unimaginable levels. As already noted, the idea of interchangeable components was as old as Eli Whitney, and large-scale production had been going on at this point for nearly a century. What Ford did was to synthesize the two for application in an exciting new invention—the automobile—a move whose complexity until then had been found in only sophisticated industrial products such as locomotives. Brilliantly using applied engineering to both simplify and accelerate the manufacturing and assembly process, Ford was then able to deliver these complex products—or more accurately, one product: the black Ford Model T—to the emerging consumer class at an astonishingly low price.

By accomplishing this, Ford justly became the most powerful industrialist of the new century. But the individual most closely associated with this era, for good or ill, was a mechanical engineer and professor named Fredrick Winslow Taylor.[10]

Taylor, like many brilliant young students of business, recognized the structural flaws in the industrial model and set out to fix them. Taylor's genius lay in his realization that businesses of his era had *two* basic weaknesses. At the factory level, while workers were becoming increasingly specialized at doing sophisticated work, the process by which they learned these skills—usually by word of mouth or hands-on instruction from veterans—was uneven, inefficient, and little changed from the old guild system. Meanwhile, the newly emerging profession of management was undisciplined, subjective, and anecdotal, more of an art than a science.

Taylor decided to attack both problems at once, believing that they were mutually dependent. And if he could solve them, corporations would not only be able to vastly increase their output, but internally they would find a new equilibrium in which management and labor would work in harmony toward a common goal; consequently, the need for unions would disappear.

At the management level, Taylor believed the solution lay in converting management from an erratic art form into a rigorous academic discipline, one in which both past practices and new ideas could be tested in the crucible of scientifically observed field tests, best practices could be collected, analyzed, and disseminated, and management itself could become a true, self-regulating profession. In many ways, this was Taylor's most important contribution, and every modern MBA might be considered his direct descendant.

But it is for the other half of the problem, and Taylor's singular solution, that he is most (in)famous. If for Taylor the key to improving the quality of management was professionalism, the key to improving the productivity of workers was *efficiency*. Taylor believed that there was "One Best Way" for any task, and set out to find it.[11]

For history, the defining image of this new so-called "Taylorism" is the time-motion study film. Taylor and his followers used these films to deconstruct the nature of factory work, identifying and stripping away superfluous steps and inefficient actions. In his most celebrated application of this technique, Taylor determined that the most efficient shovel load for a human being was 21.5 lbs, yet workers in different factories were using basically the same shovel for a wide range of materials of different weights. So, Taylor designed different shovels for different materials, all sized and shaped to carry the proper weight.

At its most obsessive, Taylor's time-motion studies broke tasks down to less than a second per step, to the point where he and his adherents could determine how a worker should best place his feet, how far his arm should move on a task, and how much he should turn to pick up the next component. And it worked: at progressive companies like Ford, workers achieve unprecedented levels of efficiency and productivity.

Ultimately, Taylorism came down to four tenets:

1 ≫ **Replace** rule-of-thumb methods with scientifically proven practices.

2 ≫ **Systematically train** workers in their task, rather than leaving them to learn on their own.

3 > **Provide** workers with detailed instruction and supervision in the performance of their task.

4 > **Divide** the work equally between managers (who would scientifically plan the work) and workers (who would perform the task).

There was one other rule that Taylor also believed: that increased employee pay and reduced work hours should be commensurate with their productivity. Tellingly, this last factor was the one that most companies largely observed in the breach. So too was the fact that in almost every place—from Bethlehem Steel to the American Society of Mechanical Engineers—where Taylor personally implemented his theory, the result was usually internal dissension followed by Taylor being fired. And while other companies did successfully implement the Taylor Plan, often to great competitive advantage, these new systems not only didn't quell labor strife, it they actually seemed to exacerbate it.

A clue to why labor hated Taylorism can be found in a quote from Taylor himself, who notoriously told Congress that the worker who is "physically able to handle pig iron and is sufficiently phlegmatic and stupid to choose this for his occupation is rarely able to comprehend the science of handling pig iron." (The reason Taylor had been called before Congress was because his system was being blamed for having precipitated a strike at the Watertown Arsenal.)[12]

Taylor had made the most common error of scientists and technologists: he had treated human beings as just one more component in the production process. So had his predecessors, but at least the bosses of the Industrial Era had allowed workers their own culture and social hierarchy of apprentice, journeyman, and master. In many ways, Taylor had improved the lot of most workers; he'd given the better educated and more talented a shot a professional positions, and for the everyday worker life on the job was much cleaner, safer, and fairer than ever before. But the cost to these workers had been their individuality, and for most of them, that cost was too high.

Taylor had bucked the already-centuries-long path of greater employee liberty and empowerment, and history would never forgive him.

In his *USA* trilogy, John dos Passos branded Taylor forever as the demonic figure "who couldn't see an idle lathe or an idle man. . . . Production went to his head and thrilled his sleepless nerves like liquor or women on a Saturday night."[13] Taylor's reputation has never fully recovered.

DIVIDE AND CONQUER–*PROGRESSIVISM*

In retrospect it's apparent that Taylor was very much a product of his era.

The early years of the twentieth century were a time of extraordinary scientific achievement. Rutherford was modeling the atom, Einstein was developing his special theory of relativity, Mendel's work on genetics was rediscovered and tested, chemists were inventing one hydrocarbon plastic after another, and Freud was plumbing the human brain—not to mention the explosion of new inventions, from the automobile to vacuum tube to radio.

It's not surprising then that clever people in almost every field began looking for a "third way" that escaped both the rigidity and fear of innovation that characterized conservatism and the anarchistic and anticapitalist philosophy of contemporary liberalism—a different path that used the clear-minded, objective techniques of the scientific method to rise above the petty and political to achieve real, measurable progress in the quality of human existence.

This new political philosophy came to be called "Progressivism" and it quickly resonated with forward thinkers around the world, and continued to do so for nearly fifty years. In politics, it became the watchword of the presidency of Theodore Roosevelt and his Fair Deal, and continued through the beginning of the administration of his cousin, Franklin Roosevelt, thirty years later. It resurfaced one last time, in an evolved form, a quarter-century later in John Kennedy's New Frontier and Lyndon Johnson's Great Society.

Progressivism was, in many crucial ways, Taylorism writ across society as a whole.[14] Like Taylorism, Progressivism believed that there was one best solution to every social problem, which could be discovered and fixed with the careful and objective application of scientific tools. It also held, though didn't always publicly state, that working people were largely incapable of making the best decisions for themselves and needed the help of experts to make the best choices.

Not surprisingly, Progressives were also believers (at first, then later during the New Deal) in centralized planning, be it in Washington or at corporate headquarters. And if Progressives believed in free-market capitalism, they also weren't afraid to constrain it with a host of new regulations, often spurred by a burst of newspaper investigative stories by the new "muckrakers."

After the dark days of the late Industrial Era, Progressivism came as a breath of fresh air. And its victories are still celebrated today: child labor laws, worker safety, minimum wage, income tax, anti-trust laws, conservation and national parks, and woman suffrage are among the most famous of its achievements.

To this list can be added, despite its manifold flaws, Taylorism. Taylor may have made the fatal mistake of forgetting human nature in his model, but he did bring systematic scientific thinking to the world of business, and in the process set off a virtuous cycle that would eventually rectify his error. In the end, efficiency did make work safer, fairer, and more rewarding for the average person. And at the management level, it kicked off a true revolution. It was the Progressives who dubbed it *"Scientific Management."*

Progressivism, combined with the rise of an educated consumer market, and the invention of fast new transportation and distribution systems, produced a brief golden age in the Western World—one that would die in the mud of Passchendale and on the barbed wire of the Somme.

World War I remains perhaps the most horrifying example of technology outstripping social evolution. Millions of soldiers, armed with machine guns, airplanes, artillery, tanks, and poison gas, faced each other along the Western Front in an endless and bloody stalemate. Yet when soldiers climbed out of the trenches and raced across no-man's land, their wire radio communications with headquarters were usually severed in a matter of seconds, leaving them on their own—resulting in the deaths of hundreds of thousands of soldiers who were sent out to support attacks that had already failed. In other words, a twentieth-century war was fought largely with a nineteenth-century command and control system, and the result still haunts us to this day.

Progressivism survived the Great War, but with most of its optimism and confidence gone. By now, too many of its internal contradictions were becoming apparent. Workers, furious at the dehumanization of Taylorism, were joining unions and going on strike, and worse. The May Day parade in 1919 in Cleveland turned into a riot that left two dead, forty injured, and 116 arrested.[15] The darkest moment came on September 16, 1920, when a bomb, probably placed by anarchists, went off in the middle of a lunchtime crowd on Wall Street. Thirty-eight people were killed, four hundred injured.[16]

Scientific Management wasn't doing much better. Not only did the labor unrest destroy Taylor's illusion that great efficiency would obviate the need for unions, it was becoming obvious to almost everyone that it was actually provoking them. Just as disappointing was the fact that people were turning out to be just too frustratingly unpredictable and quirky to fit into any empirical model. And in the minds of a growing number of these "experts," there grew the gnawing fear that perhaps there *wasn't* one best way, or if there was, there was no way to find it.

Managers weren't the only people heading toward this realization. At the cosmological level, Einstein's new General Theory of Relativity was positing a universe that seemed inexplicable. Planck was suggesting the same thing was true at the atomic level. And though some of the smartest minds in the world were at Vienna University—the so-called "Vienna Circle"—working to explain the natural world entirely in empirical terms and using logical analysis ("logical positivism"), they weren't making much headway. They soon would run aground on the rocky shoals of the Heisenberg Uncertainty Principle.[17]

The world wasn't proving to be as predictable as people had hoped, a fact well known to business executives trying to make their way through the minefield of business life in the economic recession immediately following the Armistice.

A FAILURE OF CERTAINTY—*THE CORPORATE ERA*

One of these harried businessmen was William "Billy" Durant. Though born a blue blood (his grandfather had been governor of Michigan), Durant dropped out of high school and found his true love in building carriages and wagons. By 1904 he had made such a name for himself that he was asked to become the general manager of young horseless carriage company, Buick. A classic maverick entrepreneur, within four years he had grown Buick to the point where he could sell stock in the firm, found a new holding company—which he called General Motors—then turn around and in quick order buy the Oakland (later Pontiac) and Cadillac motor companies.

But he moved too fast, and by 1910 Durant was seriously overextended with the banks and facing bankruptcy, and he was forced out by the board of directors.

But Durant was one of those extraordinary and slightly crazy entrepreneurs that had always and would continue to characterize every hot new industry in America (and as we will see, America itself in the twenty-first century). A year after he went bust, Durant turned around and formed a partnership with another automobile start-up, Chevrolet. Within a couple years Durant had a falling out with the founder, Louis Chevrolet, so he bought him out, keeping the original company name.

Chevrolet made Durant rich, rich enough to buy sufficient stock to regain controlling interest in General Motors, of which he again became president in 1916, pulling Chevrolet into GM a year later.

Through all of these machinations, Durant never wavered from his original vision: what we call today a multibrand (or multiplatform) holding company offering a range of products (in this case automobiles) across the full spectrum of price and customer desires. It was a brilliant, even historic, vision, but in trying to execute it, Durant, propelled by his eccentric style, ran smack into the other contradiction of Progressivism.

A central tenet of Taylorism was that in light of the One Best Way and the objective nature of scientific management, decision making inside an organization needed to be top-down and centralized. The Progressives took this notion a big step further by arguing that government itself should exhibit a similar centralized decision making, determining what was best for the population (wages, wealth, behavior) and enforce those measures with punitive regulations. Offering evidence in support of this notion were the reported miracles taking place in the controlled economy of the new Soviet Union under Lenin and the Bolsheviks.

But Durant and the talented men who surrounded him at the top of GM were quickly discovering the problems with vertical organizations and top-down command. As one of the first great holding companies, General Motors was proving just too complicated to run strictly from headquarters. The company would have found this out in time anyway, but the pace to disaster was quickened by the mercurial nature of Durant himself.[18]

A salesman by nature, and a born speculator, Durant kept his vice presidents cooling their heels on important decisions while he pitched customers or bought and sold stock using one of the dozen telephones reportedly on his desk. Conversely, at other times, Durant seemed to make snap judgments on crucial matters—such as the location of the new GM headquarters, which would determine the future of Detroit—with almost no information and as casually, one historian would write, as if he was buying paper clips.

It didn't work, as it hasn't for generations of pure entrepreneurs ever since. One senior executive, Walter Chrysler, couldn't take it anymore and walked out to create a powerful new competitor. Meanwhile, General Motors swung back and forth from prosperity to near disaster, building up debt again with new acquisitions—and again and again being pulled back from bankruptcy by some brilliant stock market speculation by Durant using company money.

This crapshoot couldn't go on forever. In 1920, GM chairman and leading shareholder Pierre du Pont couldn't take Durant's erratic behavior any longer and fired him, made himself president of General Motors, and set out to find his own replacement.

He found him in the next office. Alfred P. Sloan had been vice president of operations for GM. Du Pont made him first his chief assistant, and then, in 1923, appointed Sloan as GM president and chairman of the executive committee. It was a brilliant move, as Alfred Sloan would prove to be perhaps the most influential businessman of the twentieth century. Sloan would be the presiding figure over the *Corporate Era*, and his most powerful tool would be *decentralization*.

Once in power, Sloan moved quickly to restructure General Motors along the lines of a business philosophy he had been privately pondering for years. In 1920, not long after Durant's departure, Sloan presented his "Organization Study" to du Pont.

According to Sloan biographer Allyn Freeman, the study's radical plan for a new business model for GM included the following precepts:[19]

<> Facts and data are the main and only determinants of decision making.

<> The company should encourage dissent and differences of opinion.

<> Organize via committees a decentralized system with centralized power and control.

<> Staff the most competent people without thought to friendship.

<> The president or CEO acts as the absolute ruler through consensus.

To this, according to Freeman, Sloan also set down four strategies for GM's future success:[20]

1 > *Offer* wide customer choices.

2 > *Promote* a positive corporate image through institutional advertising and public relations.

3 > *Realize* the need for international sales and marketing through overseas manufacturing or export.

4 > **Find** ancillary businesses beyond the corporation's core product or service.

If all of this seems self-evident, it is only because business has spent the last nine decades thoroughly assimilating every one of these rules. But in the autocratic, crony-driven, and fiat-directed world of business in 1920, Sloan's ideas were radical indeed.

What we can see now that wasn't evident to most observers at the time is that Sloan's seemingly diverse ideas actually dovetailed together with a marvelous logical consistency. For example, if you began, as Sloan did, with the belief that a company as big and unwieldy as General Motors must begin to decentralize its operations, several secondary truths became clear.

First, such a decentralization would inevitably lead to conflict and competition between the individual divisions, forcing them to scheme for the limited resources and attention of headquarters. Sloan realized that if this wasn't going to turn into a charm campaign by divisional courtiers, all executive decisions would have to be made purely on "facts and data."

By the same token, the nature of decentralization—combined with the sheer size of the company—meant that headquarters would depend on the divisions to provide it with the information needed to make key decisions. But could those divisions be trusted to provide information that didn't reflect upon them positively? Just as important, wouldn't they naturally want to present to headquarters a united front on every decision they made, acting as if every new plan had unanimous support?

Sloan was a pragmatist and a synthesizer, not a theoretician or an absolutist. And his greatest skill as an executive may have been his ability to understand people. On top of that, he had learned the biggest business lesson of the previous decade, which was that there was no One Best Way. At most, there was one path that might stand out above the others as having the greatest chance of success, and the only way to see that was to know the best also-ran ideas as well.

All of this came together in Sloan's enshrinement of dissent as central tenet in his philosophy. By this, Sloan didn't mean protest against General Motors itself—as we'll see, he wasn't as good at handling that—but rather, the free and open competition among ideas themselves. Sloan even showed how this was done: In 1920, when he was still VP of Operations, Sloan learned that President du Pont was planning on shutting down poorly performing Chevrolet. Sloan quickly requested a meeting with his boss, and then made a well-researched presentation arguing that Chevrolet's problems were a matter of execution, not the lack of a market. Du Pont relented, and Sloan thus saved the single most successful automobile marque of the twentieth century. Remarkably, given the era, Sloan also kept his job despite his insubordination.[21]

Under Sloan, General Motors was that anecdote writ large over the entire company. Managers were encouraged to present opposing views without consequence to their careers. In the most famous case, Sloan allowed a junior engineer named Nicholas Dreystadt to go before the general manager and argue for the survival of the troubled Cadillac division.

Dreystadt won his argument (which was to market to professional class African Americans), but the single most famous moment dealt with the topic of the young engineer's own career:

> One of the directors said, "Mr. Dreystadt, you realize, don't you sir, that if you fail there won't be a job for you at GM?"
>
> "Of course I do, sir," Dreystadt replied.
>
> But then Sloan stepped in. "But I *don't*," he announced. "If you fail, Mr. Dreystadt, there isn't going to be a job for you at Cadillac. There won't be Cadillac, but as long as there is a GM, and as long as I run it, there'll always be a job for a man who takes responsibility, who takes initiative, who has courage and imagination. *You* worry about the future of Cadillac. Your future at Cadillac is *my* worry."[22]

Dreystadt's strategy paid off handsomely for General Motors. But something even more remarkable had taken place in that board meeting: Alfred Sloan, the CEO of one of the world's biggest corporations, had not only allowed a junior manager to aggressively challenge his seniors all of the way up to the board of directors, but even more incredibly, had guaranteed to protect that young man's job *even if he failed*.

It was such an incredible break from the usual style of corporate management up to that moment that another young man, this one an academic turned consultant, would use this story as a case study in his vision of new type of enlightened manager. This was Peter Drucker, and he would become the most influential business theorist of the century.

By enshrining "dissent," Sloan greatly improved the likelihood that top management, now further removed from the daily activities of the company, would have access to accurate and complete information about company operations.

Then the final step, the capstone in the Sloan philosophy: headquarters, now freed from dealing with the quotidian problems of everyday operations, could focus on long-term strategic planning, distribution of corporate resources, corporate marketing, and shareholder relations. In the perfect scenario, the executive board would make these decisions dispassionately and objectively, with no bias for or against any one operating division, but only with an eye on maximizing profits and return on investment, increasing shareholder value, and improving the long-term health of the company.

As we all know, that didn't quite happen; human beings are creatures of ambition, jealousy, and pride, especially when most of the men and women on a typical executive board have come up through one division or another and remain loyal to it. But Sloan's model was a quantum improvement in functionality over anything that had come before. And there's every indication that Sloan himself didn't have a utopian view of his model, which is why he added one last factor: the CEO, which though he operates through consensus is ultimately the absolute ruler.

CHAPTER
‹ 4 ›

PACKARD'S WAY

THE TECHNOLOGY ERA

SLOAN'S INNOVATIONS, systematized and expanded upon by Drucker, would resonate for decades, and would come to be adopted by most large corporations throughout the world. Even Ford Motors, which under Henry Ford still had barely moved out of the previous era (some would even say the Industrial Era), found itself having to hurriedly restructure and divisionalize as General Motors, once an also-ran, blew right past it.

By the advent of World War II, in part because of greater competition and in part because of the desperate need for increased flexibility and ef-ficiency demanded by the Great Depression, most major banks, manu-facturers, industrial corporations, transportation companies, and utilities had moved to divisional organizations with a strong headquarters and a separate research laboratory.

The Corporate Era had arrived just in time to help the business world survive its greatest direct challenge of the century: the Great Depression. Sloan's model, adopted and adapted by thousands of large companies around the world, gave those firms the resilience to deal with a nearly complete collapse of the world's economy, and the civil strife that came from it. It is hard to imagine how traditional, single-minded, top-down companies of the Industrial Era could have survived 25 percent national unemployment (in the U.S.), rioting across Europe, hyperinflation in Weimar Germany, and ever growing movements in support of (and, as we now know, funded by) Soviet communism.

The Great Depression raised in the minds of millions the specter that, as Marx had predicted, capitalism was a failure, and that the only solu-tion was state-owned and -run economies. And in every country of the industrial world, statist movements arose to replace market economies with state-controlled ones. The challenge came from both the left (the IWW, the Workers Party, Fabians, national Communist parties) and the right (Nazism, America First, Italian black shirts, the British Union of Fascists), all offering a vision of renewed order in the face of industrial collapse and social chaos.

That most (though hardly all) of the world's great enterprises survived the Depression played a crucial role in both staving off complete eco-nomic disaster and serving as a bulwark against social revolution, though few people at the time would have seen it that way. On the contrary, business, especially Big Business, was generally perceived as the bad guy in the story, its greed the cause of the Depression, and its inflexibility the reason the hard times lingered so long.

Just as bad, in all but the most evil states (Germany, in particular), business was also seen by government as the enemy, an impediment to their efforts to enact sweeping emergency regulations. In the United States, for example, Big Business almost inevitably sided with the Republicans against the statist moves of Roosevelt's New Deal Progressives. In almost every Western country, businessmen were seen as enemies of the working man, while big government was seen as his only defender.

We know now that almost none of this was correct. The Great Depression was caused as much by rising international tariffs, combined with weak rules on stock speculation, neither created by business. And while FDR's statist New Deal policies played a crucial role in restoring hope to the nation, and held off the dangerously statist and collectivist policies of more extreme groups, they also likely attenuated the Depression by years. Hoover's policies, though much crueler in the short term, probably would have been more successful, had America survived the violence that would have ensued.

American industry, while in some ways the hero of this era—its ability to come out of the Great Depression and go right into the massive ramp-up in production for World War II is one of the miracles of business history—did little to help its case. The policies it proposed to get out of the Crash may have been correct, but they were also cold-blooded. And this was entirely in keeping with the general lack of understanding of the average worker that still characterized corporate life.

The corporate world had come a long way from the smokestacks and Bessemer furnaces of the Industrial Era. Thanks to scientific managers like Taylor and corporate managers like Sloan, power had been widely decentralized from the era of the owner sitting in his office micromanaging every phase of the business. Indeed, the owner now was hardly ever at the company, and just as often now there was no owner, but rather a board of directors representing thousands of individual shareholders.

By the same token, the days of the head boss running every aspect of his enterprise were almost over as well. Those who tried—and it was usually entrepreneurs, because it was in their nature to do so—almost always succumbed to managerial overstretch and pulled their companies down with them.

World War II was a war defined by technology: military, communications, manufacturing, and organizational.

There were three other vital factors to the Allied victory that are of interest to us in this book. The first was *information processing*. The success of the British code-breaking program at Bletchley Park in breaking the German Enigma Code was an enormous (and at the time, secret) victory against the Axis powers, which would provide a powerful advantage against the enemy for the rest of the war. Not only would Alan Turing's bombe computers prove hugely influential in the creation of other, more sophisticated computers—notably the first true electronic computer, the University of Pittsburgh's ENIAC—but his invention, combined with the 1s and 0s of Boolean algebra and the cybernetics work of John von Neumann, would usher in the digital age.

Henceforth, almost all great economic success would come from the ever-improving ability to gather, manage, and manipulate information.

This is precisely what happened throughout the 1950s and 1960s, and though largely completed now in most of the world's industries, continues into the present. Test and measurement instruments, computers, finance, telecommunications, computation, games, automotive, appliances and capital goods, personal record keeping, telephony, television, pharmaceuticals, agriculture. One by one, these industries, along with a thousand other smaller businesses, migrated to digital.

The second great postwar factor was *organizational*. The world's great corporations staggered into World War II, bruised and battered by the Great Depression, labor unrest, and a growing inability to manage their own operations. Now, they had to ramp up, almost overnight, to unprecedented size, then design and get into full production a host of brand new products—jeeps, bombers, ships—at what had until then been impossible speeds.

They did it, and by arming not only the United States but England and the Soviet Union through Lend-Lease, American industry won the war. Neither Germany nor Japan could ever hope to defeat an enemy that, despite massive material losses, still grew more powerful and better equipped each day.

The now legendary success of American industry during this era would not have been possible strictly using the established Corporate model, for all of its efficiencies. Rather, executives were forced by the extreme circumstances into a kind of management triage. With skilled laborers being lost to the war and women suddenly entering the workforce, with multiple shifts being added throughout the night to meet impossible production goals, and with a vast array of different products being produced at different company divisions, all bets were off. Whatever worked was adopted, whatever failed, no matter how established a tradition, was largely abandoned. Abetting this kind of organizational Darwinism was the synthetic wartime reality of guaranteed contracts, a committed workforce, and almost no union activity.

The third factor was *technology*. Historically, war has always spurred innovation. But there had never been anything like World War II. It began with most of the world's armies still using horses, biplanes, and telegraphs, and ended with jet fighters, radar, computers, tanks, and jeeps—and the atomic bomb. Only the semiconductor was put on hold until after the war.

Increased and highly predictable demand was only half of the equation. Just as important, faced with unskilled workers and undermanned manufacturing lines, manufacturers were forced to apply ever more design engineering and factory automation to their processes. What had still, despite Taylor, been a business largely of rule of thumb, now became a world structured by the slide rule and the micrometer. In many industries the implementation of new manufacturing technologies became a crucial competitive factor, and in time the pursuit of the latest and greatest new technology became an end itself.

This was the beginning of the *Technology Era*, and its driving force would be *information*: its acquisition, manipulation, and application. Its defining moment not only went all but unnoticed at the time, but was essentially forgotten for almost sixty years, until discovered by a filmmaker preparing a corporate history.

In 1948, at a gathering of corporate CEOs and senior executives—ostensibly to discuss corporate responsibility, but really to plan industry strategy for the postwar world—a young businessman found himself listening in disbelief as one of his peers after another announced that his company's sole responsibility was to make a profit. "Looking back," he would write later, "I suppose I shouldn't have been surprised. During the early decades of the twentieth century, profit was the businessman's sole objective. Labor was a commodity that could be bought and sold on the market."[1]

But this young man, David Packard, knew better. He had just come off a decade of brutal work in which he and his partner had started a company in a dirt-floored garage. Then, when that partner, Bill Hewlett, went off to war, Packard had spent four years, much of it sleeping in the company's offices, running three shifts of workers building some of the world's most sophisticated test and measurement instruments. When demand had crashed after the war, he had been forced to lay off some of his most loyal employees, an experience so heartrending that he swore he would never do it again. At that moment, Packard and Hewlett were still struggling to keep their company alive long enough to participate in the anticipated postwar boom.

If Dave Packard had learned anything from these experiences, it was that his little company would have died long ago if it hadn't been for the creativity, the hard work, and the loyalty of the employees. During those long war years, Packard, running the company almost alone, had discovered the incredible power of letting the employees themselves make decisions, to assume control over their own careers, and to take it upon themselves to keep the company healthy and successful. So, as Packard sat at this gathering, listening to his counterparts deny almost every bit of Packard's own hard-earned wisdom, he grew increasingly angry. Finally, he could take no more, drew himself up to his full 6'4", and told the gathered executives that they were completely wrong, "that we had important responsibilities to our employees, to our customers, to our suppliers, and to the welfare of society at large."

Young Dave Packard at that moment was forty years ahead of his time. His comments were met that day with silent bemusement. But Packard would have the last laugh: before he died, as perhaps the most admired business leader of the century, he would live to see his argument proven correct, and to see every other company represented in that room judged by the lofty standards set by Hewlett-Packard Co. during the "Bill & Dave" era.

Even as Packard was speaking, the invention that would drive this new era toward a pace of change that would have no precedent in human history was being launched: the transistor.

The transistor would win the Nobel Prize for its inventors. But even

more important than the device itself—arguably the most important invention in a century of great inventions—was the high-speed path it
placed industry (and ultimately society itself) on. It would be nearly
twenty years before the nature of the path would be described, by another great technologist, Gordon Moore of Fairchild Semiconductor
and Intel Corp., and given the name Moore's Law in his honor.[2]

What Moore's Law said was simple in its elucidation and profound
in its implications. Memory chips, Moore noted in his milestone 1965
industry speech, seemed to be doubling in capacity every 18 to 24 months.
What we can see now in retrospect is that the clock on Moore's Law really began at Bell Labs with that first transistor, and it has been ticking
ever since.

In the early years of the transistor industry, while the distinct advantages of using a solid state switch over its vacuum tube and electro-
mechanical antecedents was widely celebrated, the sheer power of the
structural force (Moore's Law) operating behind it was all but unnoticed. Still, among the most forward-looking and technology-oriented
companies—IBM, Motorola, Hewlett-Packard, Ampex, Digital Equipment, Tektronix, Siemens, Philips—there was a growing realization
that change itself, in the form of perpetual *innovation*, was becoming a
crucial competitive advantage.

Ultimately, this led companies to restructure around innovation itself.
Until then, corporate laboratories typically developed new products in
response to proven demand, and the challenge was to create but not get
too far ahead of the audience. But in a world of continuous change, waiting for the customer was often a recipe for failure. Rather, you had to
march out ahead of the market, and then draw the customers (themselves increasingly addicted to change) toward you. The corporate design of the previous generation wasn't entirely abandoned, but into this
structure the R&D department, now consuming 10 percent or more of
annual company profits, moved to a privileged position, setting the pace
and direction for the rest of the organization.

As I noted earlier in this book, tech revolutions inevitably force organizational transformations, and together they ultimately provoke sweeping social and cultural change.

Thanks to advertisements and other ephemera, we can track this organizational change through the decades, and in the process begin to understand the change in mind-set that accompanied it.

The typical corporate office of the late 1940s contains, in terms of technology, a telephone, an adding machine, and a manual typewriter. The company R&D lab likely features a dozen test and measurement instruments (with dials and meters) and a lot of slide rules. The manufacturing area is stocked with mechanical tools and, if the company makes electrical products, perhaps a few voltmeters and other testing aids. The company mostly keeps track of its records using file cabinets and perhaps microfiche. Its bookkeeping is done by hand, using adding machines.

Go forward just a decade, and the same company office features an electric adding machine and typewriter, the lab uses digital instruments, the factory floor features a primitive electronic process control system; and most transformed of all, the bookkeeping department has now turned over much of its operation to the new Information Processing center, which devotes its day to feeding thousands of punched cards, containing all of the company's financial (and sales, payroll, customer, and quality control) data into a large mainframe computer. Much of this information goes to senior management to monitor the company's performance, but some of it is also distributed to field sales, to supervisors on the factory floor, and to other employees throughout the company.

This is an extraordinary metamorphosis, greater than anything seen in the earlier eras of business organization. And given the continuous, relentless pace of change, is it any wonder that companies began to define themselves around the technology that was not only transforming their products and giving them a competitive advantage, but also changing the very nature of daily work? Nor should it be surprising that the companies that took turns at the center of this technology revolution—IBM, General Electric, Memorex, Intel, Sony, Apple, and Microsoft—would be seen as archetypes of how a modern business should be organized and run.

Hence the *Technology Era*, characterized by the adoption and implementation of ever-newer technologies, the race to get aboard Moore's Law, and the rise of R&D and information processing as the heart of almost every important company in the modern economy. Each of the emblematic technology companies of this era contributed in some way to the redesign of corporate organization. For IBM, it was the company as industry standard and the culture of absolute commitment; Intel, the company as one giant R&D department; General Electric, the company as technology-based conglomerate; Apple, the company as innovative maverick.

But no company contributed more to business reorganization in the Technology Era than Hewlett-Packard under its two founders. Bill Hewlett and Dave Packard seemed to understand, almost intuitively, and years before anyone else, that in a world of constant change, the old rules had been turned inside out. Those enduring factors in business (products, customers, and markets) had now become ephemeral, while that great variable cost of business (employees) had now become a company's single greatest asset.

With that realization, Hewlett and Packard embarked on a business strategy that had little precedent, and would prove to be hugely influential. At its heart, made explicit in the HP Objectives, and implicit in the mysterious heart of the company culture known as the "HP Way," Hewlett-Packard made its products expendable and its employees vital.[3] In practice, that meant a company built on perpetual innovation, which jettisoned even its most famous products without a second thought once they matured, and which implemented a string of personnel policies— profit sharing, employee stock options, employee recreation camps, morning and afternoon coffee breaks, flextime, on-site graduate programs affiliated with local universities, beer busts, college tuition programs. In one form or another, nearly all would be adopted by progressive companies throughout the world, but at the time HP introduced them they were revolutionary.

The high-water mark of the HP Way culture came in 1974, during the worst recession the high-tech industry had ever experienced. While almost every other company in the industry resorted to massive lay-offs, Hewlett-Packard alone chose to adopt the "nine-day fortnight," in which every employee in the company, including Bill and Dave, donated one free day of work to the company every two weeks. The result was that HP had no lay-offs (maintaining a record it had sustained since just after WWII), and surveys found that company employees exhibited the highest levels of worker satisfaction ever measured in a large company.[4]

Hewlett-Packard under its founders would become the gold standard for the generations of companies that followed, most notably Apple, Tandem, Sun Microsystems, and Silicon Graphics, as well as many of the first-wave dot-com companies such as Google. But none could match it, and few even came close. In fact, once the founders departed from day-to-day management, HP itself struggled to maintain its old culture.

There were several reasons for this failure. First, the Hewlett-Packard culture was philosophical, not structural, and it depended on the characters of the founders more than anyone knew until they were gone. Second, part of that character involved a level of trust—a willingness to pass decision making down through the organization—that was second nature to Bill and Dave, but almost antithetical to the personalities of most other corporate top executives (i.e., you don't accumulate power just to give it away). Finally, HP's commitment to the welfare and permanent employment of *all* of its employees ran smack into a changing world of "free agent" employees, part-timers, class-action lawyers, government regulations, and all sorts of other factors that have increased corporate volatility in recent years.

Still, Bill Hewlett and Dave Packard had seen something vital and far-reaching regarding the organization of companies in the technology age. The two men were on to something, and American industry still feels the void of their departure. We'll return to Hewlett and Packard and the HP Way when we begin to construct the Protean Corporation.

In the meantime, the Technology Era moved on. Corporations, like people, prefer to do what they do best. And in the digital age, that expertise was in information: its gathering, processing, collation, aggregation, and distribution. By the 1970s, the typical mid-sized company, whether or not it was in the tech business, was processing billions of bits of information—on customers, markets, employees, finances, taxes, manufacturing, design, and on and on—every year. A decade later, it was in the trillions of bits. And thus, in a fundamental way, companies themselves became information edifices.

Thanks to Moore's Law, as well as advances in software, how this information was processed evolved over the course of the Technology Era. What began in the 1950s with giant mainframe computers run by teams of experts evolved by the 1980s into networked personal computers sitting on employee desks.

What this meant in practice was the decentralization of information throughout the company, and given that companies were increasingly defined by information, this meant an unprecedent leap in that centuries-long process of empowering individual employees. And these new ultra-empowered employees were engaged employees. For the first time in the four-hundred-year history of corporations, rank-and-file workers found themselves active decision-makers in the fate of the companies they worked for.

Meanwhile, concurrent with this change in the infrastructure of corporations, there was a far-reaching shift in the culture of those companies. Led by the example (and the competitive and public relations threat) of progressive firms like Hewlett-Packard, companies throughout the industrialized world began to culturally and economically engage their employees to a degree never before seen: stock options, profit sharing, employee product discounts, ultimately even health clubs and gyms, specialty restaurants, tuition support, and day care centers. Just as important, these same companies also began to institute merit-based pay, a fairer system of bonuses and incentives, and career migration paths that, in theory, enabled any employee to one day reach the CEO's office.

This combination, because it identified employees as individuals for the first time, and customized their relationships with the employer, was ultimately what broke the back of unions in the commercial sector, especially in the United States. For good or bad, from now on employees would be judged largely upon individual performance, their relationship with their employer one-to-one, and they would be responsible for their own career; *Waiting for Lefty* was now to be replaced by *Dilbert*.

It's difficult to overstate the importance of this change. For a generation, businesses had spoken of companies "being" their employees, but now for the first time this was actually becoming true. The rank-and-file, which had long been treated (except when they caused trouble) as a bookkeeping entry, had now become a sea of individual faces, each with its own expectations, and thanks to stock options, each with a vote in the future direction of the company.

Social change is always a two-edged sword, and this growing empowerment of employees in the fifties, sixties, and seventies was a classic example. "Employee-oriented" corporations were typically more responsive to the marketplace, better places to work, and just all-around smarter. But the new attention being paid to these employees came at a cost, not least of which was the "ratchet-effect": better-treated employees quickly saw any improvements as standard procedure and raised their expectations to an even higher level of power, pay, and perquisites.

In prosperous, highly competitive industries and regions—for example, among the semiconductor companies in Silicon Valley in the early 1980s—the result was a kind of benefits arms race, offering everything from on-site exercise course to employee rock concerts to giant Christmas bonus raffles: good news for employees until these added costs drove their employers into an earlier and deeper downturn than usual, the lay-offs more sweeping, and, of course, a quick shuttering of all these extra benefits.

But one employee demand didn't go away: *autonomy*. Employees wanted to define their own work lives—their schedules; their relationships with customers, bosses, and fellow employees; even their work location. Companies resisted the notion at first—not surprising, given centuries of top-down management and the human reality that few people ever voluntarily give away power.

However, three factors worked to convince corporate management to experiment, if gingerly at first, with the idea of "inverting" the corporate pyramid and empowering rank-and-file employees:

1 › The realization that modern products and services had become so sophisticated that it was very likely the folks in the middle, even at the bottom, of the org chart who actually understood what was going on better than the folks at the top.

2 > It seemed to work. While few had the courage to go all of the way and adopt the Hewlett and Packard trust model, none could argue that HP's organizational model was producing anything but spectacular results.

3 > It saved money, and there's nothing like improving both sides of the balance sheet to get a CEO's attention. Unfortunately, this wasn't apparent at the beginning. On the contrary, most companies saw employee empowerment as only added expenses for training, tools, and (frankly) cleaning up after mistakes. That would soon change.

The lesson came, appropriately enough, from Hewlett-Packard Co. In 1979, at an industry gathering, an HP division manager got up and presented the most influential graph since Moore's Law. It showed, with devastating and irrefutable evidence, that the semiconductor devices being fabricated by Japanese electronics companies were cheaper, more reliable, and almost in every other way far superior to those offered by their more veteran, and certainly more celebrated, American counterparts.[5]

The news landed like a bombshell on not only the U.S. semiconductor industry but all of American industry—creating an unprecedented outburst of anger, soul searching, and self-recrimination. How could a nation that until recently was synonymous with cheap consumer products, suddenly become a world-beater?

In their desperate search by U.S. companies to understand Japan's success, two things soon became clear: their Japanese competitors had built a philosophy of quality *into* their corporate cultures (a lesson learned, ironically, from two American consultants, Deming and Juran), and perhaps even more important, they had enlisted *all* of their employees into this culture, making them its purveyors and guardians. In other words, even in traditional, socially rigid Japan, employees were being enlisted into the decision-making process, and their companies were now beating the daylights out of their American and European competitors.

Now there was no excuse. If they were going to survive this onslaught, Western companies were going to have to empower their employees to help with product design, customer relations, manufacturing quality, and service. And that is exactly what smart companies did over the next decade: catching up close enough in quality to their Japanese competitors that they could pull ahead through category-busting innovation, Japan's one weak spot. But in the interim, Japan became one of the wealthiest countries in the world, and some of its companies among the largest—a lesson to others about the power of enlisting a population's combined intellectual capital.

CHAPTER

THE CENTER CANNOT HOLD

THE VIRTUAL ERA AND ITS FADING RELEVANCE

THE *VIRTUAL ERA* might be said to have begun at the West Coast
Computer Show in 1976 when Steve Wozniak and Steve Jobs first
showed off the Apple II.

It was certainly underway by the early 1980s with the introduction of
both the IBM PC and the Apple Macintosh. Now, for the first time, computers were being placed, in huge numbers, in the hands of everyday consumers and workers. And, in one of the most sweeping transformations in

business history, within a decade the personal computer would become a standard tool sitting on almost every office desk in the developed world.

That transformation made PC companies among the fastest growing enterprises ever recorded. It also did more to change the nature of everyday work than perhaps any other invention short of the telephone. Now the very symbol of employee empowerment was sitting, glowing, in ten million offices. In some companies, the entrenched IT departments tried to staunch this loss of control, but they were doomed to fail. Personal computers meant personal freedom, and employees would never again give them up.

But personal computers, for all of their power as computational, word-processing, and record-keeping tools, were still limited in application within companies if they could not share their information with other computers in any but the most mechanical ways (i.e., passing diskettes from machine to machine).

Luckily, the answer was already there in the form of computer *networks*. Historically, these networks were designed either to manage time-share systems of multiple terminals surrounding a big mainframe, or later, to link multiple minicomputers. Some of this technology could be adapted for PCs, notably modems, which could convert one computer's digital data into a form that could be transmitted over a dedicated wire, or more commonly, a telephone line. But the process was exceedingly slow, made worse as personal computers got ever faster and more powerful.

Still, as crude as these systems were, they still made possible the beginning of electronic mail systems and the rise of community chat sites such as The Well. And that was impetus enough to keep working toward even more powerful solutions. Once again, it would be two forces, one academic and the other practical, that would drive this movement, in this case to a full-blown technology revolution.

The first of these was *Metcalfe's Law*. Not as celebrated as Moore's Law, it has proven to be as influential. And, unlike its semiconductor counterpart, which is really more of a covenant between the chip industry and the rest of the world, Metcalfe's Law is an actual empirical law. And though its exact formulation has been much disputed, its essential truth has long since been validated. Bob Metcalfe, who was the creator of one of the first and still most influential networking protocols, Ethernet, stated his law as, *The overall value of a network increases proportionally as a square of the number of users.*

In other words, the more users you add to a network, the *much* more valuable it becomes. It was an astonishing claim—and even as Metcalfe was formulating it, a new phenomenon was emerging that would put his Law to the ultimate test, and prove it true.

This was, of course, the Internet, which began in that miracle year of 1969 as DARPAnet, a means for the government agencies, contractors, and academic institutions to quickly and securely share reams of information and e-mails. The early incarnations of the Net were klugey and difficult to use; nevertheless, they more than proved the truth of Metcalfe's Law.

The turning point came with the 1989 creation, by Tim Berners-Lee of the CERN laboratory in Geneva, of the World Wide Web, a way of linking together individually created Web pages through a simple addressing system and a "browser" tool. The impact of the Web cannot be overstated: within a decade of its general adoption, the number of Internet users leaped from a few million to a billion people—a number that will triple again by the end of this decade. The story of the high-tech revolution is filled with superlatives, but nothing in that story has ever matched the sudden impact and rapid global adoption of the Web.

A lot of the early growth of the Web came from the corporate world. After forty years of the digital revolution, most companies had learned the value of adopting important new innovations rather than resisting them. And with several million computers now sitting on office desks, the transition to being Web-enabled was an easy step. Indeed, the single most limiting factor was not employee demand, management interest, or even capital investment, but the inadequate ability of the networks to keep up with the growing power of both the servers and the nodes (that is, the personal computers) in the network. Despite that, and even though thousands of office workers were reduced to getting onto the Web using dial-up modems, the near-vertical adoption rate of the Internet continued apace.

By now, the modern corporation was as much defined by, as controlling, its digital infrastructure: computer integrated manufacturing,

computer aided design, management information systems, mass customization, integrated supply chains, customer-aided design and service, multimedia marketing. And from all of these various initiatives a
new kind of company was beginning to appear: *Virtual Corporations*.

These Virtual Corporations:

<> Featured a strong digital component

<> Enlisted outside participants up and down the distribution and
supply channels

<> Exhibited higher levels of adaptability to change than what they
supplanted

<> Seemed to accelerate away from their competitors, stealing huge
percentage points of market, and to basically leave mere leftovers
for everyone else

Though the idea of the Virtual Corporation preceded the Internet, it
was the general adoption of the Web that made this new kind of company possible.

Meanwhile, a second career phenomenon had appeared: the Road
Warrior. These were the men and women, typically working for a global
national company, who found themselves almost continuously on the
road, visiting distant customers, suppliers, and their own company divisions. The Road Warriors were, not surprisingly, the early adopters and
drivers of most new portable electronic devices. What made this cohort
particularly interesting was that it increasingly began to include senior
managers. Indeed, at the dawn of the century, in Fortune 500 companies, it was often the CEO who was the most traveled employee—and
the least often seen at headquarters.

Virtual Corporations, in an unexpected secondary effect, began to
atomize almost from the beginning.

Reward structures started to change, as did capital investment. When

companies began to realize that they could cut overhead, and reduce facilities costs, by sending employees home, they began to reward just that
kind of behavior. It was a lot cheaper to give telecommuter employees a
laptop and broadband cable than to pay for office space, cafeterias, security, and parking lots. There was even further incentive when it was found
that home workers often put in more productive time than their office
counterparts. No one expected office workers to stay and take a call from
a fellow work team member at midnight or five a.m., but they could ask
that sacrifice of home workers, because their time was far more flexible.

The result was the most curious, yet pragmatic, transformation in business history. For more than a century, it had been one long bitter battle,
fought by labor unions, scientists, and enlightened business leaders, to
convince corporate managers to surrender some of their power and give
up a little bit of trust to their workers, to empower them with greater decision making, and to allow them to direct their own careers. Suddenly,
in less than a generation, all of those goals were being achieved. Senior
management was now struggling to convince the rank and file to take on
more responsibility and *greater* control of their jobs, *assume* more flexibility
in their work environment, and *accept* greater ownership of the company.

Furthermore, this revolution wasn't a one-way street. Management
wouldn't have allowed this diminution of power if it hadn't had tangible,
measurable results. And the good news came by the bushel: the first real
gains in worker productivity in decades, employees *voluntarily* working
longer workweeks (with a sizable fraction even taking their computers
with them to work on holidays), and greater amounts of voluntary sign-
ups for training. Even giving employees ownership in the company, via
stock options, proved to be an unexpected boon: not only did it increase
loyalty and reduce turnovers, but, contrary to the fears of a century before, employees not only didn't use their equity to vote for radicalism or
outright mutiny, they actually became a bulwark against perceived outside threats, from shareholder suits to unfriendly acquisitions.

With so many incentives, it's not surprising that the pendulum swung
so far the other way. And with the bottom line seemingly boosted by almost every initiative to empower employees and move them outside the
walls of the company's buildings, by enlisting stakeholders up and down

the supply/distribution ladder (including customers) in product design, manufacture, and service, and by wherever possible jettisoning full-time employees in lieu of contractors, freelancers, and "permanent part-time" workers—is it any wonder that many companies simply went too far? Or that the newest generation of start-ups—the so-called dot-com companies of the late 1990s—became so detached from traditional business practices that many convinced themselves that even such traditional concepts as "profit" and "loss" were obsolete in the Internet age?

WITHOUT A MAP

The bursting of the dot-com bubble in 2000—with its destruction of several thousand new start-up companies, hundreds of thousands of jobs, and an estimated $1 trillion in wealth—was a wake-up call. Clearly things had gone too far.

The young companies seemed to have developed no structural integrity and had collapsed at the slightest competitive challenge. Meanwhile, the big, older companies seemed to be lacking in cultural integrity; no one had been minding the store while senior managers at companies like Enron had wandered off into criminal behavior. Even that celebrated source of employee empowerment, stock options, had been widely abused to enrich senior management.

Coming off the wild abandon of the 1990s, the early years of the new century—industry collapse, recession, 9/11—proved to be very serious and sobering times indeed in the United States. These shocks, coming one after another in quick succession, consumed every second of management time; companies (and every other institution in American life) were intent on survival. They had little time for dealing with destructive underlying forces in their own organizations or with new ways to attack them.

And those forces are steering the modern company at the beginning of the twenty-first century into very dangerous waters. Let me repeat again what I wrote in the introduction of this book. I think the reader will now find these words less alarmist, but much more alarming:

Every trend in the corporate world—technological, managerial, financial, and cultural—is pushing companies toward ever-greater virtualization, of the dismantling of every traditional organizational structure, and their replacement with networks of free agents. At the same time, mounting evidence is warning us this model *doesn't work*.

In other words, we are in a locomotive racing down the tracks at full speed, watching as every bolt and rivet is starting to loosen, but we don't know how to get off the track or slow the engine down—nor do we want to because there's a big bonus waiting for us if we arrive at the station early.

This is not something you can simply patch. As we've just explored, three centuries of business history have taken us down a nearly continuous path toward ever-greater employee autonomy and empowerment, an ever-greater dependence on technological innovation at the heart of the organization, and toward ever more detached remote-control management (with an emphasis on "remote").

These are not trends that are going to be stopped—we've seen the chaos and violence that result when someone has tried—nor, in many respects, do we want to. But we can't go forward either, at least not in the direction we are heading, because that leads only to anarchy and the kind of impermanence that is repellent to human nature.

And thus, we find ourselves facing the defining business paradox of our age:

Do you want to build a fast-growing, successful company with a very high risk of imploding quickly or a slower-growing, ultimately just-as-successful company, which may last for generations but at every moment risks being rendered obsolete?

The bad news is that these are rapidly becoming our *only* two choices. The worse news is that the second choice—building an enduring company—is also being taken off the table. In our fast-moving, Internet-driven world of day traders, twenty-four-hour cable business channels, and time horizons that rarely look ahead more than a couple quarters, the very notion of building a slower-growing company is anathema.

So what do we do now?

The answer, I believe, is not to make the equally catastrophic mistakes of either blindly tearing ahead along the same path or trying to turn back. Rather, we need to keep moving forward (because we have no choice) but change our trajectory. Not radically, but just enough to arrive at a very different destination, and survive the journey.

That destination is not just the Protean Corporation, but a society that is hospitable to these new kinds of organizations.

That's a tall order, but it beats the alternatives. Now, bear with me as we explore two other important trends that will help us shape this new trajectory for our society.

COWBOYS IN THE WILD WEST

The story of entrepreneurship is usually buried within the story of enterprise. And yet, they are very different things, especially when one speaks of entrepreneurial start-ups versus large corporations.

They are, in fact, almost natural antagonists. Of course, nearly every company begins as a small start-up. But those enterprises that do become large and successful, often by challenging the status quo and pulling down the existing industry leader, are naturally motivated to try to close the door behind them to keep from suffering the same fate.

They do so in a number of ways. They use an army of lawyers to create patent barriers and sue any new competitors for any potential infringements, real or not. They do the same with their employees who leave to join those start-ups. They also (often illegally) threaten customers with a loss of delivery—or at least reduced priority in delivery—if they deal with the new competitor. They steal away key employees with tantalizing employment offers. They spend large sums to outpromote and outdistribute their smaller new competitors. They use their financial strength to try to price-bomb the new competitor into nonprofitability and, with luck, bankruptcy. And when all else fails, they go to the government; it's a surprisingly short step from being the happy recipient of venture capital and complaining to legislators and regulators about the pernicious effects of "vulture" capital.

And yet, like clever little mammals darting beneath the feet of dinosaurs, entrepreneurs and their start-ups manage to not only survive, but thrive. And thank goodness they do, because for the last half-century at least, they have been responsible for most of the innovation and the new job creation in the U.S. economy and in most economies in the developed world, including even those with resolutely antientrepreneurial cultures.

There is an extraordinary alternative—entrepreneurial—business history of the twentieth century, one intimately tied with the expansion of human freedom, that has never really been told in detail. Someday that story will be written, but for now consider the story of the high-tech revolution.

The first generation of high-tech entrepreneurs—the men of the 1930s and 1940s—were basically scientific or business geniuses. Shockley, Hewlett and Packard, Litton, Watson, Galvin, Haggerty, the Varian Brothers: the kind of extraordinary talents that appear just a few times in any given generation.

The second generation of tech entrepreneurs had its geniuses too, but the entry requirement was now expanded to include PhDs in solid-state physics, chemistry, and electronics; thus Shockley's "Traitorous Eight," who founded Fairchild (and later Intel, AMD, National Semiconductor, and scores more chip companies). Essentially, to start a technology company in the 1950s and 1960s, you had to have a deep understanding of the physics at the heart of your product; the business side was second.

But by the 1970s, the combination of Moore's Law, networked mainframe computers and minicomputers, cheap logic and memory chips, and available venture capital opened the door to creating new companies based upon "consumerizing" what had until then been the province of corporate IT departments and university computer centers. Now it was possible for an entrepreneur with some technical acumen (or a brilliant technologist partner) and a deep understanding of the market to start a high-tech company. This was the era of the "T-Shirt Tycoons," exemplified by Nolan Bushnell at Atari, Steve Jobs at Apple, and Jack Tramiel at Commodore, as well as, in software, Bill Gates at Microsoft, Gary Kildall at Digital Research, and a bit later, Mitch Kapor at Lotus.

The incredible success of some of these individuals (several became billionaires) further opened the door to high-tech entrepreneurship. The 1980s, though largely a decade of stunted high-tech start-up creation due to onerous capital gains taxes and stagflation, still saw the creation of a number of new companies, most of them oriented toward the corporate market (ROLM, Sun Microsystems, Oracle, Autodesk) and many founded by entrepreneurs who, for the first time, were less technologists than accomplished businessmen and businesswomen.

But it was in the 1990s when the door of entrepreneurship was finally flung wide open to almost any businessperson with the desire and the commitment of time and energy to create a new company. Several factors made this expansion possible: (1) the by now highly sophisticated infrastructures (venture capital, banks, real estate, consultants, executive placement firms, PR and ad agencies, suppliers and distributors, etc.) in places like Silicon Valley specifically designed to take inexperienced young entrepreneurs and build companies around them; (2) a new medium, the Web, appeared with an extremely low cost of entry, cheap scalability, and instant access to a worldwide market of billions of potential customers, and best of all, requiring comparatively little technical aptitude; and (3) a new generation that had never known a time without the personal computer, with a sizable number of their parents working at home, and raised in an era in which entrepreneurs such as Steve Jobs were as much cultural heroes as any rock star.

The result, as we remember, was a land rush, as hundreds of thousands of young would-be entrepreneurs created thousands of companies seemingly overnight. That most of these "dot-com" start-ups had unrealistic business models, quickly turning the Internet "bubble" into the Internet "bust," is of secondary interest here—an 80 percent mortality rate of companies in a hot new industry is pretty standard in tech; this boom/bust just happened to get more attention than most. So too is the fact that this boom also created a number of very successful and very important

Web-based companies, such as Amazon, Google, eBay, and the various travel sites.

What we're interested in for this narrative is the *perceptual* impact of this wave of "e-commerce" start-ups. That is, for perhaps the first time in human history, it seemed possible that *anyone* could become an entrepreneur, and that such a person would actually be honored in society as opposed to, in the past (and still in many places in the world), treated like a hustling shopkeeper. The new universality of entrepreneurialism was visible in almost every business story of the era.

This new wave of entrepreneurs didn't even look like the traditional image of the start-up founder—neither a brainiac scientist nor a buttoned-down number cruncher or even a tie-died nerd. Now the stereotypical image was the twenty-five-year-old with an MFA or a classics degree, dressed all in black, sitting on an Aeron chair in a minimalist office—in other words, like every smart young college grad in America.

Most of the new start-up stories of the era didn't end well. But then, they never do, which is the nature of entrepreneurship. What did matter, as it always has in places like Silicon Valley, is that for all of the carnage of the dot-com bust, there were enough wildly successful survivors to show that the brass ring was still there for the taking. And just as important, a whole generation had gotten a taste of the entrepreneurial lifestyle, and wherever they found themselves afterward, they would now dream and scheme to get back there.

Meanwhile, even as the Gen-Xers, the dot-com generation, was enduring its rite of passage, yet another generation was coming on. The Gen-Ys, or Millennials, as they are called, had never known life without the Internet. And just as their older brothers and sisters had known the PC intuitively, this next generation lived and breathed the Web as if it was the very air itself.

This generational cohort, the biggest since the Baby Boomers, grew up in a world in which there had always been the Internet, the Web, and broadband and wireless access. Few had ever seen a dial phone, and a sizable percentage owned their own cell phones before they finished elementary school. They spent more time on video games on computers and game machines than watching television, and spent much of their adolescence as de facto criminals for illegally downloading music and video files: an experience that will leave many with a lifelong belief that all content should be free to the user, ultimately forcing the creators and providers to find other sources of compensation.

But most of all, this generation, unlike perhaps any before it in human history, grew up with the widespread belief, based on what they observed among their parents and older siblings, that no one really needs to go to an office to work. And what's more, *no one ever needs to have a full-time job working for someone else.* This shouldn't be too surprising given the sizable percentage of this cohort that has never seen one or both of their parents commute to any office other than the one down the hall.

The business heroes of this generation are almost all entrepreneurs, current ones such as Twitter's Evan Williams, Facebook's Mark Zuckerberg, and Slide's Max Leuchin; or business magnates who still carry the trappings of a legendary earlier entrepreneurial success, such as Steve Jobs and Larry Ellison. And every day, this new generation is given the message—from Mom and Dad working as freelancers and contractors, to Grandma selling items on eBay, to stories of their own peers already starting their own businesses and making money from Second Life or the Sims, or just for playing online games like World of Warcraft—that you can create your own career and control your own life, and flourish in the process.

Even more remarkable, this generation is, mostly unconsciously, being *trained* to entrepreneurship. Consider community sites, the best-known phenomena of the so-called Web 2.0 era. Nearly a quarter billion people, most of them young, now have their own pages on Facebook, My-Space, or a related site. Several million more have set up an alternative existence on Second Life. They construct these pages, maintain and embellish them, and grow and refresh them through regular upgrades. In some cases, as in Sims mods or Second Life "real estate," they actually create new items to sell to others, or make speculative investments in hope of long-term gain.

Now, as Web 2.0 evolves into Web 3.0, the monetization of these social networks, this advanced training in small business capitalism is about to take off in earnest, especially when the shrewder sites realize that even better than selling to these millions will be empowering them to sell to each other—and pay royalties for the right to do so.

Needless to say, this is teaching small business skills on a scope and scale that is orders of magnitude beyond anything ever possible with Junior Achievement or 4-H clubs. And the result is likely to be an entire generation of twenty-five-year-olds with a decade or more of entrepreneurial training setting up businesses in regions of cyberspace where there are few barriers to market entry and start-up costs are almost nothing.

What comes out of this de facto social experiment will be unlike anything we've ever experienced before. In the United States, where this is likely to happen first (with the Four Tigers nations close behind), we could see the creation not of several thousand new companies, as in the dot-com bubble, but millions, with thousands disappearing each day only to be matched and more by new ones emerging at the same time. And all of it will be driven by tens of millions of self-proclaimed entrepreneurs perpetually hopping from one business opportunity to the next.

The implications of all of this, good and bad, are rather shocking. And we'll close the book by looking at some of them. For now, however, consider what we've seen in the history of high-tech-driven entrepreneurship over the last half-century. If we were to present it as a Venn diagram, it would look a lot like a bull's-eye, with each generation of entrepreneurs encompassing all that came before, but also further democratizing the process. So too would a diagram showing the active participants in corporate decision making over the last century, beginning with an owner and a handful of lieutenants, then incrementally moving out to include middle managers, rank-and-file employees, shareholders, customers, and even competitors.

What had begun as an endeavor for only the most brilliant, in twenty-five tech generations but only three human generations, is now an opportunity available to almost anyone, no matter what experience or age.

It has often been said that as goes Silicon Valley, so goes the electronics industry and, ultimately, the nation. Well, this is the U.S. economy as a kind of souped-up Silicon Valley, soon to be followed by other industrialized nations. It's all rather heady to contemplate, and offers the potential for extraordinary economic growth, but also for levels of innovation, wealth distribution, and cultural adaptability unlike anything we've ever seen before. And on the personal, it offers the kind of mobility, merit-based reward, control over one's destiny, and economic freedom only dreamed of just a few years ago.

But it is also going to play hell on the corporation. If you think managing today's independent and mobile workers is a challenge, imagine when *most* of your employees resemble the most maverick employee you have right now. How are you going to build a stable and enduring company out of a population of workers like *this?*

BILLIONS AND BILLIONS

If that isn't enough, there is one last factor at work on the twenty-first century organization, and this one is so titanic that no one knows where it will lead—and likely no one will for a century or more.

The easiest way to appreciate this force is to take that first bull's-eye diagram I described, the one representing decision-makers in the modern corporation. If we imagine a typical Fortune 500 company of fifty thousand employees, we are probably looking at about one million participants, including shareholders and strategic partners, but not competitors or the employees of those partners.

Now, multiply that number by *one hundred*. If you will be working in a successful global company a decade from now, that's the number of fellow employees and "participants" in the company's daily life you will have around you. If you are CEO, that's the number of stakeholders you will have to represent, serve, and be responsible for.

The number of nations in the world with this many citizens almost can be counted on two hands. And what that means is that in this new century, the biggest companies will be bigger and more numerous than all but a dozen or so of the world's most populous nations. We have never seen anything quite like this before, and the implications for sovereignty, taxation, and foreign policy are worthy of a hundred dissertations and government white papers.

But what lies behind this is even more mind-boggling. The best explanation I've seen is in the recent book *The Jump Point*, by high-tech marketing expert Tom Hayes. As we noted earlier in the book, Hayes shows that it took eight thousand years—basically from the dawn of the agricultural era in human history and the rise of the first cities till about 1980—for the world to see a total of one billion consumers participating in the global marketplace. Needless to say, most of these consumers came from the Developed World, the remainder from the enclaves of wealth and higher education found in some of the major cities of the Developing World.

After that, it took only twenty years, around the turn of the millennium, to bring the next billion into the global marketplace. This cohort has been largely individuals living in the Developing World near cities where they can take advantage of advances in local infrastructure—reliable telephony, Internet cafes, cable television, global package delivery services such as DHL and Federal Express, and platforms such as eBay—to participate (albeit in a low-level way) in international trade.

We are already beginning to feel the impact—both good and bad—of their arrival. The world's richest man now, Carlos Slim Helu, is from Mexico. India's Bollywood movie industry is now nearly the size of Hollywood—and much more productive—and the sheer size of the international market has begun to have a highly visible effect upon the content of American and European film. The same is true for music.

Meanwhile, certain Web communities, such as Orkut, are thriving despite having almost no Western participation, because of enthusiastic supporters in Brazil. The world's most popular online game is Cyworld, which is all but unknown outside South Korea, but is more popular there than television. Indeed, a 2007 survey found that the game engaged 90 *percent* of all South Korean teenagers, and 50 percent of the nation's population.[1] Global news, once monopolized by the West, is now being challenged by newcomers such as the Qatar-originated Al-Jazeera, while established Western news networks such as CNN are accused of censoring the news to cater to its expanding Middle Eastern audience.

India produces more computer scientists and electrical engineers than the rest of the world combined (if you exclude China). And, as already noted, even mighty Intel, on the very cutting edge of semiconductor technology, has found itself in a battle for supremacy against Samsung. Osama bin Laden, ostensibly speaking from a cave in northern Pakistan, reaches an audience of billions of people. China demands, and gets, Google and Yahoo! to acquiesce to self-censorship, even (in the case of Yahoo!) assistance in rounding up dissidents. And we are no longer surprised to find Nigerian "419" solicitations in our e-mail, or that the piece of jewelry we just ordered on eBay isn't from Hawaii but Botswana.

It almost goes without saying that this process has just begun. Doubling the number of participants in the world market can't help but lead to massive redistributions of goods and wealth, or create giant corporations where there never were before. Less obvious, but even more important, is the likelihood that the doubling of the number of participants will also lead to a doubling of the total intellectual capital being brought to bear on the world's business challenges, meaning an efflorescence of new inventions, products, and fads.

All sorts of other new phenomena associated with this doubling of the world market are also starting to appear. For example, we are likely to see in the next decade the first companies with market capitalizations of more than $1 trillion, sales of more than $500 billion, and more than five million employees—and with that, the world's first private citizen trillionaires. But it will also be possible to see (and it has already begun) far-flung terrorist and/or criminal organizations coordinating their activities via the Web, as well as massive virtual communities organizing around everything from racism to child pornography.

For business, the addition of this second billion is already creating some real and immediate challenges. These take two forms and both grow in magnitude by the month, and will likely continue to do so for generations.

First, *the market created by this second billion is not as virtual as we thought.* Sure, we can communicate with this next billion via the Web or wireless, even market through those media, but once the transaction is made, things start getting very concrete and complicated. Where do you build your products? Domestically, exchanging greater control and quality for higher costs? Or near the customer, and create whole new levels of management, quality control, and HR? And once the product is built, you need a sophisticated distribution infrastructure—and where DHL and FedEx fail, you may have to build one of your own, including local shops and trucking. And don't forget service: the less wealthy the customer, the more likely he or she is to see a product as a valuable durable good needing repair, rather than as a comparatively inexpensive disposable device.

In other words, the doubling of the global market cannot be answered inexpensively, remotely, and solely through greater virtualization. It requires boots on the ground, perhaps not nearly as many as would have been needed a half-century ago, but still enough to represent a massive expense for any company, a huge management and human resource task, and a life-threatening challenge to existing corporate organizations.

Second, *there is no longer such a thing as "local" business*. The message of this is that you can't simply opt out of competing on this global scale. One obvious reason is that this second billion is where most business growth will occur in the next few decades, and shareholders and investors will simply not allow you to choose not to fight for these potential revenues.

But even more important, if you don't go out and compete in the world, the world will come and compete with you. This is the other side of the globalism coin. The same technologies that make it easier for you to sell your products in Sri Lanka and Mozambique from, say, Enid, Oklahoma, also make it possible—and ever more likely—that emerging enterprises in those countries will start selling their goods, and especially their services, in Enid.

We have already experienced the beginnings of this, with the Chilean blueberries in the supermarket, the newest video game from Estonia, the small press books printed in China, and, of course, the automobile, television, computer, and game console composed of parts manufactured all over the planet. But that's only the beginning; we're not talking here about out-sourcing, but *in-selling*, not just about encountering a new wave of competitors on the international scene, but being attacked by them in one's home market.

What's even more amazing to contemplate is that *no one* is immune to such competition, especially in services. There's no reason in the age of broadband Internet for the tax accountant down the street not to be challenged by his or her counterpart in Bangalore armed with the latest

U.S. tax code information. The local barber may still cut your hair, but a technician in China may be looking at your latest chest X-ray—and eventually, using a remotely controlled robotic arm, your dentist may be in Jakarta.

Put both of these forces together and it is apparent that you will have to compete on the international stage, whether you want to or not. And when you do, you will have to not only expand your cyber-presence, but also begin hiring or contracting talent around the world, if not as employees then as sales reps, service technicians, or local marketers.

And if that sounds challenging, consider this: many of those people you hire will have never worked for a real company before, come from societies that are heavily dependent upon barter, or even graft, and have very low levels of both education and literacy (though they may be quite computer savvy). These people will be the "face" of your company in large regions of the world; they will be responsible for increasingly large segments of your business; and in time, many will expect from you the same benefits (medical, dental, retirement) you currently offer your employees in the United States and other parts of the developed world.

How are you going to find the right people from this second billion? How will you train them—not only in your products or services, but in simple business transactions, record-keeping, tax withholding, and so forth? How will you inculcate them with the culture of your company so that they don't put you at risk of scandal, litigation, or criminal charges? And, finally, how are you going to match their benefits to that of the rest of the company's employees (and they will know what those are, thanks to the Internet), when their own societies lack adequate healthcare, education, and safety?

It is a mess, and it is going to be an even bigger mess as this second billion becomes further assimilated into the global marketplace. No organizational scheme we have today is equipped to deal with this new world: traditional organizations can't scale up in this way, can't afford the communications infrastructure that would be required to turn all of these folks into full-time employees, and don't have the flexibility they need to deal with this kind of culture shock.

Virtual organizations *can* scale up to meet this new reality, and they have the flexibility, but without any real center they are unprepared to deal with the complexities of divergent societies and mores. And because they have no real centers, no way to imbue those new Second Billion employees with the company culture (often because the company has no culture in the first place), they are dangerously vulnerable at the fringes of a kind of brutal, twenty-first-century Hobbesian corporate environment of renegade employee behavior, malfeasance, even criminality. Care to have terrorist cells growing inside your company?

What's needed is a new kind of corporate organization that manages to balance some kind of enduring structure at its center, which develops the strategic direction of the company and maintains and enforces the company's core philosophy . . . yet still allows the kind of global extension, scalability, and rapid-fire adaptability that will be required to compete in this new world.

And so, once again we find ourselves at the gates of the Protean Corporation.

And if all that I just wrote didn't scare you into accepting the need for the early adoption of the next era in corporate organization, I suspect that this will: according to Hayes, waiting just behind the Second Billion is a *Third Billion*, yet another giant cohort of global consumers—and it is expected to begin arriving around 2011. And this Third Billion will make the Second look easy. These are the people in the developing world who are either the poorest of the poor in large cities or people living in remote villages that are currently off the grid. As they are almost all illiterate and have few representatives or spokespeople, we know next to nothing about them. But what we do know is mind-boggling: according to Hayes, this Third Billion has never seen an airplane close up, much less flown on one; has never ridden in an automobile, though has been conveyed on a truck or bus; is more likely to have eaten monkey meat than a Big Mac; and its dominant religion is not Christianity, Buddhism, or Islam . . . but Animism.

This Third Billion may even have a *lingua franca*, a common language, that we don't speak and which may give them a unique advantage in trading with each other. Here's the *International Herald-Tribune* describing what might be a common event in the future:

... during an airport delay the man to the left, a Korean perhaps, starts talking to the man opposite, who might be Colombian, and soon they are chatting away in what seems like English. But the native English speaker sitting between them cannot understand a word.[2]

One candidate for this universal language is "Globish," a simple 1,500 word language based on English. Another is some variation of "Franglais," or perhaps the English/Afrikaans/Swahili variants found throughout southern Africa, or the pidgin Englishes of the Caribbean or Southeast Asia. English may be the world's new dominant language, but that doesn't mean it will be spoken the same way everywhere—and its homophonic replacement may already be in the process of being coined in some distant corner of the world by a member of this Third Billion.

Per capita, this Third Billion makes only a couple hundred dollars per year, but more and more of that income is being spent on cell phone time and other electronics. None of these people will likely ever use a computer, but they will soon be pouring by the millions onto the Internet via cheap cell phones, and they will begin selling their services and their wares on the Web. Per customer, they mean nothing to your business, but multiplied by a billion, they will mean a whole lot, and once they join the global economy they will inevitably grow more prosperous and loyally support those vendors who were there with them in the beginning.

Not only do we know almost nothing about these people, we don't even know where many of them *are*. But they are coming, and within the decade they will become important to your business—within a generation, they will be vital.

How will you reach them? The obvious—and scary—answer is that you will hire the Second Billion to help you reach the Third Billion, the city folk selling to their country cousins. If you think you are flying blind now, just wait until you have to hire or contract thousands of people you can't control to represent your company to millions of people you don't know. And that day is less than a decade away.

Any entrepreneur or company that figures out how to reach these next two billion consumers is going to quickly be among the most successful and wealthy in history, enjoying an unprecedented jump in sales and profits. Those companies that don't come up with a workable strategy—or fail to imitate those that have—will not only fall behind, but will be beset by uncounted new competitors, and will be crushed under a billion feet of those rushing elsewhere.

RIPE FOR REVOLUTION

We've spent a lot of time in this section looking at the historical trajectory of a number of forces.

The story of the corporation is one of ever greater decentralization, the pushing downward through the organization of ever more decision making and employee independence, and of the ever-expanding scope of company owners and stakeholders.

The story of technology has been the path set by Moore's and Metcalfe's Laws toward ever greater virtualization and digitalization, as well as the ongoing increase in the size, power, and value of networks.

The story of entrepreneurship has been the increasing democratization of the eligibility of talented individuals to create important technology-based enterprises, from a handful of technical geniuses to millions of motivated individuals from every walk of life and every age group.

And finally, the story of consumerism is the explosive tripling of the population, in less than a lifetime, of individuals actively participating in the Internet-based world economy.

In studying the history of corporate organizations, we have seen that rather than a continuous evolution toward ever more sophisticated and democratic models, these changes have occurred as a series of incremental jumps. Over a finite period of time, historically about once every twenty to thirty years, the current model—itself a competitive breakthrough over the one it supplanted—becomes obsolete. It no longer fits with the changing marketplace, with new technologies, or the expectations of the surrounding society.

That's when some new organizational scheme appears, often in a hot new industry, or in the mind of a business theorist, or someplace else in the world. This new model usually seems radical and risky, but in short order it produces spectacular results. Smart, progressive companies adopt this new model and, if they can successfully work out the kinks and implement it properly, quickly accelerate away from their more reactionary competitors. Those competitors either die or adapt, and if the latter, almost never catch up to the early adopters.

I believe the forces that I have described in this section fully represent a radically changed business environment. I also believe that no currently practiced business organizational model is prepared to deal with this new world, at least not if it plans to be both successful *and* enduring.

If you agree with me, then you also must agree that the time is ripe for a new business era, and a new business organization to meet it.

Now, let's figure out what that organization should look like.

BUILDING THE PROTEAN CORPORATION

CHAPTER

 **‹ 6 ›**

THE CLOUD, THE CORE, AND THE BOSS

WE'VE NOW SEEN THE FORCES at work and the stakes involved in forcing the creation of a new organizational model for companies.

We've also taken a first look at how such an organization would need to be designed if it is to meet the changing economic, technological, structural, and culture demands of the next few decades.

The rest of this book is devoted to investigating the details of such a

"Protean" Corporation, how it will work, and how to get there from where we are today.

A TIMELY NOTION

We begin with the overall *idea* of the Protean Corporation. I found it very interesting that several months after I began writing this book, *BusinessWeek* magazine devoted a cover story to a new kind of computer environment at Google Corp:

> To thrive at Google, he told them, they would have to learn to work–and to dream–on a vastly larger scale. He described Google's globe-spanning network of computers. Yes, they answered search queries instantly. But together they also blitzed through mountains of data, looking for answers or intelligence faster than any machine on earth. Most of this hardware wasn't on the Google campus. It was just out there, somewhere on earth, whirring away in big refrigerated data centers. Folks at Google called it "the cloud." And one challenge of programming at Google was to leverage that cloud–to push it to do things that would overwhelm lesser machines. New hires at Google, Bisciglia says, usually take a few months to get used to this scale. "Then one day, you see someone suggest a wild job that needs a few thousand machines, and you say: 'Hey, he gets it.' "[1]

And a more specific explanation:

> What is Google's cloud? It's a network made of hundreds of thousands, or by some estimates 1 million, cheap servers, each not much more powerful than the PCs we have in our homes. It stores staggering amounts of data, including numerous copies of the World Wide Web. This makes search faster, helping ferret out answers to billions of queries in a fraction of a second. Unlike many traditional supercomputers, Google's system never ages. When its individual pieces die, usually after about three years, engineers pluck them out and replace them with new, faster boxes. This means the cloud regenerates as it grows, almost like a living thing.[2]

A *cloud.* How interesting that at almost exactly the same moment that I was using the metaphor of a cloud to describe the future organization of the organization, *Business Week* was using the same term to describe the information processing architecture at the world's hottest new company. (And the image was cropping up elsewhere as well, not just as a "cloud" but as related forms—i.e., "blog swarm.") By the end of 2008, just months after it first appeared in a public forum, the phrase "cloud computing" had gained common usage to describe a vast array of computers that could be instantly reconfigured, typically using the Internet, to meet individual users' needs. Companies committing themselves to a future in cloud computing include Amazon, Cisco, HP, Sun, and others.

Was this a coincidence? No, I don't think so. We've already discussed the notion of a prevailing metaphor. And historians are very familiar with the concept of an idea whose time has come. Of the latter, you need only look at all of the worthy applicants for the title of inventor of the automobile, radio, television, and computer. Of the former, history is filled with clusters of scientists, philosophers, and artists all building their work on the same underlying theme: think of the role of "the New World" or "Arcadia" during the Age of Exploration, of mutability and Darwinism in the second half of the nineteenth century, or of relativity and the distortion of time in everything from Einstein's theories to Duchamp's *Nude Descending a Staircase* to Proust and Joyce, all within the first few decades of the twentieth century.

I've already noted how first the computer and then the Internet have been used to describe everything from the human brain to the underlying structure of the universe to the Matrix movies. But other metaphors are at work today as well: note how I unconsciously relied upon "punctuated" evolution (with a little bit of Kuhnian paradigm shift) to explain the "eras" of business organization. And notice as well how nanotechnology—itself related to clouds when we speak of swarms of microscopic devices working in concert—is beginning to insinuate itself into our language, film, and imagery.

The metaphor of the *cloud* as something that combines a certain level of chaos operating within loose, but very explicit, rules of organization has been surfacing for decades. It began with the first powerful telescopes, through which astronomers saw distant galaxies, with their billions of stars looking like mist in the comparatively low resolution, and noted their resemblance of clouds.

The quantum cloud model of the atom, which we are using as our visual analogy to the Protean Corporation, was first elucidated after World War I, when the more structured Rutherford model of the atom—the classic electron orbiting like a planet around the solid nucleus—ran smack into the Uncertainty Principle. Suddenly the atom became much more complex, with the only way to accurately represent the location of the electron at any given moment as a "cloud" of probability.

"Cloud" also appeared in the 1950s to describe the mist-filled vessels used to amplify the tracks of short-lived subatomic particles, the so-called "cloud chambers."

But the idea of a cloud as a semi-organized, but largely inchoate, mass of activity or information really came into its own in the 1990s. One reason was the impact of Moore's Law: as "smart" devices became highly miniaturized, it became possible to imagine creating clouds of sensors tossed up into the air or dropped into the ocean or pumped into the bloodstream to provide massive and dynamic measurement in real time. A second reason was field theory, holography, and chaos theory, all of which posited large macro-effects created by vast numbers of independent agents. A third reason was the rise of massively parallel computers, capable of doing spectacularly sophisticated modeling using trillions of data points. And finally, the Internet made it abundantly clear that billions of people going about their everyday business could create huge secondary "network effects," including fast-spreading viruses, memes, and fads.

This was the heart of Dee Hock's theory of "Chaordic Organizations," with its belief that chaotic structures could create their own orderly metaeffects out of that chaos. In some respects, this is the Protean Organization in reverse.[3]

"Clouds" were showing up elsewhere as well. In everything from mobile computing (iClouds) to wide area networks to large computer server "farms," the only analogy that seemed to work for a large number of discrete, yet connected, nodes was a cloud. In a seminal paper written in 2004 entitled "Understanding the Personal Info Cloud: Using the

Model of Attraction," author Thomas Vander Wal described a hierarchy of four types of information clouds:[4]

1 > **The Global Information Cloud**, the best-known being the Internet, which was not organized by the user and offered unlimited access

2 > **The External Information Cloud**, such as a corporate intranet, which offered access only to members

3 > **The Local Information Cloud**, such as a local area network, which is not controlled by the user and requires membership

4 > **The Personal Information Cloud**, which is all of the information we carry around with us, in our computers, cell phones, etc., and to which we have complete access and control

I list these to point out the crucial role of access and control by the user in defining each of these levels.

Yet another type of digital cloud is the "Data Cloud," an idea very familiar to most readers, even if we don't know the term. Data clouds are those representations of information, keywords, or other ideas that are typically presented in a box on a Web page as an array of words. Typically, these words vary in font size or color to represent one or more other weightings. Thus, a Data Cloud on a busy website might list all of the story subjects for the day, then vary their size by the amount of traffic each story has received, and color by the department in which that story is found. Data Clouds were devised to be intuitive to understand and to quickly portray more than one axis of measurement at a time. But in doing so, they also capture the growing shift from monovalent presentations of information (price, color, valence, etc.) to a recognition that the world is a much more complicated place, with many events occurring simultaneously and creating larger phenomena than merely the one at hand.[5]

As we've already seen, "cloud computing" is becoming, especially after a trend-maker like Google adopted the model, the hottest new idea in information processing.

Less well noticed is that the most important new tech trend of the twenty-first century, social networks, are also clouds, this time of millions of individuals, each operating as a free agent, yet constantly linking and de-linking with hundreds of others, all of them operating under a fairly well-defined body of rules, standards, and common tools.

Thus, despite this term surfacing into everyday consciousness in only the last three years, technology-driven clouds of various forms may already be a (largely invisible) part of the lives of more than one billion people around the world. This ought to put to rest any notion that a cloud model of corporate organization is far too radical, too far out, or too extreme to be taken seriously. The real question may be why this paradigm has not been noticed and applied to organizations sooner.

One answer may be that when we look at these other types of technology-driven clouds we don't see them as they really are—and in disguising their real nature they lead the observer to the wrong conclusions about their underlying structure.

Take the Google Computing Cloud. At first glance, it would seem to be homogeneous and without internal structure, represented graphically as just a big ball of interconnected computers, without any real center or change of density throughout. But that is only the case if we focus solely on the hardware, and see the data whipping around that cloud as being undifferentiated. The reality is much different: For one thing, there are people involved, managing the servers, fixing them, writing new applications, fixing old codes, and setting rules of operations. The outside world is involved too, from equipment suppliers to code writers at other companies that sell software, right down to the hackers who threaten the Computing Cloud with their viruses and other forms of nuisance. What this means is that, whether we notice it or not, a Computing Cloud both has a fairly solid center and is more nebulous on the edges than we might assume from the term.

Moreover, the data itself has different values. Most of the user queries passing through the Google Cloud may be silly, obscene, or meaningless, but others may have enormous value to their users. So too may some of Google's own IT operations, embedded in the Cloud, be of considerable financial value to the company. What this means is that at any given moment, different nodes and even regions in a computing cloud may have more value and importance than others. The Cloud is not as homogeneous as it seems.

These features become even more evident when we look at a human cloud, such as a Web 2.0 social network like Wikipedia or Facebook. The clouds created by these entities may have millions of nodes, each representing an individual contributor or participant. And when we think about these social networks we tend to concentrate on the individuals out there in the clouds: the earnest Wiki contributor filing entries and correcting others, or the teenage girl filling her MySpace page with photographs of her girlfriends and prom dates. Once again, it's easy to forget that these are in fact businesses—and though the core team of employees who manage these enterprises is shockingly small compared to traditional companies, they do run their operations and form a very solid core that sets standards, maintains the technical (and increasingly the cultural) quality of their sites, establishes rules and punishes offenders, and provides tools to users.

To appreciate the difference between this small core and the vast cloud around it at one of these enterprises, just note that when Google bought YouTube and News Corp bought MySpace, the billions of dollars that changed hands were not doled out in small checks to the tens of millions of users of those sites, but to a few hundred employees of each. Clearly, their relationship to these sites, and their stake in its success, was far different from those legions who merely *participate* in those sites.

By the same token, within the vast user clouds surrounding these cores—as with the Google Cloud—some nodes are more important than others. Among the millions of user pages on MySpace there are several thousand that might be called "Power Pages," created by particularly gregarious individuals with hundreds of "friends" who play a crucial role in the dynamic of the entire website. They act as matchmakers, traffic cops, tour guides, and friendly way stations to the myriad of less committed MySpace users. Other similar "magnet" pages are run by particularly creative people who locate and disseminate news about interesting new books, movies, or music, advance the language and culture of the overall website, and, ultimately, keep the place cool.

There are others as well who deeply influence the nature of MySpace, including celebrities who are drawn by the cool and who stay as long as the site remains, and predators who are always attracted to dynamic areas where they can hide and still be near the action.

To appreciate the power of these "Cloud Players" one need only track the fortunes of MySpace over the last two years. Despite the fact that it is the biggest social network on the planet and its nearly 200 million members form a larger population than most nations, MySpace is already beginning to noticeably fade from the industry leadership. Upstart Facebook began as a social network largely for college kids, which fact alone made it appealing to high schoolers. It wasn't long before it became cool for high school and even junior high school kids—especially boys, who often lead these fads, with the girls in hot pursuit to be near them—to set up Facebook pages.

These pioneers were soon followed by many of the aforementioned "power page" MySpace users, who, though initially reluctant to leave their power base, recognized that it was more important to be part of the Next Big Thing. Their departure sucked much of the excitement out of MySpace, which in turn made that site less attractive to celebrities. Before long, at least among the cognoscenti—that is, with the under-twenty-five-year-olds who originally made social networks a mass phenomenon—MySpace was being dismissed as a virtual landscape of thirteen-year-old girls and the forty-five-year-old male perverts pursuing them. This was obviously not true given the sheer size of MySpace, but in a world where loyalties can change with the tap of a key, perception is almost everything.

Meanwhile, Facebook became the new social network darling and that company, perhaps learning from MySpace's mistakes, has been far more of a participant in the activities of its users, constantly introducing tools and applications to enable its millions to hide content from one audience while showing them to another, clean up their sites, even start businesses. In other words, Facebook's core isn't simply creating an environment for the cloud and then letting it run without control or interference. As a result, Facebook seems to be escaping much of the overnight obsolescence of MySpace.

That's not to say that Facebook hasn't made mistakes of its own, and big ones to boot. Not least is the fact that Facebook regularly gets low marks for being the slowest running of all of the big social sites, a breach of an unwritten trust between the cloud and the core in which the former expects the latter to always maintain a top-notch operating environment. But a far bigger breach, indeed an outright betrayal, surfaced in late 2007 when, thanks to user complaints, the media first uncovered the true nature of Facebook's so-called "Beacon" program. In operation, Beacon automatically registered any user purchase from one of Facebook's corporate clients and then notified that user's entire "friends" list of the purchase.

Beacon was presented by Facebook as a service to its users but the truth quickly became apparent: it was a revenue generator for the company in which users were automatically "opted in" to the program and only allowed, via a brief (and tiny) message, to click out of it.

It wasn't long before the scandal erupted: recipients finding out about their birthday/Christmas/anniversary gifts ahead of time, friends finding out about very personal purchases, wives discovering their husbands were buying gifts for mistresses—and spilled out into the national media. Facebook CEO Mark Zuckerberg found himself on *60 Minutes* trying to justify Beacon as "a really good thing" and as desperately needed to help the company pay its four hundred employees.[6] It was an ugly moment that broke faith with Facebook's users and all but guaranteed that they would be a little less loyal when the next hot new social network site came along.

The short, but exciting, story of social networks and the Web 2.0 world offers, I think, some very important lessons about the future of organizations and serves as a test case for the rise of the Protean Corporation.

What the stories of Facebook, MySpace, and all of the others tell us is that, despite the historic trends of the last two centuries toward ever-greater decentralization, employee empowerment, and dependence on technology, *there is a point beyond which human beings cannot go.* A purely Virtual Organization—that is, one that is only a homogeneous cloud of undifferentiated, equal employees—as appealing as it may sound, simply does not work in the real world, no more than pure communism or pure anarchy does. It will spin out of control, or turn on itself, or collapse into fiefdoms—or most likely in the twenty-first century economy, simply evaporate as all of the stakeholders depart for better opportunities elsewhere.

Real, human-based organizations need some kind of structure. They need a purpose. They need an identity. They need direction and goals. And they need an organizing philosophy that manifests itself as a culture. They can only do this, and yet still remain sufficiently agile and adaptive to cope with a rapidly changing world, if some part of that organization remains permanent, enduring, and committed to the overall health of the organization itself.

There is a theorem in topology (the Brouwer fixed-point theorem) that states that if you place a sheet of paper on a tabletop and, without lifting it, wad that paper up, some point on that sheet will remain exactly where it was, unmoved.[7] For a company to succeed in this new world, it will have to accelerate its activities, and stretch and twist and fold its operations in an endless attempt to stay competitive. But somewhere in that organization, like the eye in a hurricane, something has to remain clear, calm, and unchanged. And that center will have to spend its days worrying not about the latest new product or market thrust or intrapreneurial venture, but about the meaning of the company, its rules of behavior, its values, and its goals—and providing the tools (and, on occasion, the punishments) to help employees to reach those goals.

We will start at that fixed point in the Protean Corporation—the Core and its inhabitants—and work our way outward through the various concentric rings until we reach the edge of the bull's-eye, the equivalent of the heliosphere at the farthest reaches of the sun's influence on the solar system, where the boundaries of the Protean Corporation meet the larger economy and society.

A NEW KIND OF BOSS

Why the Core and not the traditional center of the company, the CEO? Because, in a departure from the traditional corporate model, the chief executive is not the heart of Protean Corporation: he or she is in fact the only figure in the organization who inhabits (indeed, directs) the Cloud but has limited access to and control over the Core.

Though this may seem counterintuitive at first glance, it is in fact congruent with modern corporate life. The days of the CEO who rises from the ranks of the company after thirty or forty years to take over and run the organization with an unmatched depth of understanding about its culture and operations are just about gone. In fact, in many modern companies, being a patient and loyal lieutenant is almost grounds for *not* getting the corner office, as it is presumed to be symptomatic of narrowed experience, a lack of ambition, and some character flaw that has made such a person unattractive to executive recruiters and raiders from other companies.

Though statistically this is not entirely accurate, it does seem that the only companies today run by long-time employees are those who still have their founder CEOs (who, as we'll see, actually do belong in the Core). For almost every other ambitious CEO-wannabe, the career path in the twenty-first century is an ever-upward zigzag from one company to another, learning different skills and managing different types of teams along the way. This new career path certainly produces skilled executives with the breadth of experience and the portfolio of skills needed to run a competitive company in a fast-changing global economy.

But this shift from experienced company veteran CEO to sophisticated corporate gunslinger CEO has come at a cost: a general lack of knowledge about the culture of the companies they lead. As a result, these "carpetbagger" CEOs can often do a brilliant job of shaking up a moribund company, leading a static company into dynamic new market opportunities, and, most notoriously, restructuring a company through cost-cutting and layoffs to make it more competitive.

The great risk, however, with this new type of CEO is that of a corporate catastrophe, of which there have been a number in recent years.

In too many of those cases, a superstar outsider CEO has come in and, with limited understanding of the company's culture or capabilities, has launched the firm into a new market for which it is, if not technically then culturally, uncompetitive; or adopted a new organizational model for which the company is culturally incompatible, or just introduced a management style that produces widespread resistance, sabotage, or mutiny.

Thus the *Core*, a body of individuals whose understanding of the company's philosophy, history, and culture is unmatched, and their enduring commitment to the firm stands in contrast (and counterpoint) to the comings and goings of transient CEOs.

So, who are these people: where do they come from, how do you find them, and how many should there be? Most of all, what should they do?

Let's take the last first:

The role of the Core in a Protean Corporation is to establish standards of behavior in the company, preserve the company history, and nurture and grow the company's culture. Its primary operating task is to advise and consent on all cultural decisions made by the company chief executive and management. Its secondary task is to maintain and upgrade the company statement of purpose, corporate objectives, and all other documents, regulations, and standards reflecting the company's culture and philosophy. The Core reports directly to the Board of Directors and indirectly to the CEO.

In other words, the Core of a Protean Corporation is a group of employees, representing no more than a small fraction of the company's total employment, who, by dint of their experience, knowledge of the company's history, and culture, are rewarded with a unique and influential role in the company—one that guarantees them unmatched influence, permanent job security, and considerable honor. In this new role, they are the protectors of those unchanging, or slowly changing, features of the company in an otherwise rapidly evolving and changing business environment.

To do that, these individuals need to be protected, and insulated, from the pressures and vagaries of daily business life. And that needs to be done not just by removing them from most of the day-to-day workaday life in the company (though not all, as they must appreciate the current environment inside the company for their fellow workers), but also shielded from the influence and pressures from powerful individuals within the company with their own agendas, not least the CEO. This is done by guaranteeing them, with some exceptions for egregious behavior, almost perfect job security. It is also done by pulling the Core out of the reporting structure of the organization and placing it as a direct report to the only other theoretically independent organization in the company: the board of directors.

This is hardly a new idea. The concept of a specialized group of wise people empowered to protect the enduring interests of a larger group is as old as mankind. Priests, elder councils, judges, and tribunals have fulfilled this role for thousands of years. The notion is, of course, enshrined in our own U.S. Constitution, which establishes in the Supreme Court a deliberative body of people experienced in the law, who hold lifetime seats, and who judge the constitutionality of legislation and lower court decisions. These august groups are inevitably created to provide consistency against haphazard change, and durability in the face of rapid change. The fact that mankind has turned to this solution for as long as there has been mankind would seem to recommend this model for dealing with the anarchy of the twenty-first-century global economy and the Protean Corporations that will be needed to compete in it.

Other people have begun to notice the same thing, and not least because most of these vaunted social networking sites are proving to be not as decentralized and flat as their image suggests. One such observer is Chris Wilson at Slate.com:

> According to researchers in Palo Alto, 1 percent of Wikipedia users are responsible for about half of the site's edits. The site also deploys bots—supervised by a special caste of devoted users—that help standardize format, prevent vandalism, and root out folks who flood the site with obscenities. This is not the wisdom of the crowd. This is the wisdom of the chaperones.[8]

It has become increasingly obvious that while Web 2.0 was originally perceived as vast, unstructured masses of individuals contributing willy-nilly to these great social networking sites, policing and editing ourselves, and somehow producing a structured, fully organized result—it has in fact turned out to be something very different: a comparatively small coterie of individuals hidden away at the center of these immense mobs, devoting enormous amounts of time, setting content standards, and acting as gatekeepers, devotedly serving as Keepers of the Flame.

In other words, even in the most seemingly virtualized and unstructured giant new cultural phenomena of our time, there still exists a Core. Our Digital Democracies turn out to be a lot more like Digital Republics.

So what do we call these people who dwell in the Core? When I first pondered the people of the Core, the word that immediately came to mind was *Immortals*. That term has a very long history, and almost always connected with highly esteemed individuals at the core of a larger organization: from the original Immortals, the bodyguards, and most-respected soldiers of the kings of ancient Persia who faced the Spartans at Thermopylae, to the current members of the French Academy, the guardians of French culture, literature, and language.

Unfortunately, "Immortal" is a little too patrician—even pretentious—for our more casual, and democratic, modern world. And most of the alternative titles I came up with—Corporate Treasure, Company Mentor—were either equally highfalutin or just too familiar in the business world.

So in the end, I'm going to use *The Core* to describe both the enduring heart of the Protean Corporation and the employees who inhabit it. This may cause some confusion on occasion, but I think that will be counterbalanced by the semantic reminder that the entity and the people are, in the end, synonymous.

CHAPTER

‹ **7** ›

DENIZENS
OF THE CORE

FOREVER AND EVER

WHO ARE THESE CORE EMPLOYEES, these denizens of the Core?

The fact is, you already know most of their names.

As I've already said, a Core Employee can be anyone in the company, holding any title from janitor to chief executive officer. Indeed, if there isn't a secretary or two somewhere on that list you are probably doing your search wrong and allowing your own bias and prejudice regarding class and education to slip in.

As I list the characteristics that I think make up a potential company Immortal, I'll wager a half-dozen names will pop into your mind:

1 > A *company veteran* who has been with the firm for most of its history (or if the company is venerable, seems to have been with the company longer than anyone can remember)

2 > A *survivor*, better yet a key player, in at least one of the major crises in the company's history (not necessarily a leader during that crisis, but perhaps a foot soldier)

3 > *Synonymous* with the company. When you think of a person who "bleeds the company's colors," this is the person who comes to mind, even if only for amusement and awe

4 > The *go-to* person at company headquarters or in one of the divisions or sales offices. If you need to know how something is done in the company, where corporate resources are, how to circumvent company bureaucracies—this is the person you go to

5 > *Connected*, often at levels far higher or lower than his or her pay-grade: the VP who is friends with the guys in the tool shop or the secretary who can talk directly with the CEO

6 > Generally seen as *irreplaceable*, who is so embedded into the organization of the company that it is almost impossible to imagine the place without him or her being there

If that list of criteria doesn't provoke a list of a dozen or more names, your company is either very young or very dysfunctional (likely with a lot of recent lay-offs), or you aren't doing your job as a manager. Even if you do come up with a sizable list of candidates, perhaps the best and easiest way to vet them—and to come up with names you may have missed—is to study the internal communications traffic of your company. Wherever you encounter a major communications node, that is, people who spend far more time on interoffice e-mails, instant messages, and phone calls (especially incoming) than anyone else, those people are people worthy of your attention. Either they are horrible gossips or overexploited employees, or they are precisely the people whom everyone else in the company goes to for advice or help.[1]

Once you find these people, the biggest challenge will be to overcome your own preconceptions. That's because these will likely *not* be the kind of people you would normally consider for great advancement or great power. A person who wants to spend a lifetime with a company, who feels a great sense of personal responsibility for that company's success, and who is willing to make personal sacrifices out of a deep and abiding loyalty to the company, is likely to have a personality very different—almost antithetical—to that of the modern career-oriented, entrepreneurial, gypsylike executive. It is quite possible that you won't even *like* some of these people, as they will seem to occupy a universe very different from your own. Others may remind you of your grandmother, or the friendly clerk down at the hardware store, or the teller at the bank. Others may have once been what you are now, but they have mellowed and lost the fire of ambition that still burns within you. And a few may be individuals, an industry legend or perhaps the founder of the company, before whom you are quite properly humbled.

This may seem like a pretty motley crowd, composed as it is of people with education ranging from correspondence school to Ivy League PhDs, personal wealth ranging from equity in a tract home to billions of dollars in stock, collectibles, and real estate, and lifestyles running the gamut from den mother to master of the universe. But the common thread that ties this group together is something that you yourself may not share: an enduring love for, loyalty toward, and identification with the company. That commonality is important enough to these individuals that they can leave their differences behind to work for the company's long-term good.

Undoubtedly there will be communications challenges within this group, class differences, and variations in intelligence, but the lingua franca will be the story of the company itself, its stories and legends, and its rules of proper behavior. In those matters, intelligence is not necessarily an advantage, while experience and common sense are. Wisdom is not confined to PhDs, or to Executive Row.

APPOINTMENT WITH IMMORTALITY

How should these Core Employees be selected? My sense is that early in a company's history they will be self-selected: employees who are willing to do their regular jobs and then devote *additional* time and energy to serving on the committees and boards that are the precursors to the formation of the Core.

Assuming that the founder(s) of the company are still present, it is they who should select the Founding Core Employees. After all, the founders typically are the major shareholders in the company, and thus have the greatest financial stake in its success. But even more, the company is their legacy, it may even carry their names, and thus they have the greatest emotional stake in choosing the best people as Founding Core Employees. As these founders will also be able to choose themselves as Core Employees (the only CEOs who retain that right), they will also have personal stake in choosing people with whom they can work best, and who have the closest congruence to themselves in their understanding of the core philosophy of the company.

In my experience, entrepreneur/founders are also far more likely to have the "common touch"—the natural tendency to stay in close contact with fellow employees up and down the org chart—than their more detached and professional successors. It's not unusual to see a wealthy and famous company founder still staying in regular contact with a security guard or secretary or machinist who has been with the company almost from the beginning, something almost never found in a second or third generation CEO. As a result, the entrepreneur/founder is almost uniquely suited to make those initial selections and to continue to do so as long as he or she is chief executive of the company.

Once a founder leaves the CEO (or other senior) position to join the board of directors, he or she would automatically be invited to join the Core Employees. Unique to the Protean Corporation, a founder CEO might even choose not to sit as a Director but devote full-time to membership in the Core Employees alone. This would, in fact, solve a long-standing problem in the business world, especially in high-tech companies: what to do with the founder who is more of a technologist or entrepreneur-impresario than a real businessperson.

A classic example of this type of person is Steve Wozniak, cofounder of Apple Computer. He is widely considered the heart and soul of Apple, but is not really a corporate type. So, for two decades he has inhabited a kind of limbo in relation to Apple: kept at arm's length most of the time, but occasionally brought in when the company spiritually loses its way. He is a classic candidate to become a Core Employee.

Another perfect example was Al Shugart, who founded *two* great computer disk drive companies—Shugart Associates and Seagate—only to be fired from both of them. Still another is Nolan Bushnell, founder of Atari and Pizza Time Theater, a flamboyant character who could create successful companies but ultimately couldn't run them.

Another well-known type that would likely make a good candidate for the Core is the Genius—the scientist or engineer (think Nathan Myhrvold at Microsoft, Bill Joy at Sun Microsystems, Ray Dolby, Robert Metcalfe) whose genius and contribution are so great that the company is all but obliged to put them on or near the top of the org chart, where their gifts are often misdirected on management or budgeting or some other duty for which they have little talent.

But there are also numerous other, less-celebrated categories from which Core Employees might be recruited: the "salesman's salesman" in field sales, the marcom veteran who writes all of the company's annual reports, the "go-to" guy in the factory who knows how to get the product out the door, the unofficial company historian, hostess, social director, record keeper . . .

This raises the interesting question: can a *nonemployee* become a Core Employee? There are obviously lots of former employees who moved on in their careers: retirees, and strategic partners who might be a real asset in bringing knowledge and experience to the Core. But I think the answer is *no*. To be a Core Employee requires a complete commitment to the company, not a part-time one. These individuals are better as candidates to join the Board of Directors.

One part of the process that should remain unchanged in both the founder/entrepreneur and the professional CEO eras is that all new nominations to the Core need to be approved by the Core Employees themselves and by the Board of Directors. This provides a necessary check on any efforts to subvert the Core's role in the company and its independence.

Once the founder/entrepreneur leaves the CEO chair (or other founders leave daily roles in the company), the selection process for Core Employees will need to change. Henceforth, as with other such organizations—the Légion d'Honneur, the American Academy of Arts and Sciences, and the American Academy of Arts and Letters—membership in the Core would be managed by the Core Employees themselves, nominating and electing replacements for fellow members who have retired, died, or simply gone back to work in the company. Total membership in the Core for a given company would be fixed, and, to prevent "packing," could only be changed by a vote of the Board of Directors, or, conversely, a shareholder proxy vote at, say, the annual meeting.

Removing a Core Employee should not be a simple process, but require considerable deliberation and unanimity. One possibility might be that it would only be possible to remove a Core Employee from office with a two-thirds vote of other Core Employees, followed by a special hearing and vote by the Board of Directors. The difficulties in accomplishing this would motivate Core Employees to be very careful in selecting their compatriots.

ROUNDING OUT THE CORE

The Core Employees are the only citizens of the Core, but they aren't its only inhabitants. The Core needs some sort of infrastructure, as it is asking too much of the Core Employees not only to take on such major responsibilities, but also to assume their own housekeeping as well.

At the same time, when it comes to the bottom line of the company, the Core is an expense and makes no immediate contributions to revenues. Therefore, its overhead must remain as low as possible.

In terms of salaries, this suggests that the Core Employees should be paid in some combination of wages and stock options, and heavily weighted toward the latter as they not only will provide long-term stability to company shares (they are less likely than almost any other type of shareholder to suddenly liquidate their stock holdings), but, given their commitment to and work for the company, their reward should be linked to the long-term health of the company. Having an executive secretary or division marketing manager or factory supervisor, after twenty devoted years on the job, become a Core Employee and serve the company in that capacity for a dozen years more before retiring a multimillionaire, is precisely the scenario that most smart companies should desire.

By the same token, if we are to keep the Core costs low, support staffing for the Core Employees should be bare bones (which also is a way to keep the Core from trying to extend its reach beyond its charter). Exactly what the ratio of Core Employees to clerks and secretaries should be is something that will be unique to each company, and probably can only be determined in actual practice, but the following seems reasonable:

<> 10 Core Employees, none full-time: No staff

<> 20 Core Employees, none full-time: Two staff members

<> 20 Core Employees, all full-time: Ten staff members

<> 100 Core Employees, full-time: Fifty staff members, including Chief of Staff

<> 1,000 Core Employees, full-time: 500 staff members, including Chief of Staff and lieutenants

In other words, once the Core becomes a full-time and distinct organization within the company, the total number of staffers should stay at about 50 percent of the total number of Core Employees, or roughly one assistant for every two Core Employees. Needless to say, in practice this may not be sufficient, and as the Core grows with the company, this ratio is certainly an approximation: beyond 100 Core Employees, the staffing will require some kind of a structure itself, mostly likely a Chief of Staff of some kind. And as the Core approaches 1,000 Core Employees, a management apparatus will be necessary not only to take care of the 500 staffers, but also to organize and direct Core plenums, task force meetings, company visits, and other events.

It is important to state once again that the Core staff is *not* part of the Core. Its members are members of the Cloud, albeit with rather unique job responsibilities and access to the very heart of the company. Nevertheless, they do not enjoy the privileges (job security, immunity from executive oversight, stock options) given to the Core Employees. They can be fired, transferred out of the Core, etc., while at the same time they can move on to other career opportunities and have a highly valuable and portable skill.

An interesting question is: We know that the Core Employees are answerable only to the Board of Directors—but who do the Core staffers report to? The obvious answer is to the Core Employees themselves as direct reports. But the Core Employees aren't going to pay the salaries of these staffers, advise them on their 401(k)s, or track their training classes. Moreover, as already noted, these staffers are citizens of the Cloud, not the Core. So the most likely candidate to serve as their manager is the Corporate Vice-President for Administration, or at least someone in that person's office.

It may seem that I'm dealing with minutiae here, but in fact this is not a minor matter, as it raises the question of influence. I've been a reporter for too many years, and been involved with too many companies, to believe that a good organization chart, no matter how well designed, can protect a company from the dark side of human nature.

The biggest fear most companies will have about creating a Core filled with independent, job-secure Core Employees who report to only the Board of Directors is that it will result in a group of Illuminati who secretly run the company to their own ends and do not really have to answer to anyone. But that threat can be mitigated by severely circumscribing the duties of the Core Employees and of the Core, that is, by restraining them from participating *in any way* in the line operations of the company. The Core Employees can advise and consent on personnel policies, corporate objectives, and benefit programs, as well as adjudicate disputes involving employee behavior or conflicting long-term organizational (but not business or marketing) strategies. Cross that line and they can be called in front of the Board by the CEO.

A far more likely (and more subtle) danger in creating a Core is not that it will become too powerful, but that what power it has will be subverted. This subversion can come from two directions: from the top down, which we'll deal with in a few pages, or from the bottom up. By the latter, I mean that a senior executive or CEO, feeling threatened by the independence of the Core, might try to plant staffers in the Core as listening posts on the debates and decisions taking place there, and then try to influence them.

This is a real danger; after all, nobody fights their way up to executive row in order to give *away* power. Most CEOs and senior managers will be clever enough to appreciate that a Core can be a powerful tool, not just in freeing the executive offices from what is generally considered a distraction from the real job of making money, but also as valuable ally in legitimizing the company's long-term strategy and reining in destructive elements. But a few will find the very existence of the Core to be a challenge to their authority and hegemony. Having a spy or two inside the Core will seem like a good insurance policy.

For this reason, selection of staffers for the Core will have to be done with great prudence, the independence and privacy of the Core impressed upon them as paramount, and any violation of this code of secrecy must be grounds for immediate termination.

THE HARD WORK OF STABILITY

What then will daily work life be like for a Core Employee?

We've described the creation of the Core and both the selection and population sizes of Core Employees. We've also discussed the scope of work expected of the Core, in particular, what the Core Employees are *not* supposed to do. But we have not yet described the actual activities that will fill their days.

I see six overall categories of work:

‹ 1 ›
Benefits and work environment

Advising on salaries; establishing nonsalary benefits; managing the employee stock option program; advising on profit sharing; establishing standards for retirement and pensions, oversight on medical insurance and 401(k) programs, administering flextime and other workday programs; establishing and overseeing employee events (holiday parties, picnics, specialty events); overseeing employee facilities; establishing guidelines for workplace environment; oversight of in-house services (restaurants, executive training, day care, gym, etc.).

‹ 2 ›
Infrastructure and security

Establishing guidelines for equipment (laptops, wireless modems and hubs, cell phones, etc.) provided to employees and contractors at different levels of connection to the company; setting minimum communication standards for networks, software suites, and hardware for computers; determining the level of security for company networks; setting minimum standards for the equipping of home offices; oversight on all firewalls, protocols, and security codes; determining levels of employee access to secure information, outside sites, etc., on the Internet via employee networks.

‹ 3 ›
Exposition and training

Creation and regular updating/maintenance of all corporate documents relating to company philosophy, mission statement, objectives; oversight of editorial in corporate annual report and public documents (brochures, videos, advertisements, press releases) relating to company image; oversight of, participation in, and possible management of new employee orientation programs; management of employee/management (lunches, etc.) and large-scale employee team-building (to maintain cohesion and morale among the diverse elements of the Cloud); management of new Core Employee training and orientation programs.

〈 4 〉

Standards of behavior and adjudication

(a) Establish and codify official company rules of engagement regarding company secrets, operating in other nations, bribes and graft, conflict of interest. Codify standards of behavior in the workplace, especially between superiors and subordinates. Set worldwide company rules regarding discrimination by sex, religion, age, and orientation. Determine accepted salary variability between comparable employees in different countries. Establish official company rules regarding acceptable national laws under which the company can and cannot operate.

(b) Establish boards and tribunals to rule upon violations of these company rules and to adjudicate disputes between employees. All employees called before one of these boards will be allowed to self-represent or be represented, and all decisions may be appealed to the Board of Directors. Serve as court of last resort for terminations and transfers. Approval of Board of Director salaries, benefits, and options.

〈 5 〉

Strategic planning

Early identification of phase shifts in the company's development (start-up to established, IPO, global operations, etc.) and preparation of responses in company organization and employee relations; development and regular upgrading of contingent responses to potential company crises; regular surveys of other companies to identify, analyze, and potentially implement similar employee, workplace, and compensation/benefits programs; oversight of company advertising and publicity to reflect anticipated changes in corporate message; assisting in the search for new Directors and CEO when needed.

‹ 6 ›

Corporate associations

Oversight of all company lobbying and political advocacy (determining boundaries of behavior, regulatory goals, budget); serve as company representative to Industry and Trade Associations and regional groups; serve on state and national government committees and task forces; assist in representing the company at all regional and local zoning, new construction permitting, etc.; represent the company in all "executive loan" programs to non-profit organizations; serve, upon invitation, on the board of directors of the company's subsidiaries and strategic partners.

THAT LIST SHOULD disabuse you of any notion that the Core will be a corporate country club for aging but still-loyal executives or a secure sinecure for faithful retainers—or that Core Employees will be buried inside the company with little contact with the outside world. In truth, the Core Employees are going to work hard and spend considerable time away from the company, and many will bear responsibilities of a magnitude they've never before known.

The nature of these duties, you'll also note, in almost every case requires wise judgment and a deep understanding of the company's philosophy and culture, rather than any particular professional expertise. This is why it is possible to draw the Core Employees from the top to the bottom of the company organization chart. And while the veteran janitor may be less eloquent than the veteran corporate attorney or veteran regional sales manager, he may very well be a better judge of proper behavior and have a much better sense of employee morale.

One need only glance at the job description listed to appreciate that it will require a lot of meetings and sitting on commissions. This will not appeal to everyone. The machinist or corporate attorney or facilities manager may decide to eschew all of the advantages conferred by becoming a Core Employee and stick with the profession he or she knows best and perhaps loves. This is as it should be: to become a Core Employee in a company requires a commitment to that company that supersedes one's commitment to profession or career. To turn down such a position will of course also mean sacrificing the ultimate job security that comes only with joining the Core, but as we'll see, there are still jobs in the Cloud that offer significant job security.

CORE QUESTIONS

Before we leave the Core, there are a few concerns that still need to be raised and answered:

Does permanent job security really mean what it says? What if the company gets in serious trouble? Are the Core Employees' jobs still preserved when everyone else is losing theirs? Given their power and influence in the company, shouldn't they be held at least as responsible as everyone else for the failure?

"Permanent job security" means what it says. That is the heart of the contract between the company and the Core. The Core Employees sacrifice their options, all but rendering themselves unemployable anywhere else, and the company rewards them for this sacrifice by guaranteeing their employment until retirement in all but the most egregious cases of personal misbehavior. Figuratively speaking (but just barely), should a great company go under, the Core Employees will be the last people to turn off the lights. Realistically speaking, there is some point in the collapse of a company at which its actual survival is at stake, employment shrinks, and the ratio between employees and Core Employees becomes untenable. At that point, the Core Employees must be offered the opportunity to return to their former jobs.

What happens in the case of a merger between two companies? Will the two Cores merge as well? How about an acquisition by another, larger, company?

This is a tough one. The ultimate disposition of the Core of a company merging or being acquired will have to be negotiated by the Board, but cannot violate the conditions of the contract with the Core Employees. There seem to be three possible resolutions:

1 > **The acquiring company absorbs the Core of the purchased company** and uses the latter's Core Employees to expand its own Core to match the increase in size of the now larger company.

2 > **The merging companies also merge their Cores**, using this new amalgam to help smooth the transition, meld the two cultures, and help with the new strategic planning.

3 > **The acquiring company chooses not to absorb the Core of the acquired company.** It then buys out the lifetime employment contracts of the smaller company's Core Employees through the end of the working careers.

One possible concern in all of this is that the Core Employees, seeing a threat to their own position, will use their power to sabotage any potential merger. But once again, the Core is restrained from actively involving itself in any company business activities, including M&A. Indeed, in a company that is being acquired, the Core's very last act may be to prepare employees for the transition and preside over its own evaporation.

What is the danger that Core Employees will become so detached from their former careers at the company that they will lose track of how the company really operates, where morale really stands, and how managers are painting a false picture of the real state of their operations? Just as important, what is the danger that they will use their power and position to hijack the company?

This is the Pharisee question, which has haunted me ever since I first devised the idea of a Core filled with Core Employees: what is to keep these men and women, secure in their permanent job security, and answerable to almost no one, from growing detached from the reality of daily work life, of setting standards for employees that are simply unachievable in the real world of business?

Equally, what keeps the Core Employees from enhancing their own power by actively undermining the authority of the CEO?

Once again, we're talking human nature: the Core Employees are very likely to believe that the company belongs much more to them than some hot-shot carpetbagging Chief Executive who is hanging around just long enough to post some good quarterly financials and then trade up to the CEO job at an even bigger company. Only a fool would entrust such a vital question to human goodwill and respect for others.

For the answer, we have to fall back on the example of Madison and the Framers of the Constitution: *checks and balances*. The Core cannot interfere in the business operations of the company, which are directed by the CEO, but they can set the tenor of the company in light of these operations. The CEO cannot veto Core decisions, nor influence the Core Employees through career intimidation, but does have under his or her jurisdiction the job of executing the Core Employees' decisions. For both, any infringement must go to the Board of Directors for adjudication, which is only just, as the Board is itself a body created to represent the interests of the real owners of the company, the shareholders.

Meanwhile, as we already know, the Board has oversight powers on the CEO and always carries in its back pocket the ability to fire a CEO for nonperformance. By the same token, the Board also has the power to circumscribe all actions of the Core, rendering those that exceed the Core Employees' charter as null and void. (An interesting added possibility, though experience would be the best indicator for this, might be to also give the Board the power to "fire" a Core Employee, or even dissolve the entire Core, for behavioral, rather than policy, reasons, such as an inability to get along with the rest of the Core or irresolvable differences of opinion.) Needless to say, in keeping with the contract, any such Core Employee would have the right to be compensated at full pay until retirement.

A Fine and Final Point

One final comment before we leave the Core and head out into the Cloud: Even if you are highly skeptical of everything I have just presented in this chapter, there is still one vital fact that I hope you take away from this section.

It is that whether you know it or not, your company already has a de facto Core of people who are absolutely vital to the long-term success of the enterprise. They sit at key nodes in the company, not just because they have migrated there voluntarily, but because their coworkers, recognizing their value, have put them there and surrounded them with numerous lines of communications.

These de facto "Cores," whatever name they've been given, have long been a celebrated part of great organizations: the "Whiz Kids" at post-WWII Ford Motor Company, the intensely loyal veterans from scientists to secretaries at Apple Computer, the "Crotonville" grads at Jack Welch's General Electric, the cadre of Vietnam veteran officers and senior noncoms that formed around Colin Powell and Norman Schwarzkopf, the generation of NFL coaches that emerged from Bill Walsh's San Francisco 49ers and its "West Coast Offense."

In each case, a small cohort of individuals, imbued with a common vision of what the organization should be and where it should go, served not only as leaders but as protectors and missionaries of that vision, and achieved historic results. The fundamental difference between then and now is that those organizations were distinct, bounded entities, and thus the "Core" could also serve as line employees. As I've tried to show, in today's world of edgeless, rapidly changing organizations, that kind of dual role no longer works.

As the modern business world—and by extension your company—has become more volatile, markets less predictable, and employment more fluid, the de facto Core Employees have become ever more important to everyone else in the company. They provide continuity, wisdom, and stability. Whatever their job titles, these individuals are advisors, mentors, and facilitators. Their fellow employees, and their immediate supervisors, appreciate the value of these individuals and often go to great lengths to keep them, reward them in informal ways, and protect their jobs. As such, these treasured employees already enjoy a kind of permanent job security.

By the same token, most of these individuals know who their counterparts—their equivalents—are in other parts of the organization. And though they rarely have direct contact with each other through their jobs, these individuals almost certainly have indirect—almost sub rosa—connection via intermediaries, e-mail routings, encounters at company social events, stories that circulate around the company (often circulated by these individuals), and retirement luncheons and other milestone moments. When a crisis hits the company, these are the folks management turns to for help and organizational stability. Thus, they regularly find themselves on committees and task forces at major turning points in the company's history. These employees know their role in the organization, even if their superiors (especially the newly arrived ones) don't, and though they are often zealous protectors of their turf and their reputations, they typically hold each other in mutual respect, if only because of their common loyalty to the firm.

In other words, these honored employees are not only already ersatz Core Employees, but they also constitute a nascent but still very real Core. And as important as they may be to the company in their current positions, they are even more important to the organization in this larger, yet undefined, other role they play.

Institutionally, your company knows this even if it has never either elaborated on the nature of the Core or identified and honored its Core Employees. As such, even if you don't choose to adopt the design of the Protean Corporation, you already have at least this component of it in place.

That's the good news. You can call on your Core Employees if you need to, and they are already working together in some limited way for the company's long-term health. The bad news is that because they are unidentified, they are vulnerable. Until you secure and protect them through some organizational scheme, these vitally important employees are at risk of being lost through indiscriminate lay-offs, budget cuts that focus on the highest paid employees, forced "golden parachutes" for older employees, and shutdowns of entire product groups or divisions. It should be apparent by now that in saving the salary expense of one of these employees you could be losing many, many times that in institutional value and intellectual capital.

If you take nothing else away from this book, I hope you recognize that your organization does have these unique individuals embedded within it: that they are absolutely critical to its long-term success, that you already know who many of these people are, and with a little effort you can identify the rest of them, and most of all, that once you identify these individuals, you must protect them, even if you do nothing else, and whatever you do, *do not lose them.*

As long as you have your Core Employees, anything is possible. Anything can be fixed.

CHAPTER

RETHINKING
THE CEO

THERE IS ONLY ONE INDIVIDUAL who may freely move from the
Core to the Cloud: the Chief Executive Officer.

Even now, the Board of Directors is usually constrained, except in
emergencies, from directing operations inside the company. And in the
Protean Corporation, the Core Employees are forbidden from acting
on the line operations of the company. Employees in the Cloud are not

allowed to participate in Core activities; and even the staff of the Core, though it may operate there, is still officially part of the Cloud and may not participate in Core functions.

The President of the company, if that task is de-linked from the CEO position, typically is also the Chief Operating Officer of the company, and is therefore the executive in charge of the Cloud. Sometimes, however, the Presidency is more of a titular position held by an older executive. In that case, in the Protean Corporation, such a figure may move into the Cloud to become its managing officer, still holding the title of President.

The one place where this rigid separation of church and state (or the sacred and the profane) in the Protean Corporation is breached is in the person of the CEO. But even then, that access, if properly designed, is severely circumscribed.

As noted earlier, the CEO in the Protean Corporation is formally constrained from influencing or impeding the activities of the Core. Nor may the CEO fire a Core Employee without a full hearing before the Board of Directors. By the same token, if the CEO has any dispute with the decisions of the Core, he must adjudicate the conflict before the Board (by the way, this will likely lead to the kind of active and engaged Board that both the federal government and industry observers are currently calling for).

This would seem to severely limit the CEO's freedom of action—and that, on first glance, would not be a welcome development in a twenty-first-century marketplace that demands rapid change and unprecedented flexibility. However, the CEO has a couple cards of his or her own and, given human nature, will no doubt make full use of them.

For one thing, as noted earlier, the Core Employees cannot influence the *business* operations of the company. Therefore, nearly all of the daily activities of the CEO are untouched by the actions of the Core. Perhaps even more important, the CEO remains the Chief Executor of the company, meaning that whatever the Core decides regarding benefits, training, and so forth will still have to be implemented via the CEO and the administration of the company.

In theory, this would mean that the CEO could always "pocket veto" any decision, plan, or strategy emerging from the Core, but that would likely lead to a quick hearing before the Board.

So, a more likely scenario is that the CEO, whose task it is to smoothly integrate these initiatives into the company with the minimum of interruption, confusion, or collateral damage, will *modify* the program to better fit his or her interests. The result will be the kind of push and pull, debate and compromise that will only be salutary for the company in the long run. It will force the CEO, even if he or she is new to the job, to always consider the culture and history of the company; while at the same time it will force the Core Employees to make sure their decisions are not only proper, but pragmatic.

As both Adam Smith and the Founders taught us long ago, the surest path to success is to bet not on human idealism, but its basest instincts, and then to pit those instincts against one another to create a higher good. There is no doubt that the CEO and the Core will occasionally clash—they *have* to if they are doing their jobs—so the challenge is not to avoid that conflict, but to keep it both balanced and channeled toward resolutions that ultimately benefit the enterprise.

The most likely result of all of the countervailing forces, acting as checks and balances, within the Protean Corporation, is that the Core Employees will invite the CEO to make presentations or give testimony regarding proposed initiatives, so that the final draft of the initiative will have the best chance of being implemented by the rest of the company. Conversely, the CEO will be motivated to achieve some sort of compromise with the Core Employees early on in the process so as not to be stuck with a program he or she does not want to implement, or perhaps worse, be called to a hearing before the Board (which is, one remembers, the CEO's boss). In the latter case, the CEO will hardly fail to notice that should there be a showdown, the Core Employees have more job security than the CEO does.

Once again, a shrewd CEO will recognize that good relations with the Core Employees can bring enormous benefits. What might seem an arbitrary or self-serving decision by the CEO (reducing benefits, changing the pension plan) gains considerable cover if it comes from the Core, and smart CEOs may just choose to defer those tough decisions to the Core Employees. Moreover, with the Core in place, the CEO can escape some of the most time-consuming "secondary" activities of the office—like determining it is time for a new set of Corporate Objectives, then determining (and dealing with the politicking that inevitably follows) who should sit on the committee, then accepting and studying the committee's decision—and, should the results need to be thrown out and rewritten, or a committee member replaced, dealing with the bad internal publicity that ensues. All of that now sits squarely on the shoulders of the Core Employees, and they get to take any resulting flak.

In fact, the prototype for this structure is the Corporate Objectives program at Hewlett-Packard Co. Every few years for a half-century now, a committee of veteran HPers gathers to revisit the company's famous list of Objectives and determine if each is still valid and is properly phrased. This process, begun under founders Bill Hewlett and Dave Packard, has continued now long after their deaths, and has been supported by four other CEOs (John Young, Lew Platt, Carly Fiorina, and Mark Hurd) whose management styles could not be more different from one another.

Why has this program endured through good times and bad? Because of precedent, employee expectation, morale, and most of all, because each CEO in turn has realized that this is how HP defines itself, how it brings the employees together in common cause, and more pragmatically, because it enables those executives to point to some other justification for their decisions besides their own judgment.

Once CEOs realize they can offload such matters on the Core— duties for which CEOs increasingly have little inclination or expertise— and devote more time to the real business of increasing revenues and profits, market share, and stock price, they may quickly abandon any early objections and work to get the Core to take on even *more* company activities. When that happens, the Core Employees will find that the ban placed on their involvement in the noncultural "business" of the company also wisely protects excesses in both directions.

CEO QUESTION TIME

There are some questions that still need to be answered about the role of the CEO in the Protean Corporation:

Will CEOs accept the presence of this new, largely untouchable organization—the Core—inside their companies?

The quick answer is that they will have no choice; the presence of the Core will be part of the new status quo of the companies that employ them, and excising it will be even more difficult than removing one or more Core Employees.

But the simple fact is that new CEOs are *always* dealing with unique structures and patterns of behavior at companies they inherit. That's their job: they take what they're given and try to make the best of the situation. And I believe that new CEOs will find that the existence of a Core will prove to be a major advantage. For one thing, instead of having to search the company blindly for experienced advisors to explain how the place works, that reservoir of wisdom will have already been assembled and will be easily accessible.

Moreover, one of the leading causes of failure by new CEOs is their inability to understand or maneuver within the existing corporate culture. Too many new chief executives blunder in this way at the very beginning of their tenure—Sculley at Apple, Fiorina at HP, Bill Agee at Bendix, Al Dunlap at Sunbeam-Oster, Ed McCracken at Silicon Graphics, Phil White at Informix[1]—and end up creating a legacy of employee resentment and damaged morale that can take years to cure (if ever). The business media is filled with stories of failed CEOs who alienated their employees almost from the first day on the job, and soon found themselves with an angry, truculent company that quietly sabotages any of the CEO's new initiatives.

The presence of the Core enables the new CEO not only to hit the ground fast and focus upon the operations of the company, its competitive health, and its long-term market strategy, but to do so within a structure that protects that CEO from making dangerous cultural faux pas. Instead, even with the new boss, the company still maintains the continuity of its corporate style.

But what if the company's culture is all wrong, toxic, or obsolete?

In other words: what if the corporate culture itself is dysfunctional? What if the Core has failed to create and nurture a healthy company environment? Why then should it be allowed to maintain its position of power and immunity within the company? And why would a CEO ever join a company without the power to toss out the Core and build a new one?

These are all very good questions, and it would be absurd to assume (once again in light of human nature) that every Core will have a salutary effect upon their surrounding organizations. But let's not forget: the Board of Directors also has added powers in the Protean Organization, not least of which the ability to reconstitute the Core. Part of the negotiations between the Board and potential new CEO hire will, if both parties are smart, include discussions of the Core and its composition.

At the same time, we don't want the revamping of the Core to be *easy*: arbitrary restructurings, wholesale firings, and casual comings and goings of Core Employees defeats the entire purpose of this organization structure, which is designed to be enduring, contemplative, and detached from the vagaries of daily operations.

The best defense against this, I believe, is *expense*: by the nature of their employment contracts, Core Employees must be bought out for the rest of their career. That won't be cheap, and will require both the Board and the new CEO to give serious consideration to precisely which Core Employees need to go. It will also force the CEO to recognize that there is a cultural legacy at the firm that must be dealt with by something other than the usual solution: laying off the accumulated wisdom of the company. Finally, it forces the Board to fully commit itself to the cultural and financial consequences of the new CEO's proposed strategy. (In some cases, it may also buy some time for the new CEO to learn that the *real* problem with the company's culture is not bad employees, but bad management; not a sick culture, but a misguided business plan.)

How will the job of the CEO change in the Protean Corporation?

The job of the CEO is already changing in traditional corporations. A few years ago, I spent some time with an old acquaintance, Eric Schmidt, in his new role as CEO of Google. I had known Eric as a scientist at Sun Microsystems, as the CEO of troubled networking company Novell, and as a director of Siebel Systems. Now he was in the cockpit of the hottest and most exciting new company on the planet.

The Eric Schmidt I met that day, which was early on in the Google story, was the same guy I'd always known, and yet very different. He still dressed like a division general manager and talked like a college professor, but instead of meeting in an executive office, we met in one of Google's conference rooms—at a Ping-Pong table.[2]

When I kidded him about the change of work environment from Fortune 500 to frat house, Schmidt shrugged, as if to say, "It's what the kids want."

But when I pressed him further, Eric launched into an explanation of how he saw the role of the CEO changing in the modern, fast-moving technology company. In retrospect, I realize that he was in fact describing what it will take to run a Protean Corporation.

What Schmidt said was that the modern CEO must become a *chameleon*. The Chief Executive must change management style and attitude with each company constituency he or she meets through the day. As Schmidt explained it, that might mean meeting in the morning with code writers at a Ping-Pong table in a room filled with Pilates balls and lava lamps, at noon with the finance guys in suits in a traditional boardroom, and in the afternoon in the game room with artsy creative types dressed in black and sipping herbal tea. But it is more even than wearing the uniforms of these various constituent groups: the modern CEO must also share the thought processes of these groups, understand the argot, and ultimately, *think* like the members of these different groups.

In other words, the modern CEO, as described by Eric Schmidt, must become *Protean* himself.

This is a mind-boggling notion, because it turns all of our existing notions of what it means to be the chief executive—to be the *boss*—on its head. The standard image of the CEO as Master of the Universe, who has battled to the top of the corporate pyramid in order to be the captain of his or her own fate, who sets the tune to which everyone else in the organization must dance, now needs a major revision. If Schmidt is an early bellwether of what is to come on executive row, and I think he is, then the next generations of chief executives will have a very different relationship with the rest of the organization, and the people they nominally control.

This shouldn't be surprising: anyone who has studied the corporate world over the last couple of decades can't fail to notice that the nexus of technology, democracy, and mass culture—not to mention the accelerated pace of modern life—has forced even the most hidebound organizations to shift ever greater quantities of responsibility and decision making down through the organization.

You simply cannot hand away power in an organization and expect your job to remain unchanged. The traditional chief executive of a rigidly structured, top-down organization was expected to put his or her stamp on the entire organization, not just because of ego, but because it is the most efficient way to get things done. When everyone marched in lockstep, the enterprise enjoyed its maximum market impact. You toed the CEO's line not just because he or she had the power of life or death over your career (and changing jobs wasn't easy a half-century ago), but because, like the offensive line in football, if you surged forward together you could push the competition backward and gain yardage.

But modern business is no longer "two yards and a cloud of dust." In a worldwide market, linked at light speed, change is beginning to happen so fast that there is no longer time to send almost *any* information back to headquarters and the CEO for judgment, not because the information transfer takes so long (it doesn't, not in a wireless broadband world), but because the decision cycle itself takes too long. By the time the CEO sufficiently verses himself on the matter at hand, the opportunity is likely to be lost.

A decade ago, a lot of people predicted that this was coming, but almost no one really considered what it would mean for the man or woman at the top of the company. While it seemed self-evident that the CEO could no longer micromanage the firm, what couldn't be imagined was that the CEO would quickly thereafter reach the point where he or she barely managed *at all*. Instead, modern CEOs increasingly—and in the Protean Corporation will almost entirely—focus on creating the ground for their company's operations, choosing the best talent to run those operations, resolving disputes, and breaking logjams, and in almost every other way, *serving* his or her employees. The CEO will be amply rewarded for this work, and the job itself will require incredible intelligence, empathy, focus, and versatility but also—contra the business books of the 1990s—a whole lot less of the CEO as warlord.

Think of it as Packard's revenge: sixty years ago he warned those old-line CEOs that they were dinosaurs, and then he created the business model, and the technology revolution, that has now made their kind extinct.

That said, please don't get the impression that the new kind of CEO that will characterize the Protean Corporation is some kind of sensitive, passive soul. Dave Packard was a giant of a man, a table-pounder, and no one who ever faced his wrath ever forgot it. The unwritten subtext of the HP Way was that while Bill and Dave may be entrusting you to make decisions for the company, you had better not make any stupid decisions. Jack Welch, another prototype of the CEO of the future, this time the impresario setting the stage for a hundred different activities and coordinating them all, was legendary for sweeping in on a GE division president and interrogating him into a puddle of jelly. And Eric Schmidt, the prototype of the CEO as chameleon, is always the smartest guy in the room and will blow right past you if you are not prepared to keep up.

Surprising as it may sound, the CEO of a Protean Corporation will have to be *more* authoritative—or at least more persuasive—than the CEO of the traditional company. When you can't manage by fiat, you have to manage by charisma, character, and competence. That's not easy, as proven by the wrecked careers we've seen in recent years.

Worse, as companies lose all of their rigidity and become fluid, and then cloudlike, the onus will be on the CEO to regularly visit—physically or virtually—all of those many diverse operations around the world. We are already seeing that: anyone who envies the salaries and benefits enjoyed by modern Fortune 500 CEOs should take a closer look at their lives, which are largely spent on airplanes visiting one company division and sales office after another. The CFO may be able to do most of his or her business via telephone and e-mail, but the CEO needs to be there in the flesh. For that reason, the days of "Executive Row" at the company headquarters are over as well: the only person there is the executive secretary, who serves as traffic cop to her ever-in-transit boss.

This is already creating a spiritual and structural vacuum at the very center of the modern company. And it was recognition of this, and its potential for disaster, that first led me to ponder the notion of establishing some kind of new and solid corporate Core.

Will the presence of the Core make CEOs even less loyal to the companies that employ them? Will it make them even more gypsylike than they are today?

The snarky answer to that question is: How could they be any *less* loyal than they are today? Since the 1990s, CEO superstars have behaved much like their sports counterparts: less loyal to any one employer than to their salaries and public image; often rewarded more for their reputation than for their actual performance; and perpetually in search of the next opportunity to trade up, no matter what their current commitments.

It's unlikely that this behavior will change with the advent of the Protean Corporation. It probably won't get worse, and only a starry-eyed optimist can think it will get better. So the real question is: what can be done to mitigate the damage created by these peripatetic CEOs, while at the same time taking maximum advantage of their talents?

The answer, I believe, is not to force the CEO to assume a role for which he or she is not temperamentally suited, but to instead create a new center to the company, one that doesn't threaten the power and prerogative of the Chief Executive, but liberates the CEO to do what he or she does best.

But won't that help keep the CEO around a little longer? Maybe, but only until other companies develop their own Cores.

What happens when the plans of a CEO collide with the corporate culture being maintained by the Core Employees? Who wins?

This, I think, is the most interesting question regarding the new role of the CEO. What if the Chief Executive's long-term strategy for a company goes in a very different direction or, even more interesting, is in actual diametric opposition to the corporate culture being maintained by the Core?

For example, what if a CEO wants to take the company in the direction of high-risk market opportunities, while the Core is building a work environment dedicated to stability, or vice versa? Or if the Core is struggling to instill in the company a philosophy of superior customer service and support, while the CEO is moving the company's products toward commoditization and budget pricing. Or perhaps most likely, the CEO wants to incorporate lay-offs and rapid turnover into the corporate operating style, while the Core is instituting programs dedicated to job security and employee retention.

An already classic example of just this kind of behavior at cross-purposes can be seen in the story of Hewlett-Packard under Carly Fiorina. Fiorina, a bona fide CEO superstar, arrived at HP with a portfolio of plans for shaking some life back into what she thought was a sleepy, almost moribund corporation. But she didn't take into account that HP had a de facto Core: the so-called "HP Way," one of the strongest and most-storied corporate cultures. And, thanks to a half-century of generous employee stock purchase, which had put a near majority of HP's outstanding shares in the hands of current and past employees, this de facto Core also had real teeth, as Fiorina discovered when she embarked on a major acquisition of Compaq Computer and found herself in a proxy battle with her own employees. She barely won that battle, but came away facing widespread employee mutiny and an eventually fatal loss of confidence by Wall Street.

In the years since, some analysts have argued that, in fact, Fiorina's strategy for HP was the right one, and that her successor, Mark Hurd, merely executed that strategy and, in doing so, turned around HP's fortunes. That's a debate for another time and place (though for now it should be noted that for a half-century before that HP had always innovated its way out of doldrums merely by trusting its employees to come up with new ideas). What is important for our purposes is that, whatever the merits of her strategy, Fiorina *failed* as a manager: her employees mutinied against her, the Board of Directors fired her, Wall Street abandoned her, and most of HP cheered her departure.

Why the vehement response? Because Fiorina tried to impose a new company environment in the face of, and almost directly antithetical to, perhaps the strongest and most established corporate culture on the planet. She never learned to use HP's Core; instead, she tried to destroy it. It was a fatal mistake.

A few years before that, just the opposite occurred at Apple Computer. There, a series of Chief Executives had spent a decade leading the company away from what many loyal employees and customers believed was the true Apple culture. The return of cofounder Steve Jobs seemed almost overnight to re-attune Apple's business model to its corporate culture, and the company embarked on one of the most enthralling runs of new product creation in business history.

As we've already noted, the fact that there might be conflict between the CEO and the Core in the Protean Corporation is not *in itself* a bad thing. The task of any corporation is not to eliminate conflict (because that would also eliminate innovation and change), but to use it in a productive way.

So the real question is: will a conflict between the CEO and the Core regularly lead to gridlock and stasis?

No. For the simple reason that there is a built-in conflict resolution process: appeal to the Board of Directors for a ruling. I would go one step further: such a conflict, once brought into the open, would serve as a powerful early warning mechanism about threats to the health of the enterprise. It says that the company's business strategy does not mesh with the company's internal culture, the perfect recipe for catastrophe. It may very well be time for the CEO to go, before he or she does any more damage; or for the leaders of the opposition in the Core Employees to be retired. Either way, it is time for the Board to act swiftly and decisively. In contrast, no comparable warning system exists in today's organizations; usually it is only when the company finds itself in an existential crisis that the Board intervenes, and then usually too late.

Perhaps the best part of this is that both parties, the CEO and the Core Employees, can look ahead and see this draconian resolution to their conflict, and may very well decide not to reach that point of no return, but instead find a compromise. It is in just such negotiations that a new CEO may truly understand the soul of the company for the first time. And that can only be for the good.

CHAPTER

WHERE THE REAL ACTION IS

THE CLOUD

NOW LET'S LOOK AT THE *CLOUD*.

This is where the real action is going to be in the Protean Corporation. Everything discussed until now was merely to set the stage for the employees of the Cloud to do their jobs as effectively as possible. It will be the Cloud that determines whether the company remains competitive and successful in the new economy.

The first thing we need to understand is that, like real clouds, the

Cloud is not entirely chaotic, nor is it completely amorphous. It has structure and rules governing its behavior, and it is precisely this structure that enables it to behave in a largely fluid and fast-moving way.

First of all, we need a taxonomy of the Cloud: its structures, its governing rules, and its key agents.

Let's begin with structures. Like the quantum or nebular clouds we used as analogies in the beginning of this book, the Cloud of the Protean Corporation is denser toward the center; that is, it grows more structured and sophisticated as we get closer to the Core. If we want terms to describe this feature, à la the Core and the Core Employees, let's call this denser area of the Cloud the *Inner Ring*, and its inhabitants, the *Varsity*.

The Inner Ring is essentially the traditional corporation. It contains those infrastructural operations found in nearly all companies and other organizations: manufacturing and product management, finance and payroll, advertising and public relations, sales and marketing management, corporate communications, research and development, and administration and human resources. None of these disappears in the Protean Corporation—they are indispensable to any organization in a market economy—but they do change in certain structural ways.

These changes are subtle. For example, in the earliest forms of organization charts, the President/CEO sat at the top of the pyramid, with successive tiers below for corporate administration, corporate operations (marketing, finance, HR), division management, manufacturing, and workers. This was replaced by a more complex org chart that distinguished between "line" and "staff" operations, the former being a vertical organization from the CEO down through operations management to division management to product management to employees; the latter branching outward through diverse staff VPs to the company's various and relatively self-contained support operations.

With some variations, that's how most enterprises are organized today. Smaller companies may contract out some of the staff functions, but once they reach any real size they typically pull these functions in-house and organize in a line/staff manner. Even a company that claims to operate in an "inverted pyramid" management style—empowering the employees to a greater degree than in the past—still largely maintains this organizational scheme.

Anyone who works in the modern corporation knows that there is not a lot of satisfaction with this arrangement: line workers (rightly) believe that staff workers have more autonomy; while staff workers are convinced (rightly) that should the company get into financial trouble, they will be the first to go.

In the Protean Corporation, the boundaries between line and staff will largely disappear—not for philosophical reasons, but pragmatic ones. In an age when everything from stock option programs to customer service to the enlistment of tens of millions of users in the Web community as product designers is considered a potential edge over the competition, *every* corporate operation can become a key competitive factor. For that reason, every company operation must exist in continuity with all of the others, tapping into the Core at one end and spreading out to the entire Cloud at the other.

This process is already well underway as companies have become more virtualized. In the modern corporation, almost every company operation is now composed not just of full-time employees, but ever-growing numbers of other workers whose connection to the company range from full-time contracts to occasional piecework. Some are given desks and workstations at the company, but most just come and go, usually working from home.

In other words, most companies already have emerging clouds, and most full-time employees spend at least part of their workdays acting as conduits and intermediaries to these inside/outsiders—managing them, training them, and training them in the company's "way of doing things."

Another way to visualize this is to go back to our cosmological image. Think of comets racing down into the strong gravitational field of the sun, nosing into the solar wind, and how they grow tails of streaming particles trailing behind them. Now picture the Protean Corporation, with its solid Core and Cloud that grows ever thinner the farther out it extends from the Core. The Inner Ring is the dense area nearest the Core, and traditional corporate operations now become a necklace of even denser areas encircling the Core, nearly solid toward the center and trailing ever wider outward into the Cloud.

In the denser regions of these operational units can be found the Varsity. Conversely, as we will see, "alternative" employees with a much more tenuous connection to the company will be found in those thinner, expanding regions of these units.

If all this seems a bit too mumbo-jumbo, put yourself in the position of the business owner of 1890 being shown the first pyramidal organizational chart, or the company president of 1930 looking at Sloan's divisional model. Or, remember the first time *you* heard about the concept of virtual work teams linked around the world and handing off tasks throughout a twenty-four-hour workday. In the age of MySpace, blogswarms, and cloud computing, this new metaphor for company organization is anything but outlandish.

VARSITY CLUB

What is the role of employees in the Varsity? Well, not much different from what it is today or what it has been for the last decade.

The employees of the Inner Ring will be the equivalents of today's "exempt" employees in a corporation, or "full-timers" in other organizations. That is, they will work full-time for a salary for the company, and in return earn the benefits for that commitment in the form of profit-sharing, health insurance, education, 401(k) contributions, and employee facilities. Some of these employees will work at home part-time or even full-time; others will be required to work at the office or factory. All will show their commitment to the company through longevity, job performance, and promotions, and in doing so will migrate ever closer to the Core. In fact, future members of the Core will be recruited from the innermost regions of the Inner Ring, though some may choose to stay where they are.

What is crucial to understand is that the Varsity is not the same as Management. Though the Varsity is likely to have a higher percentage of managers and supervisors, there is not a causal link; rather, hardworking and committed employees tend eventually to be promoted into some sort of management position. But research scientists are also likely to be in the Varsity, as are a sizable percentage of factory workers and secretaries.

This is pretty much what enlightened companies do today, rewarding their best employees with higher "tracking" in terms of salaries and other benefits. The establishment of an Inner Circle just codifies the process, distinguishing those employees who have made a level of commitment to the company that earns them in return greater job security, higher pay, and better benefits.

It is quite possible that in many Protean Corporations, individuals who traditionally appear high on the organization chart—corporate attorneys, salespeople, even product managers—may not be part of the Varsity at all and have a much looser and more tenuous relationship with the company than today. This too is a trend not unknown in the modern corporation: a growing number of professional "hired guns" is choosing to establish their own entrepreneurial ventures and then contract their services—often for extended periods—to corporate clients. Companies have grown as accustomed to this as they have to employees working from home.

Another experience that has become increasingly commonplace in corporation operations—and will only be amplified in the Protean Corporation—is that a near-majority of employees in these departments and divisions aren't traditional employees at all. The last twenty-five years has seen the rise of a whole bestiary of new employee types: part-time, permanent part-time, contractor, full-time contractor, (in-house) consultant, on-site nonemployee (from a strategic partner), off-site employee (based at strategic partner), and so forth.

This list is only going to get more complex and subdivided in the years to come. For example, what do you call a person in Bangalore who is hired, off the Internet, for twenty minutes, to write two crucial lines of computer code? How about the sixteen-year-old girl in Mexico City who has volunteered to help maintain the quality of her small section of the company's Web community, and has done such a brilliant job that you want to pay her a small retainer to keep her around? How about the village chief in the Luangwa Valley of northern Zambia who is "paid" in cell phone credits for acting as the host twice per year to your regional sales director (who himself is not an employee of the company either)? Now multiply those scenarios by ten thousand or more and you have the face of the twenty-first century corporation.

One of the best places to see this future is among the Web 2.0 companies: Wikipedia, MySpace, Facebook, Twitter, LinkedIn, and YouTube. In one respect, these are gigantic operations: MySpace and Facebook have more total users than the population of the United States; in terms of contributors, Wikipedia has more "employees" than most Fortune 500 companies.

As we've already noted, by any traditional measure, these firms are tiny: most can fit their entire permanent employee staff in a modest four-story office building. But if you include "nontraditional" employees, that is, the people who (usually voluntarily) design, build, maintain, and upgrade the company's "product," the total employment at these firms suddenly jumps into the millions.

Dealing with all of this complexity will be the greatest challenge faced by the operations of the Inner Ring. The Core will do its best to create the base for these activities, but it will be the departments that execute it. And they won't be operating from afar: they themselves will exhibit the same kind of structural complexity. It can accurately be said that in the Protean Corporation (and any company model that attempts to function in the new global economy), corporate operations will function with their heads on the ground (the Core) and their feet literally in the Clouds. They will experience every day, on a smaller scale, the same challenges faced by the larger company that envelops them.

MAKING THE TEAM

What will it be like to be a member of the Varsity?

On one hand, it will be a lot like having a job in a traditional organization, or at least such an organization today. You'll have a full-time job, with all of the benefits expected from a modern company; in fact, you may even have more, given that the number of your peers will likely be fewer in number than today, and your position thus more valued and privileged. You'll have about the same job security as you do today, though in some cases perhaps a little more. You may go to an office every day, work from home, or do a little of both, much like the average business professional today.

Because of your fewer numbers, you'll probably get paid a little more than in the past, and have greater opportunities to earn real wealth through stock options and other forms of compensation. And, though you'll be able to change jobs by joining other companies, such a jump will be somewhat more difficult than today, and there is a distinct possibility that the outside job offers you receive will be for somewhat less money, but perhaps for a greater opportunity than what you enjoy now.

However, some parts of your job will be *very* different.

For one thing, at the opposite poles of your business relationships will be two groups that could not be more dissimilar. On one side will be a small group of highly privileged individuals who, though they may earn less than you in terms of salary, enjoy much greater benefits (especially when it comes to stock options) and have almost perfect job security. This group cannot tell you *what* to do in your job, but it will certainly tell you *how* you can do it. You will be motivated to work with this group in part because they are crucial to the long-term health of your employer, because they determine the quality of your daily work life, and perhaps because you dream of joining them one day.

On the other side will be a vast group of people whose connection to the company can range from ironclad to tenuous, whose understanding of the company's business and culture can be anything from complete to indifferent, and whose contact with you may last for decades or just a matter of minutes. And though these "employees" are nominally direct reports to you, most will be indifferent to your authority beyond what is instrumental to getting the immediate job done. If you aren't helping these people, they will simply ignore you or move on to another employer.

The task of the Varsity, it seems to me, is already becoming apparent in the modern corporation. In the Protean Corporation those tasks only become more amplified as the number of "alternative" employees grows to dominate the organization, in some cases—such as social Web sites—reaching up to 98 percent of the participants, but even in more traditional businesses they probably amount to 60 percent or more. (Any reader who is concerned that there will be too much overhead of "nonessential" employees, like the Core Employees, in the Protean Corporation should look at those ratios. Not only is the Core and Inner Ring, that is, the entire structure of the traditional company, minuscule compared to the surrounding Cloud, but nearly all growth in the company will take place in those outer regions.)

It's important to keep that ratio, and those relationships, in mind when we consider what will be the job responsibilities of people in the Varsity. Obviously, they will still have their basic job to do: marketing, payroll, facilities, manufacturing, product management, legal, and so forth. But the way those jobs will play out on a daily basis will be drastically different. In particular, members of the Varsity will have three basic tasks:

‹ 1 ›

Recruitment

With the vast majority of people reporting to you being "alternative" employees, whose time under your management may be measured in anything from decades to seconds, and whose monthly turnover may reach 50 percent, it will take a lot more than posting a job notice on the office bulletin board to find the right people for these jobs.

It's going to take considerable marketing skills, combined with powerful search tools and real-time adaptable contracts and payment systems, to compete against all of the other Protean Corporations trying to grab the best talent out of the transient global workforce. Headhunters and executive recruiters will be of little use: you'll save them for hiring new members of Varsity. Online job placement services such as Monster .com will help, but they will likely be inadequate to capture the really specialized, very short-timers. That will require a mastery of Google keywords, Craigslist, and specialty search bots.

The good news (and what will keep this part of the job from becoming full time) is that those same people will be looking for you, and there will be some structures further out in the Cloud that will take on much of this work as well.

≺ 2 ≻
Control

The generally accepted maximum number of people who you can closely manage effectively is about a dozen. After that, you need to incorporate an additional layer of management.

In the Protean Corporation, if you are a member of the Varsity, you may well have hundreds, even thousands, of "employees" reporting to you. And there will be much less chance that you will be able to create the requisite layers of intermediate management that those numbers would seem to require. Luckily, most of those employees will be of such brief duration that they will need little management, only an assignment and, a short time later, the acceptance of their finished work.

Of course, that too will take time and will probably require automation tools (contract generation, formal acceptance, automatic test, and payment) that are not currently in general use. Just as important, much of that resulting work will be assigned to other entities in the Cloud that we will soon describe. It is those entities that will largely determine whether the terms of the contract have been adequately met.

≺ 3 ≻
Communications

Corporate internal communications have come a long way since interoffice memos, and today's professional uses everything from e-mail to instant messaging to BlackBerrys, virtual meetings, and Skype Internet phone calls to convey information up and down through the organization. Moreover, this information can be made quite rich through streaming video and audio, PowerPoint presentations, and hyperlinks.

That's welcome news, but in the face of what's coming, it is also wholly inadequate. In fact, one can make a very strong case for contemporary institutions having, for the most part, fallen dangerously short of what they *currently* require in the way of company communications.

WITH THE ARRIVAL OF the Protean Corporation, these weaknesses can become catastrophic, and I don't use that term lightly. Should those thousands of "alternative" employees—scattered throughout the world speaking and acting in the company's name—not be well-trained in the company's culture, philosophy, and rules of behavior, they could make deals, break laws, or in a thousand other ways seriously damage the company's reputation and cost millions in litigation.

It is important to ask *why* today's companies and other large institutions haven't gotten better at communicating with their employees and members. It's not as if the technology isn't there: when almost every laptop and cell phone has a built-in camera, when fourteen-year-olds are casually loading videos onto YouTube, high schoolers hold international conference calls on Skype, and the avatars of millions of people wander around virtual landscapes like Second Life, it is false to claim that the communications infrastructure is inadequate. Neither can you claim that there is not enough talent available to fill these channels with content: not when there are thousands of hugely talented and highly trained newspaper reporters and magazine writers right now looking for work after the collapse of their respective industries.

No, this has been a failure of HR and Corporate Communications to adequately deal with a pressing matter with anything beyond a few Band-Aid solutions, such as an employee Web page, a blog or two, and (for the most adventurous) a few tentative steps into Second Life—all the while ignoring the juggernaut heading their way. If anything goes wrong in these feeble attempts—the occasional antimanagement posting on a company Web site, for example—the organization quickly retreats to the status quo ante.

In the long run, that is a recipe for disaster. Companies are going to have to develop much more extensive, pervasive, and richer communications apparatuses if they are to maintain their growing number of "alternative" employees. If they fail to do so, they will lose their ability to compete in the global marketplace. If they succeed, they will have created the skeleton of the Protean Corporation.

SPEAKING OUT

To consider this communications paradox, let's do a little thought problem: You are the product manager for a new software application product. You have about twenty Varsity employees and maybe four supervisors in your immediate team, who help you manage product development (product characterization and features, compatibility, code writing, debugging, etc.), marketing (packaging, advertising, publicity, point-of-sale, Web), sales, and admin. You will also eventually have fifty more (plus supervisors) working on your manufacturing line, overseeing the packaging and shipping of the product in-house for your major markets, and supervising contract manufacturers around the world doing the same for your specialty markets. You estimate that this will include about a thousand workers around the world.

Beyond them, you have an estimated three thousand "alternative" employees helping with this work in one capacity or another. About fifty of these are what you would characterize as permanent part-timers like Ben—who lives on a farm outside of Medford, Oregon—with whom you have worked in the past, and whom you recruited for this project at the very beginning. There are also two thousand code writers scattered around the globe in India, China, Estonia, and Israel. You have worked with some of these people before, like Santosh, who is a professor in Bangalore at IIT and a whiz at spotting logic errors, but most are very short-timers who sign up for a few days, write a few score lines of code in their particular area of expertise, take their online paycheck, and move on.

A quick check of the home locations of these "Quick Contractors" (when you can even find them; most communicate only online and by code names) yields a full-immersion lesson in geography: Dakar, Nairobi, Tuscaloosa, Moose Jaw, Addis Ababa, programmers in Nigeria (please let it be a reformed "419" scammer, not a current one, you pray), Lithuania,

Malawi, four hundred in China, Gibraltar, Paraguay. You don't have enough pins to mark their locations on a world map, and luckily you don't have to because by tomorrow a quarter of them will be gone, replaced by another global contingent.

And that's just the code writers. They're the easy ones. Not only do they carry their certifications and ratings from previous employers with them, but the work is largely empirical: either it works or it doesn't and that can be quickly tested. But there are another 950 folks under your putative control whose work cannot so easily be quality-tested. One hundred fifty of these individuals can be described as "marketers," which include publicists who specialize in either trade or business publications and work in particular national regional markets, and advertising people who do the same.

Then there is the small army of two hundred people, many of them housewives, retirees, and students, who help manage the social network that is being created around your product and who travel about the Web enlisting other people to join in. You also depend on these individuals to supplement your automatic recruitment tools and help you find quick contractors with special skills (say, a calligrapher for the invitations to your launch event in Hong Kong) that are beyond the capabilities of the search bots.

Finally, there are the "salespeople"—all six hundred of them. About fifty can be described as traditional sales professionals. That is, they work for your company almost exclusively, on long-term contracts. You know their names and talk with them almost daily. They usually provide the bulk of your sales, but not always. There are another half-dozen contract agents whom you know little about beyond some questionable facts (does the "X Man" really own an island?). But what is unquestionable is that they are demon sellers: Yokahama Tommy's clients represent a full 10 percent of your sales, all from a guy (if it is a guy) whom you wouldn't recognize if he sat next to you in a bar.

As for the rest, how do you characterize them? The guy in Dar es Salaam is apparently a government minister who uses his contacts with local business leaders to sell your products. It's legal in Tanzania. Then there's the "singing gaucho" in Uruguay who sells your product (and his

CDs) from a booth set up at his concerts. He appears to be very popular. You estimate that about two-thirds of these folks work in the countries of the industrial world, operating like classic contract salespeople, getting paid in commissions, and (if they prove their worth and stick around) some salary.

As for the other third, you know far, far less about what they do. You've heard stories about one of your "occasional" salespeople who happens to be a bush pilot in Angola and is very successful at selling to some of those secret diamond-mining operations deep in the back country. Then there's the woman with the Thai mailing address who could be smuggling your product into Myanmar, but there's no proof. And, of course, everyone in the country knows about that group of grad students at Colgate who constructed that wacky avatar "Gurundi" and set up a very popular b-to-b software store on Second Life. But hundreds of other successful sales representatives of your products remain all but anonymous, or come and go so quickly that you have neither the time nor the inclination to learn much about them. Nevertheless, *all* of these salespeople are important to you, and though you may see little of them, it is obvious that they know their customers to a degree that you could never match.

So here are the questions: How do you communicate with all of these different people, with their diverse lifestyles and equally diverse relationships to you and your operation? Leaving aside the question of how you will find and recruit these "alternative" employees, how will you bring them up to speed—give them an understanding of the product, performance specs, pricing, options, service, and support, plus the rules of engagement as determined by the company, the corporate culture they are expected to exhibit in dealing with customers, contracts, and order entry—fast enough for them to be productive in the potentially short time they have before moving on to other work? How will you know, once these individuals disappear into the field, bearing your company's name and your reputation, that they will abide by the laws of the nation(s) in which they operate, as well as by the rules set down by the company Core? And if they are successful, what are you going to do to keep them around as contributing members of the company, and retain their talent and intellectual capital?

Finally, even assuming that you have a personal staff and several score middle managers to help you, how are you going to manage this army of employees whose ratio is well beyond the traditional leader's span of control?

These are not questions solely for the still theoretical Protean Corporation of the future, but for real companies operating in the real world right now. As I write these paragraphs, the news is carrying the story about a rogue trader at France's Société Générale Bank who through improper and unchecked investing may have cost the company as much as $7 billion. The dark side of empowering employees to make their own decisions for the company is that sometimes they can make very stupid or dangerous decisions. It is a risk the modern company has to take if it is going stay competitive, but it is a risk that grows by the day.

In the business world of the future, where companies will likely have a majority of their employees not under continuous supervision, and all of them will be empowered to one degree or another to represent the company and to make important decisions in its stead, the risk becomes extreme and the danger acute. That is yet another reason for the evolution to the Protean Corporation: lacking a center, truly virtual corporations can't control the chaos on its fringes; only the presence of the Core and the Inner Ring can establish rules for and maintain relative control over the behavior on the company's outer fringes.

But that is only possible with powerful communications and monitoring tools. The first time a new "alternative" employee is hired or contracted, that person should know *within minutes* how the company works; its standards of proper business behavior; its attitudes toward local, national, and international laws; and a fair amount about the company's history and culture.

That's a very tall order, especially when you add to that instruction and databases on the company's products, options and customizations, pricing, shipping, and service—all for an individual who may work only a few weeks for the company, and thus whose stake in the firm's future is marginal, and whose interest in all this training is almost purely incidental. The "alternative" employee is primarily interested in using his or her skills to make money and enhance a résumé; you are interested in having him or her make you money but to do so only while putting the company's image in the best light.

Today, no company has in place a training program and information-sharing apparatus sophisticated enough to accomplish what will have to be a standard business activity, repeated thousands of times each day. So, the big make-or-break question becomes: How do we get from here to there—fast?

One answer, I think, is that conducting this much training in such a short time is almost physically impossible, especially with a marginally indifferent student. So we have to *stretch* that window of time.

How? By conducting some of that training even when the "alternative" employee is not actually employed by the firm. For example, a first-time contractor might begin receiving information on the company—in the form of e-mails, downloads, and videos—even while he or she is still negotiating the contract. Indeed, final agreement of such a contract might require some basic knowledge of the company, its philosophy, and its products.

Even more important, many "alternative" employees will likely migrate back around to the company on a regular basis. In fact, shrewd companies would reward this behavior—and would thus add to their total knowledge of the company with each new contract (especially if the company tracked the status of each contractor's training). They might even offer greater benefits to these contractors based upon their length of service to the company.

Meanwhile, in between these projects (and during them as well), these contractors could automatically be added as subscribers to the company's daily online newspaper—an outgrowth of the very busy employee and recruiting websites currently found at companies ranging from American Airlines to Starbucks—that would not only carry news of events at the company, but also be designed to deepen the reader's understanding of the company's operations and products. Contractors obviously can choose not to read this publication, but if they intend to work with the company again someday and want to enjoy the benefits of higher levels of training, they will certainly check in on a regular basis.

It's long been a wonder to me why large companies haven't already created sophisticated daily online company newspapers. I assume it's because they don't see themselves in the news business or want the overhead of carrying reporters and a (virtual) newsroom. Yet this is exactly what they do with company newsletters, websites, and streaming video, albeit in much slower motion. And it is what outside (and often unfriendly) bloggers do to *them*. This omission is particularly surprising, not just because the modern company so desperately needs rich, daily (even hourly) information sharing, but because—thanks to the collapse of the newspaper industry—there are literally thousands of trained reporters in the world looking for work who could slide into this slot almost instantly and produce world-class reporting and copy. The first company that figures this out is going to have a team of Pulitzer Prize winners turning out a brilliant product.

That's extending the available time for training. It is also possible to compress time. For example, in the course of thirty minutes, an "alternative" employee could watch a well-produced video about the company and its culture, all while reading a description (with charts, links, and images) of the company's businesses and markets, automatically download the company's current price list, contracts, and order documentation, as well as product demos that can be used with customers—*and* ask questions live online with a company HR trainer. All of this could be accessible from the contractor's laptop, BlackBerry, or cell phone, and in return, the contractor (especially a salesperson in the field) would be expected to Twitter his or her status every half hour while on the job. Payment would be wired directly to the individual's bank account, and, if agreed upon in advance, stock option data or a deposit to a 401(k) account or an extension on health care coverage would be done automatically.

It goes without saying that these training materials would have to be of the highest quality. We live an age of shortening attention spans, and none will be shorter than that of the short-term contract employee who just wants to know what needs to be known and then get to work converting that knowledge into money. Dreary lectures from talking heads or endless pages of text with crude line drawings aren't going to work. These training materials will have to be productions of top quality that approach the viewer through multiple learning modalities, including voice and music, animation, charts and graphs, theatrics, hands-on demonstrations, and even tactile feedback (i.e., your cell phone buzzes when you answer a question wrong). Most of all, this training has to be *engaging*—the busy, distracted contractor needs to be entranced by the presentation enough to devote the attention needed to learn in a brief window of time.

Very few companies are now capable of creating this kind of quality in their training; in fact, this kind of creative work is usually the first to be cut from the budget as too arty and extravagant. Big mistake.

The third and final way to ensure that this training takes is to incorporate feedback loops. Though occasionally subject to abuse, this system has worked surprisingly well in large community sites from MySpace to eBay. Egregious violations of company standards will bar an "alternative" employee from ever working with the company again. But infractions identified by the company, or complaints from customers or local officials, would also tally against the contractor, and may cost them a contract or two with the company in the future in favor of another contractor with a more spotless record. Such a system could be kept very simple, like eBay's rating system; or it could be more nuanced, with contractors able to erase past violations with an improved record and more training; or it could be two-tracked, using some calculus to weighing adherence versus job performance.

Whatever the process, and however many components of the above a company chooses to implement, the goal is to use rich and fast communications technology and a system of rewards and punishments to create a virtuous cycle among short-term employees toward ever more training, ever-greater adherence to company philosophy, and ever-higher productivity in selling company products and/or services.

The companies that build the best systems for doing this will be the ones that ultimately capture the best talent swimming past in the great global employee pool, that hold onto them the longest (and bring them back more often), and that ultimately enjoy the huge competitive edge by having the greatest intellectual capital assets and the highest levels of "alternative" employee productivity. That's one hell of an advantage to the company that owns it, and not something you want to face in a competitor.

WELCOMING THE NEW SUPERSTARS

If you'll remember, we asked the question at the beginning of this book: what happens to the small percentage of people who don't want to be free agents, entrepreneurs, and one-person companies?

Now we know the answer: they are the Core and most of the Inner Ring of the Cloud, two groups that have shown their commitment to staying with the company. In the case of the former, for an entire career; for the latter, likely an interval much longer than the normal job tenure in the twenty-first century.

My hunch is that even in our increasingly entrepreneurial, self-employed society, the Pareto 80:20 Rule will still apply, that about one-fifth of all workers will still want something very close to the traditional career of a generation ago. I also believe that this 20 percent, while absolutely vital to the long-term health of the enterprise, must stay as a small minority in the modern corporation for the institution to be sufficiently nimble, adaptable, and transformational to compete in the new global market.

In other words, for a corporation to be truly Protean, about 80 percent of its employees will need to have alternative relationships with the company. We have already discussed how the Inner Ring will need to improve its communications and training apparatuses to deal with these contractors, part-timers, and other gypsylike employees. Now it's time to characterize the people of this "Outer Ring" who will soon make up most of the institutional mass of the organization.

But before we do, first we need to be introduced to an extraordinary new corporate figure, all but unique to the Protean Corporation, who will soon be the most important figure in the new economy. Like the CEO, who moves back and forth between the Core and the Cloud, this individual moves comfortably between the Inner and Outer Rings, acting as the first real-life example of an old but until now rarely applicable term, the "intrapreneur."

We'll call this individual the *Competence Aggregator*, and he or she will be part of a brand new profession that will come to exemplify the age of the Protean Corporation.

Competence Aggregators will be the "company" builders inside the Protean Corporation. The organizers of new enterprises, new market thrusts, and new products and services. They will keep their companies competitive and vital, and will come to be responsible for a sizable fraction of the new job creation in the global economy. And as such, these individuals will be highly sought after, and will become among the most powerful—and most richly rewarded—figures in the corporate world.

If you've concluded so far that being a Core Employee is the best job in the Protean Corporation, you may want to reconsider. The position of Core Employee is essentially designed to motivate the most loyal and engaged employees to commit themselves to the firm for the rest of their careers. But many people—most people—in the new economy, especially the most dynamic, ambitious, and entrepreneurial, will find that kind of commitment unattractive and the work it involves stultifying.

As we've seen over the past thirty years, what these more independent individuals really want to do is *start companies*. And bless 'em for it. Entrepreneurial start-ups have been responsible for most of the new jobs, new wealth, and important new products of the last half-century. And the process has only accelerated as the infrastructure of venture capitalists, banks, consultants, and recruiters has grown ever more nuanced in its ability to serve as incubators, taking inexperienced teams with clever products and turning them into billion dollar public corporations. And what higher honor can you give these entrepreneurs and their support networks than to credit them with transforming twenty-first-century America into the world's first truly entrepreneurial society?

However, there is a limit to the number of new companies that can be created in a given year. Even if you have enough start-up teams to encompass almost every risk-taking entrepreneur, it's unlikely there's enough venture money available. And even if there were enough investment capital available, are there sufficient bank lines of credit, headhunters, marketing consultants, PR and advertising agencies, small office buildings, and all the other contributors to the creation of new companies to meet the growing demand?

Let's say there are; let's posit that there are the trillions of dollars and armies of consultants and specialty firms needed to cultivate a nationwide—even worldwide—efflorescence of entrepreneurship over the next decade. Why would established companies ever allow it to happen? If the corporate world has learned anything over the last half-century, it is that the fate of every big and successful company is to bleed creative talent until it slows, stumbles, and then is overrun by small and fast-moving new competitors.

That's the "innovator's dilemma" according to the influential book by Clayton Christensen: you start out as a hot young company full of innovative ideas, one of those ideas catches fire and you grow rich, but then that very success paralyzes you to respond to a similar challenge by some new hot young company, or Glenn Reynolds's "army of Davids"—mass movements initiated by a host of independent creators.

It's taken decades, and established companies tried every other strategy—from trying to crush innovators (until the government stopped them), to investing in big research labs (and thus subsidizing innovations for competitors), to buying up every little company they could find (and suffocating their entrepreneurial culture in the process)—but now mature companies (at least the smart ones) are finally realizing that they have to innovate from within to survive. And to do that, they have to recognize, cultivate, invest in, and support the entrepreneurs within the company, rather than lose them. And to do that, they have to create an environment of trust and freedom that allows these entrepreneurs to play, create, and even fail.

At least, that is what it's going to take. We've already discussed at length why I believe that Protean Corporations will thrive in the new economy. This is why I think traditional companies *won't*. Not that they'll die overnight if they fail to evolve, but their inability to adapt will slowly thin their ranks until they all but disappear.

Meanwhile, forward-thinking companies are already moving toward a more creative environment. Google has famously required that all of its employees devote 20 percent of their time not to their current jobs, but to coming up with new products and businesses. "Intrapreneurship," which has long been one of those buzzwords full of sound and fury but signifying next to nothing, is about to come into its own at last. Not because company executives will want it to (at least not at first), but because they will have little choice if they are to both compete in a rapidly changing marketplace *and* deal with the ongoing threat from new start-up companies.

The business environment is going to be so biased toward new companies in the years to come—even more than now—that established companies are either going to have to learn to germinate them within their organizations, or they'll watch top talent (now more free-floating than ever) be drawn away to hot new ventures. And since—as we business journalists learned long ago—innovation and success in any industry tend to follow around just a handful of especially talented, ambitious, or lucky individuals, if they go elsewhere the odds suddenly turn against your company.

You've got to keep that talent inside your company. And people of this temperament, that is, entrepreneurs, are hardly likely to be located in either the Core or even the Inner Ring, where you might be able to tie them down with salary, benefits, and job security. No, they are going to be floating around in the Outer Ring, in the far reaches of the Cloud, doing some contract work to pay the bills and looking for their main chance. Or, they are going to be outside the Cloud, floating past, looking for opportunities, building a start-up team, and chasing venture capital.

Your challenge is to identify those people—or enable them to identify themselves—and reel them in under the banner of your company. And the only way you are going to do that is to give entrepreneurs what they are looking for: autonomy, investment capital, access to talent, technical resources, ownership.

That's what VCs and angel investors do right now, and that's why established companies soon begin to bleed talent. A number of smart companies, especially in tech, have tried to respond. After attempting intrapreneurship and failing, they typically fund corporate venture capital funds that then go out and invest in independent new start-ups with products that relate to, and perhaps can supplement, the company's core competencies. That's why you see venture funds at Intel, Cisco, Vodafone, and a host of other companies.

The problem with this strategy, as even the VCs at these companies will acknowledge, is that corporate investing is neither fish nor fowl. For one thing, by their very existence they are an admission that the company can't innovate as well for itself anymore and has to search for outside innovators who are effectively quarantined from the company's entrepreneurially stultifying culture.

Second, these corporate venture operations are typically chartered, paradoxically, to be more risk-averse than their VC counterparts, yet at the same time are narrowed in their investment opportunities to specific markets, forcing them to invest in new companies with perhaps a lower likelihood of success than if they could simply chase any new opportunity for its intrinsic value.

Finally, these corporate venture capital operations usually end up reduced to two activities: making early round investments in marginal but industry-related start-ups and then trying to doll them up and convince real VCs to invest; or following the lead, as minority investors, in large investments made by those same VCs—the latter to help balance the books on the former, which are often loss leaders.

This is no way to run a corporate venture capital fund. But one can hardly blame the corporate VCs: as hard as they work, and as committed as they are to the entrepreneurs in their portfolio, they can never fully get out from under the constraints put on their work by their employers, which signals their attitude toward these start-ups and their entrepreneurs by keeping them at arm's length.

That simply cannot happen in the companies of the future, not if they want to stay competitive. Instead, they must not only support fully the creation of new entrepreneurial enterprises within their corporate operations and do whatever it takes to make the company's work environment conducive to start-ups, but even take the next step of *basing their corporate strategy on the presence of these internal start-ups.*

That is a huge psychological leap. But if a company is going to be adaptive enough to keep up with the twists and turns of the new economy, it can no longer just tack its way back and forth within its current markets. Rather, it must be able to make giant leaps from market to market, forever abandoning past success and pursuing new opportunities, no matter how incongruent to the company's current business.

We have seen just that kind of behavior, in perhaps the most celebrated business story of this new century, at Apple Computer. In the late 1990s, Apple was a dying company. Despite having a storied past and some of the best products in the personal computer industry, not to mention a cohort of some of tech's smartest inventors and designers, the company couldn't seem to execute. Its market share, more than 70 percent of the personal computer industry in the early 1980s, had fallen to single digits; and the company had suffered through a series of CEOs, each more inept than the previous one.

Yet within five years, Apple was once again the hottest company on the planet, introducing one history-making new product—iMac, iPod, iTunes, iPhone—after another.

What made the difference? The return of cofounder Steve Jobs.

Jobs is a notoriously difficult and mercurial character, but he has two gifts as a CEO that approach genius: (1) he pulls together a team of the most talented people around and instills in them the sense of a calling to change the world through technology; and (2) he creates a work atmosphere in which risk taking, even if it fails, is rewarded more than playing it safe, which can actually be punished. This management philosophy is the antithesis of what is found in most companies, where managers are usually threatened by a sense of superiority in subordinates, and *not* taking risks is the key to a rewarding and upwardly mobile career.

This unique combination has been critical to Apple's turnaround and recent success, but it needs one more factor: the willingness of Jobs to let new products and new opportunities, not the existing product line or the company's history and reputation, guide his business strategy. Apple Computers had a distinct architecture . . . right up to the moment that iMacs started offering Intel processors. Apple was a computer company . . . right up to the moment it went into the music business and dropped the word "Computer" from its name. Apple had the product of the generation in the iPod . . . until it went after the mobile business with the iPhone. The company didn't slash prices on its new products . . . until it did just that within weeks after the iPhone introduction. And, Apple was a hardware company until it became a software company until it went into the music service business.

While both admirers and competitors have largely focused on Apple's products, marketing, design, and style—all of them innovative—the real lesson Apple has to teach is about corporate dynamics. Steve Jobs has created a work environment that encourages creativity over the status quo, and honors risk over security (even if that risk leads to failure) and the pursuit of the opportunities in the future over nostalgia for the successes of the past.

Those may sound like clichés, but how many companies actually have the courage to execute them rather than merely give them lip service? And the results are indisputable; indeed, so exciting is the opportunity to work at Apple these days that talented inventors are willing even to surrender their public identities—ego being a primary driver to creative types—just for the chance to be part of Apple's next big product.

So efficient has this process become that major new Apple product initiatives are just as likely to bubble up from some distant part of the company as they are from the office of the CEO. Neither Steve Jobs nor anyone else in the senior management of Apple would have ever thought of a portable MP3 player as the company's next product.

"I don't know whose idea it was to do a music player, but Steve jumped on it pretty quick and he asked me to look into it," said Jon Rubinstein, who had led many of the company's hardware programs. Jobs was shrewd enough to see that this new device, eventually called the iPod, had enormous potential . . . and he and his senior team were prepared to swing into place Apple's vast financial, manufacturing, design, and marketing operations to make the product a success.[1]

CHAPTER

BRINGING IN TALENT
COMPETENCE AGGREGATORS

FIGHTING FOR TALENT

AS IT IS IN MANY THINGS, Apple Computer is also a pioneer in the new wave of high-tech intrapreneurship. And in the years to come, most companies will follow its lead when it comes to the development of new products and services.

Once again, this will happen because most companies will have little choice. As the population of permanent employees begins to shrink, even as the numbers of nontraditional, "alternative" employees grows, the likelihood that new product ideas—much less new *market* ideas—will emerge from the heart of the company will diminish with each year. Instead, the real action will take place out on the edges, on the frontier. That's where the cross-pollinations of ideas and random juxtapositions of events and unlikely partnerships and competitions will take place, resulting in the really good ideas.

In the Protean Corporation, that means the Outer Ring, where employees and contractors will come and go, bringing with them new ideas and new experiences from other places. Some will have forms of expertise that would never be found in the Inner Ring of the company; others will come with new ideas or inventions, drawn to the company's singular culture or to its values or to its special capabilities.

But what to do when they get there? Whom do they contact with their ideas? And how do they convert those ideas into actual business plans (if they haven't done so already) and then into action by the company? After all, they are likely to be, at most, permanent part-time employees and more likely just contractors, hired for only a brief interval. From their positions in the Outer Ring of the Cloud, the Inner Ring and the Core seem very far away, perhaps geographically as well as organizationally.

Truth be told, lots of this sort of thing goes on right now. And most companies are quite content to keep these entrepreneur wannabes at arm's length, not just because most of the ideas are lousy or impractical, but also because even the good ideas pose a potential legal threat: should the company even read the proposal, and at the same time be working on a similar idea, it could be open to a lawsuit should that in-house project ever succeed. And, of course, as anybody who has ever worked in a large corporation knows, there is also a strong "Not Invented Here" factor: every new idea that comes in from the outside is seen as a rebuke to the effectiveness of the company's in-house R&D and product development operations.

That attitude will be business suicide in the new global economy. No company will ever have enough resources to stay on the leading edge of all of the potential industries and markets it may need to enter to thrive over time. Because of that, they will have to abandon their fears and prejudices and begin to look for, recruit, and hold on to the best outside talent they can find.

Even the R&D departments of Protean Corporations will more likely resemble the new internal start-up companies they serve than the laboratory-with-faculty they typically are today. In particular, they too will likely have an Inner Ring of full-time scientists and engineers who devote much of their time to recruiting outside talent, designing tools to help those researchers, and managing the investment of department resources.

Still, even if companies learn to be receptive to these outside innovators, how will that distance be spanned between the worthy creator and the infrastructure that has been put in place to help him? And then, beyond that, how will this invention or idea then be converted into a real business for the company?

Enter the Competence Aggregator.

I have spent most of my career working in one way or another with entrepreneurs. I've reported on them, advised them, invested in them, and on several occasions, been one. As a result, I think I understand the fundamental nature of entrepreneurs better than almost anyone—a task made easier by the fact that few entrepreneurs actually take the time to understand themselves or their motives.

There are, in the heart of most entrepreneurs, two intense desires:

1 > to take control over their own destinies, and to do so successfully

2 > to avoid risk

The first may be fairly self-evident, but the second may come as a surprise. We typically think of entrepreneurs as risk-takers, who willingly embrace the possibility of losing everything (including their reputation) on the small chance of becoming hugely successful.

But most entrepreneurs don't see it that way: rather, in their minds, by taking control of their lives away from others and putting it onto their own shoulders, they believe they are *increasing* their chances of success, not diminishing them. After all, by not being at the mercy of others, and by not being forced to face directly one or more established competitors, entrepreneurs are free to respond quickly and to maneuver into new markets where no competitor yet exists. This, to them, is security.

Furthermore, entrepreneurs also believe they have greater career security than their corporate wage-slave counterparts: after all, corporate types get fired or laid-off all of the time and have to search for, and usually beg (or at least compete) their way into, a new corporate job. But an entrepreneur's life is of a piece; the different companies (successful or not) merely wobble in a single, continuous career trajectory. In their minds, it is the entrepreneurs who have job security, not their corporate counterparts.

This is a unique perspective on the world, but it grows more common by the day—especially as even corporate jobs become less predictable and workers are warned to prepare themselves for a half-dozen different careers in a lifetime, to pay up their 401(k)s, and to keep their résumés up to date. No "steady" job is that steady anymore, so, often by default, most workers and professionals are becoming more entrepreneurial in relation to their own careers.

This counterintuitive notion that entrepreneurs are risk-averse is, I think, vitally important to our understanding of the role entrepreneurs play in our society, how they relate to the company of the future, and how they make the strategic choices they do.

For example, our standard assumption is that entrepreneurs, when they are building a company, go to close acquaintances who have specific skills and from them construct the start-up team. They then approach venture capitalists (and banks) to raise the capital (and credit) they need to get underway. We also assume that entrepreneurs naturally use a combination of both cash and stock as a way to both pay and incentivize their new employees to make the necessary sacrifices to help the company succeed.

But are these actions really intrinsic to the process of new company building, or are they just the adaptations of entrepreneurs to the existing business structures around them?

I believe it is the latter: Entrepreneurs build start-up teams largely from people they know, and they run the gauntlet of angel investors, venture capitalists, and banks—losing ownership as they go—because *it is the best deal they can get.*

As evidence of that, notice how the latest generation of Web 2.0 entrepreneurs has largely eschewed VC money, choosing instead to bootstrap their companies with self-financing, even if it means slower growth and other compromises. Evan Williams, cofounder of Blogger.com and Twitter, became a hero of this generation when, frustrated with the constraints placed on him by venture capitalists, he turned around and bought his podcast start-up Odeo *back* from its venture investors and regained his freedom.

This certainly suggests that today's entrepreneurs aren't wedded to the traditional business model. And that in turn argues that there can be an important role for corporations to play in this process, if:

1 > They abandon their prejudice, based on past mistakes, against true intrapreneurship.

2 > They present a viable alternative to the existing angel/VC/bank construct.

3 > They offer entrepreneurs a better package of support and rewards than current strategic partners and investors.

What would this competitive corporate alternative look like in a Protean Corporation?

It would probably offer a number of advantages that VCs would have a hard time matching, including:

Recruitment

The company would have unique knowledge of the vast numbers of "alternative" employees who have in the past or who currently populate its Cloud. This database, especially if it is well characterized and classified by skills and experience, would be a valuable resource for an entrepreneur to gather together a team based on the *best* available talent, rather than, as now, the *most* available talent.

Development Tools and Resources

There are a number of resources that a company can provide to an entrepreneur that even the biggest venture capitalist cannot. For example, there is access to corporate research and development laboratories as well as the proprietary technologies therein. Most large companies also have an extensive inventory of largely unused (and often nearly forgotten) intellectual properties, notably patents and copyrights, which could be made available.

Funding

Venture capitalists, because they typically work from funds drawn from investors with high expectations for a very high rate of return, usually demand a major share of the company in return for their investments. Further, when funds are flush, VCs also grow increasingly resistant to investing in companies with low capital requirements (because it means more investments to manage), and also tend to force more money on start-ups than they really need (its own kind of burden). Finally, and especially when funds are flush, VCs also invest less and less in very young start-ups ("seed capital") and move down the development path to later investment rounds where the investments are larger, the return lower, but the risks less.

The result is, ironically, that during periods when the money is good, it can actually be *harder* for certain brand-new companies to find funding. Corporations can respond to this by offering earlier funding, better terms, a willingness to make numerous smaller investments, and expectations for returns that are more in line with corporate than venture capital margins.

Expertise

In the classic model, a new start-up approaches a venture capital firm not just for money, but also for wisdom and experience from industry veterans who have been down this path before. That still occurs, but it is becoming increasingly rare in the venture capital world.

Today, for every former CEO-turned-VC, there are a score of other partners and associates in the firm who have almost no experience in running a start-up company, bringing a new product to market, managing rapid growth, or even meeting a payroll. What this majority of modern-day venture capitalists has is money, an impressive degree, and/or good connections. They are typically young, very smart, and quite adept at financial—and sometimes, market—analysis. These are not negligible talents, especially when constructing a good business plan or financial strategy. But they are of secondary value when it comes to actually running a new company day to day. And so, unless the entrepreneur is lucky enough to capture the fancy of an old-fashioned ex-CEO venture capitalist, he or she is going to have to look for wisdom and experience elsewhere.

By comparison, corporations are almost always filled with experienced talent, not always interested in starting a new company but certainly in running one once it is established.

Marketing

Venture capitalists are often very good at branding and positioning, in large part because those skills are useful first in recruiting other venture investors and later in positioning the company for acquisition or an IPO. These efforts, however, are not always congruent with the company's own needs regarding establishing long-term credibility and customer awareness. Moreover, in the one area of marketing where new start-ups have the greatest need—establishing communications channels to the media, to strategic partners, and to customers—VCs are woefully deficient.

By comparison, marketing communications is the bread-and-butter of established corporations. They are experts at public relations, advertising, customer relations, point-of-sale, branding, user group management, sales support, newsletters, websites, blogs, and all of the other tools of modern marketing. It they weren't, they wouldn't still be around.

It is a small matter for a mature company to insert the new start-up into its existing programs and bring all of its marketing firepower to bear—which would cost millions if it had to be contracted to independent agencies.

Distribution

It is characteristic of VCs to be helpful upstream of a new start-up by assisting in making connections to suppliers, key talent, and infrastructure support. But downstream—in making connections to distributors, retailers, sales agents, installation, and repair contractors—most VCs are almost worthless. They don't consider this part of their duties, and other than anecdotally and in bits and pieces, they almost never do it.

Meanwhile, corporations almost always have long-established and sophisticated distribution channels into which products or services from a new start-up can be easily inserted, assuming that they aren't too different from the parent company's current offerings. And even in cases when the product or service produced by the new start-up is a departure from the parent company's core competence—which will become much more common in the Protean Corporation—the larger company will still have the trained professionals to help navigate those new channels.

Liquidation

Ultimately, this may be the biggest reason that entrepreneurs will migrate to Protean Corporations. High technology has been the heartland of entrepreneurship for the last half-century, and in high tech almost all new companies have been built on the expectation of one day (sooner rather than later) Going Public. The IPO is the classic liquidation event in modern entrepreneurship, and it has rewarded thousands of hardworking entrepreneurs—and the investors who believed in them—with riches and fame.

However, in the last few years the rules have changed. Thanks to Sarbanes-Oxley, full disclosure regulations, and other government blowbacks from the perceived financial excesses of the 1990s, it is not only more difficult, but a whole lot less desirable for successful young companies to Go Public.

These days, entrepreneurs are smart enough to know that the act of becoming a publicly traded corporation is fraught with huge new expenses for oversight and reporting (enough to consume all of the company's profits), plus all sorts of new liabilities for board members (which scares real talent away), and a level of public exposure that makes the company more vulnerable to both competitors and shareholder litigation.

It's no wonder that the business plans of most new companies these days conclude with the sale of the enterprise to a larger and more established company, even though it almost always means a comparatively lower ROI. That's why the number of new companies Going Public now is a fraction of what it was a few years ago, while the level of M&A activity is higher than ever.

Given that, the question becomes: *What exactly is venture capital good for these days?* If most successful new start-ups now end up not as independent public corporations, but as subsidiaries or divisions of established corporations, they would probably be better off working more closely with those corporations from the beginning to ensure the best fit. The fact that they aren't doing precisely that today is not due to a lack of interest from entrepreneurs, but the indifference (or active resistance) of established companies to creating such relationships.

THE MORE YOU STUDY the manifold advantages that corporations have over venture capitalists, especially in the new regulatory environment of the twenty-first century, the more apparent it is that the only thing preventing a lot more intrapreneurship from taking place now is that *corporations don't want it to.*

It is as simple as that. Just a change of attitude—merely *not opposing* entrepreneurial activities inside the organization—would probably lead to an immediate explosion of intrapreneurship. But, as we know, it is often easier to spend fortunes on new corporate initiatives, hire hundreds of new employees, and redirect vast areas of corporate resources in pursuit of one more percentage point of existing market share than it is simply to change one's mind and let natural processes unfold on their own—and perhaps pioneer a vast new market.

This attitude is already proving untenable, as we watch hot new start-ups establish and then take ownership of one huge new market after another, create most of the new wealth and essentially all of the new jobs in the economy, and capture ever-more share-of-mind of each succeeding new generation of workers. As these workers become increasingly liberated and mobile, where do you think they are going to go?

Smart companies already have recognized this, and have at least established venture capital arms to attempt to capture some kind of financial and technological interest in new start-ups. We've already noted the problems with this strategy—from keeping the start-ups at arm's length to making investments based on business congruence rather than intrinsic value. But at least it's a beginning, and is likely to give these companies a head start for the time—very soon—when companies have to embrace intrapreneurship.

In the face of this, I see two possible scenarios for companies today:

‹ 1 ›

Big Iron

They try to fuel all of their growth and new business through internal operations alone. They will fail, some sooner than others, because the rapid shifts and turns of the new global market will be impossible to keep up with solely through self-creation. At this point, these companies will find themselves in a serious crisis and will need to take drastic measures to bring outside entrepreneurial talent inside a company that still has a hostile attitude toward them.

For many of these companies, this will be too much and they will collapse, the way such giants as Wang, DEC, and Digital Equipment did when the minicomputer industry evaporated in the 1980s. Those that survive will likely do so by finally abandoning the notion of going it alone, then driving out their antediluvian management and replacing it with more enlightened figures prepared to make the company more receptive to intrapreneurship.

‹ 2 ›
Army of Davids[1]

Companies recognize the changing nature of both the marketplace and their own workforce. Realizing that they need all the help they can get in identifying new opportunities and threats and building internal operations to meet both, they will begin to make the company's work environment at first more hospitable, and later actually nurturing, of intrapreneurship.

Within a few years, far from struggling to attract entrepreneurs into the company, they will actually compete with other companies not only to attract new entrepreneurial talent, but to hang on to the intrapreneurs they already have. They will fight this competition with everything from helping to write business plans; to recruiting team members; to offering access to intellectual property and design tools; to creating special financial instruments to enable the start-up team to financially participate in its own success; to providing both corporate and agency advertising, PR, and marketing; to embedding the internal start-up into the company's established supply and distribution channels.

ONCE AGAIN IT COMES down to this: In the years to come, companies—whether or not they choose to become Protean Corporations—will nevertheless have to face the reality that the global, Internet-linked marketplace will change at a rate faster than anything heretofore experienced. New opportunities, new markets, and new inventions will appear in the most unlikely locations, and at a torrid pace. But so will new competitive threats. Every company, big and small, will have to face this challenge—and to do so they will have to accept entrepreneurship within their walls in the end, no matter how hidebound their corporate cultures.

If that is the case, this new competition will also include competition for entrepreneurs. Venture capital isn't going away—still largely funded by banks, investment funds, and already-successful entrepreneur/

tycoons—and will move to fill the niches untouched by corporate intrapreneurship, such as high-risk projects, IPO-targeted ventures, and new sectors considered too revolutionary for most corporations. They will also likely partner with corporations, even as they do now with each other, accepting a lower return for a far higher rate of success than most VC firms enjoy today.

At the same time, because of the fluidity of the global workforce, many of these new start-up endeavors will not come from "employees" more tightly linked with a single company, but "free agents," selling their idea and themselves to the highest bidder. Because these entrepreneurs will be so vital to the health of companies, firms will try to outbid each other (much as VCs do today) with financial packages, support, and cultural advantages in order to land the best projects.

All this attention can only be good news for entrepreneurs. And that is why the entrepreneur of today will want to become the intrapreneur of tomorrow. The best of them will likely want to link themselves closer to their company of choice, acting as a scout for new opportunities or projects, putting together the right team from the outer reaches of the Cloud, and acting as intermediary to the company while keeping a piece of the action. In other words, they will become Competence Aggregators.

For true entrepreneurs—and their numbers grow by the day—becoming a Competence Aggregator will be exciting work: independent, creative, and with the potential for both fame and riches . . . exactly what is available today only through stand-alone start-ups and with a much lower chance of success. Whatever form they take, and whatever they are ultimately called, Competence Aggregators will be the superstars of twenty-first-century business. The best of them will be as famous as Steve Jobs, Richard Branson, or Bill Gates, and they will never have to settle down, become bureaucratized, or take on the long-term burden of managing their creations. They will never feel obliged—by shareholders, their own equity participation, or social expectations—to stick around until they become a liability and are driven out or leave in disgust.

Competence Aggregator would be the Peter Pan of careers—with one crucial difference: as we've seen in places like Silicon Valley, and with serial entrepreneurs such as Paul Baran (one of the inventors of the Internet, founder of a four-billion-dollar company, and still entrepreneuring in his eighties), entrepreneurs can sometimes get better with age, countering any diminishment of energy with greater wisdom about human beings and their motivations, and even, amazingly, a greater willingness to take risk. It is not hard to imagine a great Competence Aggregator of 2060 having spent a half-century at two or three companies creating forty successful enterprises, and becoming a billionaire (and creating nearly a trillion dollars in wealth for his "employers") in the process.

Now picture one hundred thousand of these Competence Aggregators unleashed in the U.S. economy alone—a couple million around the world—and imagine the impact, in terms of innovative new products, new jobs, and wealth creation, that would result.

CHECKS AND BALANCES

The complete and self-contained organism called the Protean Corporation now stands before us.

Compared to the traditional organization, with its complex networks of groups, divisions, and facilities, silos and labs, direct reports and indirect reports, solid and dotted line relationships, the Protean Corporation seems remarkably simple in design. Merely a small, solid center surrounded by a large Cloud that grows thinner in direct proportion to the distance from that center.

Still, on closer inspection, the Protean Corporation is no less complex that its predecessors, merely less fixed. Its complexity is embedded in its relative chaos, rather than in its rigid patterns of control. In fact, in many respects, the Protean Corporation is actually *more* complex than traditional organizations.

For example, the Protean Corporation has a more robust system of checks and balances, whereby the CEO is constrained by the Core from interfering too deeply in the company's culture, thus ensuring continuity in the firm's operations even as the executive's life becomes more peripatetic. Conversely, the Core's operations are severely circumscribed, keeping it from interfering in the day-to-day operations of the company.

Meanwhile, the Board of Directors—long ago drifted into the largely ornamental role we see in most companies today (to the growing anger of both shareholders and government regulators)—becomes much more engaged in the daily life of the Protean Corporation, and when needed is asked to adjudicate disputes between the CEO and the Core.

In fact, there is something pleasantly Madisonian about this new design, reflecting as it does some of the basic tenets of the U.S. Constitution. Though the parallels are inexact, it's hard not to notice that the CEO and the Inner Cloud serve as the Executive Branch of the Protean Corporation, the Core is the Legislative, and the Board of Directors is the Supreme Court. Each is constrained in its powers, and each is in some fundamental way checked by the others.

Moreover, all three of these operations ultimately exist to serve, promote, and protect the freedom of action of the employees—traditional and "alternative"—who inhabit the Cloud. True entrepreneurship is about liberty: freedom of action; the chance to control one's destiny; the ability to circumvent traditional constraints of seniority, rank, and social stratification; and the opportunity to construct something new and important out of nothing. This I believe is the most important part of the Protean Corporation.

In the traditional corporation, the top of the pyramid controls the bottom. In the Protean Corporation, because the center cannot stay on top of all of the rapid market changes occurring in the world and, equally important, cannot track all of the competitive threats and new business opportunities popping up in that global marketplace, it can merely set the ground and provide tools and capital, and then get out of the way. It can only monitor events as they unfold in order to shift company assets, provide assistance where needed (government relations, service and support, targeted R&D), and make sure these efforts are congruent with the company's overall business philosophy and strategy.

The heart of the Protean Corporation may be the Core, and the executive offices the brains, but the body—the *self*—of the company is the Cloud. That body itself may be amorphous and a shape-shifter, but no matter what form it takes it still has single identity. It is the job of the Core to make sure that the employees of the Cloud, in all its forms, and in all of the places around the world where they can be found, and whatever the length of tenure they have with the company, understand what that identity is and never betray it.

Ultimately, the primary task of the Board, the Core, the Chief Executive, and the Inner Cloud is to support the efforts of the Competence Aggregators. Without question, this turns the traditional business organizational model on its head. Rather than resisting, even punishing (via de facto banishment), the entrepreneurial impulses of its employees, the Protean Corporation is all but dedicated to attracting these figures, competing to hire the best of them, and then giving them whatever assistance they need to succeed.

The result is that, in the healthiest Protean Corporations, the Cloud will be far from homogeneous. Not only will it grow thinner the further out from the Core, but it will also be mottled with regions of greater density, where new internal enterprises will coalesce around key Competence Aggregators, much like (to return to our original cosmological metaphor) planetoids form out of pockets of increasing gravitation within the gaseous cloud surrounding a newly formed star.

These new internal enterprises can look forward to one of several fates. Some may fully solidify and become self-contained. These will spin off from the Protean Corporation in their own liquidation event, or remain (like companion stars) as subsidiaries forming their own Cores and orbiting nearby. Others may nearly solidify, retaining the internal features of the surrounding corporation. These will migrate closer to the Inner Cloud, becoming the Protean equivalent of operating divisions. Finally, a third group of these internal enterprises may never evolve beyond a moderate degree of independence. These may remain in this state within the Protean Corporation, still contributing to the company's overall value, and one day, perhaps, as the situation changes, may harden into a real business or simply be reabsorbed.

This hierarchy of outcomes is not that much different from what we see today in the portfolio of venture capital firms. Among the VCs along Sand Hill Road in Silicon Valley, the rule of thumb has long been that out of ten companies in which a Fund invests, a good return is that two are Superstars (i.e., an IPO or a big money acquisition), another five or six muddle along doing moderately well until they are finally acquired, and the rest die or are fire-saled.

This ratio, remarkably, is enough to give investors in venture funds the spectacular returns they've come to expect. But in the great scheme of things it is a hugely inefficient process, and profligate with a lot of talent that is wasted on doomed enterprises. It also tends to distort the work of the VCs themselves, who, given the ROI expected by investors, tend to devote too much time to the obvious winners and too little to the in-betweens, and kill off the stragglers—sometimes not because they are outright failures, but merely because they are moving too slowly toward a distant resolution.

The results, as we have seen in the string of great new companies over the last forty years, can be astounding. But it is also inefficient. Corporate capital, if it is done right, is more patient capital. Better yet, it has a far greater capacity to absorb the worthwhile residue even of failures. Add to this a far greater depth of support, and a guaranteed exit strategy/liquidation event, and the Protean Corporation should offer a far more hospitable environment to entrepreneurs than anything found today. And wherever entrepreneurs congregate, innovation, jobs, and wealth soon follow.

At last we can see the Protean Corporation in its entirety. But we are not yet done. We still need to explore how the Protean Corporation will behave. And we also need to look beyond the outer reaches of the Cloud to even larger entities called Families, Neighborhoods, and Communities. If what you've seen seems strange so far, wait until you see what's coming next. . . .

PART IV

RUNNING THE PROTEAN CORPORATION

CHAPTER

< **11** >

WHO
MATTERS

FATEHOLDERS

ULTIMATELY, COMPANIES ARE NOT ABOUT STRUCTURE, but about *action*.

We've just spent a hundred or so pages on what the Protean Corporation looks like and explored the nuanced ways in which employees in different roles within the organization will interact with one another.

But companies sink or swim based on how well they *do business*, how effectively they increase revenues, return profits, provide employment for their employees, and most of all, add wealth to their investors and shareholders. We can debate all we want to about details of organization, what titles to give to new company jobs, and who reports to whom. But ultimately, what matters is *success*: it is the measure of all things.

Companies can experiment all they want with org charts, centralization or decentralization, employee empowerment, and virtual marketing and selling, but in the end, all must be tested in the crucible of the marketplace. History is littered with the corpses of dead companies that implemented some progressive new management or HR scheme and ended up sacrificing themselves to a failed social experiment. And no company's business strategy is ever to end up as an object lesson and warning to others.

So, we have to ask ourselves two questions: *how* will the Protean Corporation work? And more important: *will* the Protean Corporation work?

For the first we can attempt a fairly specific answer. For the second, we can only appeal to the judgment, experience, and wisdom of the reader; that is, after all you've read, do *you* think the Protean Corporation is realistic, realizable, and offers a powerful competitive alternative to corporate organizational models as they exist today?

With luck, you've probably been asking yourself that question all the way through the book. And even if you agree that this is as good a design as any for a company to stay competitive in the twenty-first century, the question still remains: What happens when you fire up this corporate engine and take it for a test drive in the real world?

So, let's take the Protean Corporation out on the road and see how it handles.

A SHARED FATE

The first thing we need to appreciate is that the Protean Corporation does not exist in isolation; neither is it wholly autonomous.

From the beginning I have tried to portray the Protean Corporation as something very like a natural system, even a living organism—growing, evolving, adapting to new conditions, and ultimately changing and learning from experience. The metaphors I've used to describe such an organization have come from the natural world—the quantum atom, the galaxy, and now that you've toured the inside of the Protean Corporation, we can add the image of an amoeba or other single-celled animal, with its dense nucleus, supporting organelles, and amorphous form that adapts to changing environmental conditions.

One of the most important characteristics of these natural phenomena is that they are, to one degree or another, edgeless. In theory, the electron circling the nucleus of the atom (as portrayed in that cloud of probability) could be on the other side of the universe, though the likelihood would be infinitesimally tiny. By the same token, the galaxy could be exerting gravitational pull on a star in another galaxy, though that pull would also be infinitesimally small.

So too the Protean Corporation is more than just the Core and the Cloud. I hesitate to use the term "edgeless" because that was applied to the Virtual Corporation. In that earlier case, it basically meant "indistinct." That is, you could no longer say precisely where the Virtual Corporation ended and the rest of the world began, given the combined effects of digital communications, enlistment of suppliers, distributors, and even customers into design and production, and because employees no longer had to be based in a company facility.

By comparison, "edgeless" in the Protean Corporation is something far more sweeping, almost metaphysical.

As we've already seen, employees and potential employees of a Protean Corporation may be as physically far from the headquarters of the company as one can get on the same planet. They may also have only the most tenuous of employment arrangements: never actually speaking to a person at the company, meanwhile signing on to, working on, and completing an assignment for the company, and getting paid online, all in a matter of a few seconds—never to interact with the company again.

But when we speak of "edgelessness" with regard to the Protean Corporation, we are also talking about "inclusiveness" as well. The Protean Corporation encompasses more people, more stakeholders, than any comparable business organization has until now. So different and important are these "other" players to the company's destiny that we need a new name for them. Let's use: "Fateholders."

Moreover, the members of this Fateholder *Family*, as we will call it, include parties who would *never* be considered part of the company in the past. This is an extremely important point, because it is already happening, and many great companies, including some that are considered among the most progressive in modern business, are already making dangerous mistakes concerning it.

What then constitutes the Family of the corporation in the twenty-first century? Who are these "Fateholders?"

The Company itself

In the case of the Protean Corporation, that means the Core and the Cloud. And the Cloud includes all full-time, part-time, contract, and "alternative" employees. It also includes every individual who has worked with the company, even for a few moments, as well as everyone who has a high likelihood to work for the company in the future.

Suppliers

The entire supply chain is part of the Family, as every company in it has a stake in the fate of the corporation, and vice versa.

Distribution and Sales

The entire distribution chain is part of the Family for the same reason as the supply chain.

Customers and Users

The last twenty years have seen a growing recognition that customers are not outsiders to a company, and merely the target of its efforts, but actually participants in a relationship with the company that is mutually beneficial. Any doubts about this disappeared as the customers themselves became increasingly enlisted in the processes of designing, building, and servicing their purchases from the company. In the new world of business, this process has now evolved to the point where, in the case of Web 2.0 companies such as MySpace and Facebook, the customers *are* the company: they create the content, establish the de facto language, mores, and customs, and monitor themselves.

Shareholders

This is largely self-evident; after all, the shareholders are the owners of the company. Moreover, in this age of employee stock options, the shareholders increasingly *are* the company. This is likely to only be enhanced in the years to come, as companies use stock as a way to attract ever more mobile, and ever less loyal, employees. As we saw in the Hewlett-Packard proxy vote of 2001—when HP employees and retirees came within a few percentage points of voting down a decision made by their own CEO with the backing of major financial institutions—we are entering an era when employees may ultimately employ their own bosses, and hold veto power of their decisions.

In the Protean Corporation, the final check on company behavior may prove to be occasional proxy battles between the Chief Executive and the Core Employees, who themselves hold equity in the company, both fighting for the support of not only the members of the Inner Ring, but the denizens of the outer Cloud as well.

Analysts

The traditional view of stock analysts is that they are outsiders, similar to business journalists, but are allowed additional access (via tours, private presentations, and quarterly conference calls) to the views of senior management, as well as corporate proprietary financial and product information, in order to set the value of the company stock and make predictions about the company's financial health and short-term growth. This is unlikely to change in the future.

However, as companies become more Protean, shifting their forms and quickly entering and leaving markets, the challenge of making accurate appraisals and predictions is going to grow much more difficult. Brokerage houses are likely to react in one of two ways: by either dedicating analysts even more than now to covering single companies, or restricting them to covering specific markets and picking up on companies as they pass through those markets.

If it is the former (which is my hunch), analysts will find their own careers even more intimately bound up with the companies they watch, becoming even more Fateholders, and perpetually resisting the pull to identify too closely with their subject and risk losing objectivity.

Financial Institutions

Companies have always had a close relationship with their bankers, if only to soften them up for the next loan or line of credit. The same is true, to a lesser degree and at different times in the company's history, with venture capitalists, investment banks, and stock exchanges.

None of this is likely to change, though a company shape-shifting from one business to another, and moving into and out of markets with unprecedented speed, is likely to need the services of financial institutions even more than today. This should be a boon for them, but it will also require them to work much more closely with their Protean Corporation clients. And their ability to speed contracts, transfer funds, exchange currency, and extend credit—or conversely, their tardiness in doing so—will greatly impact the ability of their corporate clients to compete in the new economy. We were reminded of this power during the global credit crunch of October 2008—suddenly, we saw even the highest-flying companies being pulled to earth by a shortage of credit. That makes lenders true Fateholders.

Organized Labor

For most companies, especially in the United States and even more especially in technology, this is not an issue. But it very easily could become one. An extended downturn or a particularly vicious antiunion purge by a major company, or a single NLRB vote that gets nasty, could galvanize the unionization of an entire industry.

Moreover, one aspect of working in a global economy is that you must do business in nations and work with strategic partners that are characterized by pro-union labor laws. Meanwhile, the expanding scope of your company's Fateholders is likely to also pick up a union shop or two in the Family. And though it will be difficult for a union to organize or even qualify for a vote, at a Protean Corporation, with its sizable percentage of gypsylike workers, it is highly possible that some of these "alternative" employees will belong to one union or another.

The good news is that after a century of labor-management loggerheads, many unions have already begun over the last generation to appreciate that they are members of the company Family, and ultimately share its destiny.

Community and Regional Governments

One of the most interesting and unexpected side effects of globalism has been the growing number of large corporations based in comparatively small cities and towns. Look at Microsoft in Redmond, Washington, or Google in Mountain View, California. In some cases—Wal-Mart in Bentonville, Arkansas, and IBM in Armonk, New York, to name an obvious pair—companies have many times as many employees as there are citizens of the town in which they are headquartered. This isn't a new phenomenon—DuPont was already dwarfing Wilmington, Delaware, a century-and-a-half ago—but it will be exacerbated in the years to come.

Here again, the need is not to change the company's relationship with the communities in which it finds itself—most twenty-first century companies are too sophisticated to run roughshod over their hometowns—but to recognize that their futures and their health are deeply intertwined. A great company moving out of a town or suffering massive lay-offs there can be devastating but no more so than the town deciding to pass a severe "living wage" regulation, change local building and residential codes, or rewrite environmental impact requirements.

By the same token, a regional government or body can often improve the business environment (as Joint Venture Silicon Valley did a decade ago) by bringing together industry and community leaders to agree on strategic goals, streamline bureaucracies, and establish joint business/ government task forces.

Some of the impact of the giant new corporations on local communities will be mitigated by the fact that they are so protean, with so many full-time and part-time employees scattered around the world; but that won't be enough to counter the sheer mass of these companies wherever they do set up operations.

For all of these reasons, the communities around the headquarters and major facilities of Protean Corporations should be considered not only as Family, but second only to the employees themselves—and the maintenance of this relationship should probably be one of the duties of the Core.

NOW IT STARTS GETTING STICKY. These are the relatives you wish you didn't have to invite to holiday dinners and weddings. But like them or not, they too are Family members of your company in the new economy:

The Media

For all of its marketing genius, Apple Computer made a horrible error in 2006. After a blog site dedicated to Apple products got its hands on and published an internal company document describing an upcoming product introduction, Apple went after the site with lawyers—eventually running it out of business.

Setting aside the fact that pre-announcing products is a long if not necessarily noble tradition in the electronics trade press (something to which I was often a victim in my early days as a PR person) or given the fact that the leakers are most likely to be senior executives in the victimized company itself (which I discovered when I became a journalist), Apple's behavior was a mistake in all sorts of ways.

For one thing, it violated if not the letter then certainly the spirit of the First Amendment and its enshrinement of free speech. But just as important, Apple damaged the symbiotic relationship between the media (especially the computer press) and the company. This was something Apple could do with impunity because it was the hottest company around, and the darling of the mainstream press and the general public.

But Apple had also forgotten that a decade before, when market share was slumping and the company was in a leadership crisis, it had been the trade press—including many of these same publications—that had held together Apple's true believers (even if only in their common dismay) long enough for Steve Jobs to return and turn its fortunes around. Many of those publications had been antagonistic to Apple—as well they should have been, that's what the press is supposed to do—but even that was hugely valuable to the company. They offered Apple users a breath of honesty when the company was unprepared to give it; provided an outlet for customer frustration; and served as an important source of ideas and potential solutions to the company's problems.

In its weakness, Apple Computer saw the media as a threat, when in fact it was just as much an advantage. The same was true ten years later: Apple, in its arrogance as the coolest company on the planet, saw the little website as an annoyance to its finely tuned marketing strategy and crushed it like a bug.

No doubt Apple saw this as a triumph, but it quickly had a chilling effect: never again, in good times or bad, will Apple hear the straight truth about its business. It will come to regret that.

It is true today, and will be even more true in the years to come, that the media—the mainstream press, websites, bloggers—and the companies they write about have common cause. Even when they are antagonistic—*especially* so, when it is skeptical, challenging, probing, and judging—the media plays a vital role in providing valuable feedback to the company and maintaining the health of the larger Cloud. They are true Fateholders.

Crushing the press, much like stifling dissent, is a guaranteed way to create bigger explosions down the line. Turn off your radar and you will eventually hit the side of a mountain. Smart companies in the new economy will *read* their employee and customer hate sites, and learn from them or work to change their minds, rather than ignoring them. And they will study blogs and bulletin boards to identify early the emergence of new trends, new markets, and new competitive threats; yet another reason to keep those sites independent and alive.

Even smart executives may find this idea hard to swallow. But that's why I call this larger population, beyond the Cloud, the Family. As with real families, there are always feuds popping up, black sheep, and embarrassing relatives. But they are still Family; you are stuck with them, and you make the best of your shared fate.

Competitors

Dealing with the media is good preparation for dealing with this next group of Family members. If the media are an annoyance, competitors are, well, the *enemy*. It goes with the nature of capitalism and simple human competition that one's competitors, the entities perceived as standing between you and success, are usually vilified and treated as the ultimate outsiders.

However, as anyone who has spent time in business knows, your competitors are often the people most like you; they share your interests, your ambitions, your market, and usually your technology. They consume a large percentage of your waking thoughts, and sometimes even haunt your dreams. Just behind your own good or bad judgment, your toughest competitor is also your biggest Fateholder.

As you'll see in a moment, competitors actually fit into two categories in the ecology of the Protean Corporation. This is the nearer one, the recognition that in the Family, your competitors are like rival siblings: each of you wants the Family to succeed, with yourself at the heart of that success.

Smart companies regularly use their competitors as an added source of intellectual capital: imitating your competitor's successful products, marketing techniques, and new inventions is not only the greatest form a flattery, but also sometimes the key to defeating that rival.

Finally (we are seeing this already, and it will become paramount in the Protean Corporation), a sizable percentage of your competitors' employees are also your employees: those vast outer Clouds overlap, and the freelancer or part-timer you hire today may hold the same position at one of your competitors tomorrow. They will be using the training and tools you gave them at your competitor in order to defeat you and vice versa. You won't have enough lawyers to pursue every leak of company secrets and insider information that is likely to occur in this new world, so you (and your competitor) are going to have to rethink your IP security strategies, accept the inevitable losses, and perhaps even enter into some privacy accords with those competitors.

Activists

Now we are getting to the Family members most companies wish were never born. In a real family, they'd be barred—by a restraining order if necessary—from seeing grandma. In the business world, they are considered members of the Family only because it is a good idea to follow John F. Kennedy's adage about keeping "your friends close, but your enemies even closer."

Activists are typically in the unique position of being the only owners of a company (by purchasing a single share in order to attend annual shareholder meetings) who are indifferent to a company's success. Rather, they see the company as emblematic of the dark side of their worldview, the synecdoche of all that is wrong with the status quo. At best, their goal is to radicalize and mobilize fellow shareholders to force the company to change its culture, practices, or strategy; and at minimum to obtain some publicity in hope of trying the same technique more successfully somewhere else.

Because their goals are usually utopian fantasies—global anarchy, communism—these activists are rightly dismissed by nearly all of their fellow shareholders, and their odds of victory are minuscule. But that isn't always the case: the right controversy, a sufficiently stressful economy, or the right corner of the world, and what seems the obsession of a few cranks can turn into an explosion of discontent. Just ask McDonald's: after having seen its restaurants burned to the ground on three continents, you can bet that it keeps close tabs on protesters who see the company as emblematic of Yankee imperialism. This is a case when the least of a company's stakeholders can suddenly become the biggest of its Fateholders.

Class Action Attorneys

As I type this I can imagine readers actually crossing themselves, as if to ward off evil. This is the Family member that no one talks about, or spits when doing so. Class action attorneys are destructive forces in the corporate world, but they are like woodpeckers: they only hammer holes in a tree that is already infested. Most companies prefer not to believe this, believing that these folks are bloodsuckers who trump up claims, enlist greedy fools to join the case, and pay off legislators to keep the game lucrative.

There's a touch of truth to that: after all, über class action attorney William Lerach *was* sentenced to two years in prison in early 2008 for conspiracy. But the truth is much more complicated: class action attorneys often have no trouble finding aggrieved parties willing to bring suit. The damages may be trumped up, but the underlying sense of victimization is there. That is something your company should know about, and as early as possible.

That's why the angry bloggers are part of the Family, as are the unions and the media. Long before a class action attorney can make a case, there will have been warning signs popping up among far less lethal Family members. If you ignore those signs, or choose not to address them, you end up with these guys. And if their relationship to the company is less symbiotic than parasitic, they are very much Fateholders, and as such must always be in your planning and in the back of your mind.

CHAPTER

RINGS OF
ENGAGEMENT

THE BULL'S-EYE THAT IS THE PROTEAN CORPORATION can now
be seen as a series of concentric rings of engagement with the long-term
success and fate of the enterprise: the Core, the Inner Ring, the Cloud, the
Family.

We are now well outside the Protean Corporation. Nevertheless,
those entities that the company affects—and those that in turn impact
the company—continue to radiate outward. The immediate ring outside

the Family is composed of those institutions for which the company is no longer first priority. Nor, strictly speaking, are they Fateholders, in that neither side lives nor dies based on the behavior of the other. Nevertheless, these institutions—let's call them collectively the "Neighborhood"— are in close enough proximity, and have enough impact on the health and operating conditions of the company, that they must be incorporated in its strategic planning.

Interestingly, almost every one currently exists in a comparable relationship with today's corporations:

Competitors

This is the second appearance of these entities, underscoring the complex relationship they have with the Protean Corporation. As Family members, they are important for their commonalities with the company; as Neighbors, the focus is on their competitive threat as opponents—as competition for market share, revenues, profits, and talent—and for their potential lethality.

Competition in the age of the Protean Corporation will be no less brutal than it is today, or was a century ago. And in one particular arena, recruiting talent in a world of highly mobile workers, it will likely be all-out war. Success in business, and especially in technology, has always gone to the company that can attract that small number of true innovators and leaders. This won't change: the company that can sign up the best Competence Aggregators and creative talent, and hold on to them for the longest time, will almost always win the battle.

National Governments

In one respect, the relationship between Protean Corporations and national governments will not be that much different from that with communities and regions. Nations will also be motivated to attract large companies for their employment, wealth creation, and tax payments.

But there are two fundamental differences. First, except for the smallest and poorest nations, no country's fate will be inextricably bound up with the presence and long-term success of a single company—or even a handful of companies—no matter how large. Second, nations enjoy powers of coercion unavailable to municipalities, including tariffs and duties, courts, even armies. It is in the interests of nations to attract large and successful international companies; but it can also be in their interests to restrain them from moving on, using them as a scapegoat for domestic unrest or their own incompetence, and as a source of revenues—even to the point of nationalization.

Some kind of clash between sovereign nations and large Protean Corporations (or any other kinds of multinational companies) seems inevitable: nations want to keep their citizens contributing to their domestic economies; companies, empowered by the World Wide Web, want their employees to be mobile and unconstrained by local laws and taxes. By the same token, nations want to retain the fruits of their own internal commerce, and industry wants those profits to be easily transferred, exchanged, arbitraged, and reinvested somewhere else where it is needed.

Those competing needs are so central to the existence of both that it is unlikely either will compromise much. Nations have the power to force companies to stay put, but they can't force them to exist. With money—and now labor—increasingly fungible, nations are realizing that if they press too hard they risk losing everything and collapsing their economies. But that doesn't mean they are going to give up; not when billions of dollars of domestic production is streaming out of the country through the Internet. They will try another way, and another, until they find one that works.

Regulators

To appreciate the importance of regulatory agencies, from securities commissions to accounting boards to lawmakers, let me list a few names and acronyms you'll recognize: Sarbanes-Oxley, FASB stock option reporting, Full Disclosure, NLRB, Smoot-Hawley, the American Disabilities Act, NAFTA, Sherman Anti-Trust regulations.

Enough said? Regulators typically don't have the power of life and death over individual companies; neither is the relationship with those companies reciprocal and symbiotic, so strictly speaking they are not Fateholders, and thus not Family. But what regulators can do is change the nature of the competition, rewrite the rules of engagement, and re-design the playing the field. That makes them a powerful influence in the life of the modern corporation, an influence that is very difficult to counter beyond supporting the election of their overseers (which can create its own problems).

In the twenty-first century, legislators are becoming increasingly enamored with regulations as a vehicle for changing corporate behavior. It is subtle, usually bears the seal of approval of one "objective" commission or another, and best of all, enables them to act without getting their hands dirty. For this reason, and the fact that global corporations are going to be seen as a growing challenge to sovereign nations (especially those that want to control their citizens' access to the outside world), regulators and the regulations they enact are only going to become more pervasive, aggressive, and intrusive.

As a frightening augury of the future, and a warning about the unforeseen consequences of "good" regulations, consider the impact of Sarbanes-Oxley: enacted in the U.S. in response to the excesses of the 1990s dot-com boom, it has done little to stop corporate criminality, but instead has done a brilliant job of crushing IPOs on American stock exchanges, transferring vast wealth to other exchanges around the world, and restoring power to mature companies by forcing entrepreneurial start-ups to sell to them rather than go public.

Stock Markets

As has always been the case, stock markets by their very nature have meta-effects on the companies whose shares they list. Good overall economic news, even on a distant front, can buoy a company's share price; while bad news can sink it, even when its actual financials argue just the opposite.

Markets, it almost goes without saying, can take on a momentum of their own, driven by unbridled optimism or infectious despair, pulling their companies along in train, changing their valuation almost regardless of the individual corporation's actual financial health.

That's how the dot-commers of the late 1990s got very rich (at least temporarily) with companies that had no profit and phantasmagorical business models. It's also why even good healthy companies lost much of their value in the Crash of 1929 (and very nearly did in 1987 and 2008). None of this is going to change.

What will change with the rise of Protean Corporations is the long-term relationship between exchanges and many of the companies they list. These changes will come in many forms. For example, as we will soon see, companies may be changing not only their businesses, but even their fundamental nature. If that is the case, Protean Corporations may find themselves listing, then delisting, on a stock exchange, or jumping from one type of exchange to another—or, to an even greater degree than today, operating around the world on multiple exchanges.

This will inevitably decouple exchanges from their companies, requiring of those exchanges a greater degree of flexibility, combined with a lower sense of shared fate. The kind of tension we see today between, say, NASDAQ and the NYSE, will now shift over and be repeated thousands of times, between these stock exchanges and the new companies. The exchanges will want to hang on to these clients forever, while the companies themselves will be motivated to keep from being tied down in any way.

The last time this kind of conflicting set of interests occurred, it created NASDAQ. It is very possible that the rise of Protean Corporations will force the creation of a whole new kind of stock exchange, one that combines new forms of accounting (which we'll look at soon) and a willingness not only to let clients come and go, but actually encourage it.

Community Relations

Beyond the Neighborhood lies the *"Community."* These are organizations and government entities whose scope either is international or deals with one or more of the larger sectors in which a Protean Corporation operates.

Interestingly, but also in keeping with the way the world operates today—with sovereign nations holding the high ground in terms of influence over international bodies such as the UN and World Court—the Community will typically have far less impact upon the Protean Corporation than the Neighborhood.

That, however, may not always be the case: as we will see with entrepreneurship, the very existence of a large number of Protean Corporations, not to mention the rise of mega-corporations (Protean or not), may very well provoke nations to put more teeth into international bodies in hope of reining in this perceived threat. That, of course, will be surrendering sovereignty to assert sovereignty—but still an appealing solution if the devil you empower is better than the devil you fear. The question then is: which is more dangerous? Giant international corporations or giant international organizations? That remains to be seen.

The Community consists of, but is not limited to:

Competitors

This is the third time this group has appeared; once again, that's probably appropriate given the central role they play in any company's life. In this case, however, we are speaking of Competitors as a whole: the aggregate of all of the companies with which your company competes in every market sector and every geographic region, of every size, and both brand-new enterprises and established veterans. It also includes all of the competitors currently operating, or likely to one day operate, in any market your company has the capabilities for and the will to enter.

This aggregate mass represents the field upon which you operate, the friction upon your ability to function, and potentially a mortal threat. This competitive backdrop is itself Protean: new markets appear, nova, and fade away; companies appear and disappear, some enduring, some growing large while others shrink. It is against this ever-changing backdrop that a Protean Corporation will perpetually be changing its shape to create the most advantageous fit, swelling outward into voids of opportunity, perhaps shrinking back in markets that are too mature or from competitors that are too powerful.

This, I think, is an absolutely vital point. We often describe business as war, but we never carry the analogy beyond the clash of large armies, offensive thrusts, and the capture of territory. But real combat, that fought by small units on the front lines, is far more complex: it is a thousand different command decisions made along a vast front, reconnaissance missions and probing actions searching for points of weakness, the massing of firepower, and the creation and defense of redoubts and salients.

This is how the Protean Corporation will compete, with thousands of scouts—"alternative" employees—scattered around the world, looking for opportunities, and squads and companies, led by Competence Aggregators and backed by the heavy armor of the Corporation's resources, heading out to capture targets and hold them until they can be supported in force.

International Organizations

This cohort, ranging from sanctioned bodies such as the United Nations and the World Court to international treaties such as the Kyoto Protocol to the tens of thousands of NGOs that have popped up over the last few decades, currently is part of the larger Community (and not the Neighborhood), mainly because its ability to constrain or circumscribe the actions of corporations is relatively limited (the International Law of the Sea may be the one exception).

However, this could change at any moment. For example, were the United States to either adopt Kyoto or accept the judgments of the World Court, these two entities would suddenly gain very sharp teeth and would quickly move into the Neighborhood, even the Family.

Will this happen anytime soon? Probably not. However, any major environmental catastrophe (global warming, cooling, etc.) would quickly give some of these organizations enormous power to intervene in the operations of every enterprise. Short of that, the growing influence of Protean Corporations, the World Wide Web, and the rapidly expanding armies of highly mobile freelancers and entrepreneurs around the world, will become an increasing threat to the sovereignty of nations, and, like any organization facing a serious challenge, will undoubtedly lash back. How they will do so, how severe their response will be, and to what degree they'll be successful will be among the great political questions of this century.

Industry, Trade, and Professional Organizations

By comparison, this is one group whose influence is likely to diminish in the years to come, which is why I've moved them from the Neighborhood of today to the Community of tomorrow. Many of these organizations have wisely responded to the globalization of their members by going global themselves. But this has not come without cost: in trade wars between nations (as in the U.S.–Japan semiconductor wars), these groups often find themselves with a membership divided against itself. Their task is not likely to get any easier.

But there is an even greater challenge to these groups, especially those that represent specific industries: Protean Corporations, moving in and out of industries, or operating in multiple industries, are simply not going to see these organizations as central to their business, but rather as an adjunct to one of their operations. This isn't new; the many electronics giants (IBM, Motorola, HP, DEC) of the 1970s that had "captive" semiconductor manufacturing operations were usually members of the Semiconductor Industry Association, but it was hardly as vital to them as it was for the mainstream chip companies like Intel and Advanced Micro Devices.

By comparison, the groups that chose to stay domestic, such as the American Electronics Association, have enjoyed considerable influence in their home countries, but have become increasingly parochial in the global economy. The situation isn't going to get easier for either side. In contrast, professional organizations face a whole different challenge. In the face of growing numbers of professionals becoming independent operators, do these associations begin to become essentially service organizations—providing tools, training, and wages/pricing information to their members? This would certainly keep them relevant to the changing careers of their members. But it also would likely turn them into just one more service among thousands catering to the new global professional.

Conversely, these associations could become more activist, advocating for the rights of their solitary, gypsylike members against the authority of their giant, distant employers. That is to say, they could become more like unions. But will that work? If we are indeed heading into a kind of Golden Age of Entrepreneurship, with millions of free agents directing their own careers, then there is no evidence that entrepreneurs will *ever* organize for common goals or collective bargaining. Indeed, such thinking is antithetical to everything we know about the entrepreneurial personality.

What's more, in the Internet Age, labor is fungible. Even if the code writers or publicity specialists in Bangalore or Brussels wanted to organize and strike for higher wages or better contracts, their work would just be assumed, in a millisecond, by their counterparts in Cairo or Chicago. Only talent will have an advantage when it comes to negotiating with contractors, and as with entrepreneurial personalities, top talent also rarely subsumes its interests with the masses.

What will keep wages strong (it is already becoming so today) is the massive amount of new competition between companies being created by a worldwide marketplace, and that is an arena in which professional organizations have little opportunity to play.

Global Communications and Distribution Networks

Bill Davidow, the venture capitalist, is a brilliant man, and one of the smartest things he's ever said is that whenever you find yourself in a technological revolution, one of the best places to invest your money is into home construction.

His reasoning—and after fifteen years it has still proven true—was that though we almost never expect it, or never really prepare for it, technological revolutions ultimately ignite cultural revolutions, which inevitably change the way we live our daily lives. And one of the most common ways that change manifests is through the priorities we give to the organizational components in our homes.

To appreciate how this occurs, one need only compare the typical suburban house of the 1950s and 1960s with the suburban homes being built today. The former is "outward" in its perspective—the large picture window facing the street, the big living room, the dominance of the garage or carport to the overall façade. This is undeniably the home of people living in a car culture, their lives oriented to the commute and jobs when away, and toward the solitary entertainment center (the TV and stereo) when home.

Now look at the twenty-first-century home. In contrast, it is inward directed, away from the street, and increasingly castlelike. In the more expensive homes, the garage has returned to its "carriage house" role of a century ago, oftentimes accessible only through an internal courtyard. The car itself is hidden behind automatic doors, almost as if it has become an embarrassment in the new environmentalist age.

Inside the house, the layout has changed as well, with the kitchen growing in importance (and expense), the living room replaced by the family room, the master bedroom becoming a suite, and the home office now the centerpiece of daytime life.

If there is a corollary to Davidow's notion, it is that when you find yourself in a technology revolution, you might also consider investing in infrastructure companies. The Internet revolution was supposed to obviate the need for physical transportation of both goods and human beings; but then, computers were supposed to end the need for printing and filing paper. Thirty years ago, I was in the first generation of publicists and journalists who proudly announced the arrival of "the paperless office." There have been two subsequent generations also announcing the same thing, and if today I manage to do much more communicating and filing electronically, I also produce as much paper as ever.

By the same token, the rise of the global, electronically linked *virtual* economy has led to explosive growth across the various forms of delivering *physical* objects. I don't have to tell you that Federal Express, United Parcel Service, DHL, major shipping companies, and even the U.S.

Postal Service have been among the prime beneficiaries of economic growth of the last twenty years. So too have the oil companies, which provide the fuel to power these transport systems. And when fuel costs skyrocket, the commercial rail industry enjoys its own boom times.

This is only going to increase: every new eBay transaction made online leads to one more parcel that needs to be transported from somewhere in the world to somewhere else. And when the Next Billion joins the world economy, not only is the volume of those shipments going to multiply, but those parcels will be coming and going from some of the most isolated locations of human habitation on Earth. So too will the communications traffic increase many times over; those hundreds of millions of new consumers, as we've already noted, are most likely to join the Internet Age (and thus the global economy) via their cell phones.

Meanwhile, in wireless, G4 or some other long-range protocol will undoubtedly emerge as the new standard and that will at last make possible the complete coverage of the Earth as a single giant wireless hotspot.

All of this will mean tremendous growth for cellular and wireless communications over the next two decades. That explains why communications and distribution networks will become part of every Protean Corporation's Community. But why not as Neighbors?—because I think the wide array of options, combined with intense competition in both those sectors, will keep most companies from becoming dependent on any particular provider. Instead, I believe both communications and distribution/delivery companies will become the new utilities in the twenty-first century—necessary, but widely available. Unfortunately for them, some nations may feel the same way.

WE ARE NOW VERY FAR from the Core of any given Protean Corporation. In the furthest reaches of the Outer Cloud and beyond, companies will share most resources and services, and be equally vulnerable to bureaucrats, regulators, and lawmakers. Protean Corporations may be essentially edgeless, but out here, the gravitational pull from any one company is minuscule; a company may still be a major customer, client, or supplier, but it is unlikely to have a major effect on the operations of one of these distant organizations. Though the threshold is unmarked, we can now say that we are truly outside the company. From here we can now see the entire Protean Corporation.

CHAPTER

‹ **13** ›

REDEFINING SUCCESS

WHAT A PROTEAN CORPORATION ACTUALLY DOES

BUT WE STILL HAVEN'T ENTIRELY ANSWERED the question: *What does a Protean Corporation do?*

1 › _____

2 › It establishes a corporate environment that is conducive to attracting the most talented people, and provides them with the tools to get their jobs done.

3 ▷ It manages its talent pool to obtain maximum quality and productivity from all potential employees at every level of employment.

4 ▷ It creates an environment in which intrapreneurs can construct new enterprises that pursue valuable new market opportunities.

5 ▷ It establishes mutually beneficial relationships with members of its Family.

6 ▷ It pursues common interests with members of its Neighborhood.

7 ▷ It obtains maximum value and reach from members of its Community.

Why is number 1 missing from the top of this list? When a task force at Hewlett-Packard prepared its famous and influential list of Corporate Objectives, Dave Packard approved it—after making one crucial edit: he moved "Profits" to the top of the list. He did so, he said, because without profits, a company could not survive and could not do all of those enlightened things like profit-sharing, flextime, and serving the community.

He was right. But having said that, I'm going to suggest that for the Protean Corporation in the twenty-first century, the definition of Profit is going to evolve in some very interesting ways. And like Dave Packard, I'm going to put it at the top:

1 ▷ The Protean Corporation continuously works to maximize value in *all* of its endeavors.

Why the different phrasing? Because it reflects the changing nature of what value means in the twenty-first versus the twentieth century. When Packard put Profit at the top of the HP Objectives he was, understandably, distinguishing financial profit from the other activities of the firm. But implicit in those other Objectives—Customers, Field of Interest, Growth, Employees, Organization, and Citizenship—was the maximization of the value of HP's *intangible assets*.

In 1957, when these corporate objectives were first verbalized, the financial structure and value of Hewlett-Packard Co. could be very easily identified and measured. With the exception of Growth, which rightly belonged with Profit, all of the other objectives were easily identified as nonempirical, the "soft" operations of the company. These "intangible" assets of the company amounted to no more than 10 percent of the company's value, entered under the balance sheet entry of "Goodwill."

But the world has changed considerably in the last fifty years. In retrospect, we can see that at the time even HP was wrong in its self-evaluation. The company's growing reputation for quality and innovation was already putting a premium price on HP's one-year-old public stock. By the early 1970s, that reputation (including being on all the "best places to work" lists), and fame for its many innovations, had now not only made HP's stock more valuable than the company's book worth, but had turned it into a de facto "blue chip" investment (a fact eventually confirmed by Dow Jones itself). So while Dave Packard may have famously put Profit at the top of his company's objectives, HP's value came just as much from the bottom of that list.

In fact, that has been true for almost every company in the developed world for the last quarter-century. It has been estimated that "intangible" assets now make up more than half of most companies' worth, and in the case of hot new tech start-ups, that number may reach 90 percent. This new reality is underscored almost every day on the world's stock markets: big, mature companies with strong balance sheets find their stock depressed because investors believe those firms have lost some of their ability to compete in the future, to innovate, to attract key employees, to create some ineffable "magic." Meanwhile, exciting young start-ups that have never seen a profit, but have attracted millions of users and are the talk of the town, typically see skyrocketing valuations, much of it based on the notion that someday they will find a way to monetize all of those subscribers. A classic example of this is Amazon, which grew at an astounding rate for nearly a decade without ever seeing a profit, then rewarded its loyal shareholders by doing just that.

This vast discrepancy between the balance sheet of companies and the behavior of the stock markets has created something of a crisis over the last decade, one that is acutely felt but rarely discussed. Recognizing that company financials are insufficient to capture the true health of the modern corporation, investors have turned to a vast array of other services—from analysts and cable television shows to blogs and day-trader online bulletin boards—for clues to the real health and competitiveness of companies. (It's telling that in recent years even HP has placed "Customer Loyalty" as the new number one objective, suggesting that keeping customers over the long term is now more important even than short-term profits.) But even these extrafinancial sources are still incapable of capturing all the factors creating the intangible assets of most companies—particularly the fast-moving, rapidly-changing ones—and the result is unprecedented volatility across the world's equity markets. If we are not quite flying blind, we are still far short of the instruments we need to guarantee arrival.

About a decade ago, in recognition of this growing gap between measurable value and perceived value, a number of researchers began to look into new ways to audit and present this missing company worth. The years 1996–1997 saw three books published, all with the same title, *Intellectual Capital*. One of them was mine, coauthored with one of the pioneers in the field, Leif Edvinsson of Skandia Bank in Sweden.

These books in turn set off a small land rush in research, monographs, books, and seminars about the nature of intellectual capital, and how it could be fostered within organizations. Much of the excitement for the subject was in Europe—unfortunately, for the wrong reasons. The first wrong reason was that it was perceived as a hot new business idea that could be used to leapfrog over the U.S. competitively. The second and worse reason was that in the eyes of many European business theoreticians, Intellectual Capital offered a potential escape—yet the latest form of the Third Way—from both the failure of Marxism and the grubbiness of capitalism. It was reasoned that if companies could only be measured by their intangible assets rather than their real ones, European companies would be recognized for their proper superiority over their profit-obsessed American counterparts.

The resulting decade has not so much been a failure of the Intellectual Capital movement as a kind of stasis, a movement that has stalled. What was and what continues to be needed is an empirical structure to underpin the lofty ideas. After twenty-five years of research, IC experts have pretty much nailed down roughly 80 percent of the intangible factors that make one company more successful than another. They range from the number of times the service call line rings before it is picked up, to the number of PhDs in the research department, to the number of patents in the company files. There are also an endless number of surveys available to determine employee loyalty, levels of training, and the nuances of the corporate culture.

Karl-Erik Sveiby, professor at the Swedish School of Economics and Business Administration and one of the leading thinkers of the Intellectual Capital/Knowledge Management movement, has estimated that there are currently thirty-four different Intangible Assets measuring models. Yet, as he admits, the field has still never effectively answered its "fundamental dilemma":

> ... [I]t is not possible to measure social phenomena with anything close to scientific accuracy. All measurement systems, including traditional accounting, have to rely on proxies, such as dollars, euros, and indicators that are far removed from the actual event or action that caused the phenomenon. This creates a basic inconsistency between managers' expectations, the promises made by the method developers and what the systems can actually achieve and makes all of those systems very fragile and open to manipulation.[1]

Sveiby goes on to warn that companies that attempt to use these tools for management control purposes—that is, for improving internal performance—usually end up with phony numbers manipulated by the subjects for their own advantage. By the same token, companies that use IC measurement for publicity purposes ("triple bottom line reporting") ultimately pay in the long term when their stock prices can't keep up with the short-term inflated prices created by that good IC publicity.

Sveiby ultimately admits that in its current state of development, IC is only good as a learning tool: "to uncover costs or to explore value creation opportunities."[2] This is hardly of negligible value—uncovering an important new business opportunity or cost reduction can be a very big deal—but it is hardly the breakout business nostrum that propronents of Intellectual Capital measurement had claimed it to be.

In other words, what was true a decade ago is still true now: all of these discrete measurements exist in a vacuum. Some have precise values attached to them; others are merely subjective impressions. But they have no common *metric*; they remain apples and oranges. Nor are they weighted by their individual contribution to the overall IC measurement, such as, is employee turnover more or less important than the number of hours spent training each worker in customer service? Are stock options more or less important than on-site day care and free lunches?

We have no answers to these questions—at least not yet. And because of that, we still cannot conduct a true Intellectual Capital audit on an organization. Until that occurs, Intellectual Capital measurement will always be a sideshow, forever anecdotal, unable to be fully integrated into Financial Accounting, where it could help uncover the true value of enterprises.

And that's not only a loss to the business world; one of the most far-reaching potentials of IC measurement, were it ever to become truly empirical, is that it would allow us to audit and compare for-profit and non-profit enterprises on a common yardstick. We'll soon look at why that is especially important for the Protean Corporation. But for now, the salient point is that companies today do not know their real value. Neither do their investors.

As companies become more Protean—begin to metamorphose ever more rapidly, quickly enter and leave markets, change their businesses, reorganize around new opportunities—the ability of traditional financial accounting to shed light accurately on their nature will become even dimmer than it is now. What's more, the companies themselves will increasingly find that the tools they need to measure and compare new business opportunities are also becoming duller, as many of these new opportunities, huge as they may be, are still so inchoate that they can only be measured by their intangible assets.

When that happens (and it already has—what was the potential value of the MP3 market when Apple decided to create the iPod? Or the Web search business when Google was founded? No one knew. How about the likely business for eBay in Malawi once that country is saturated with cell phones? No one can predict with any certainty), companies will be almost compelled to look for other yardsticks in order to measure success and reduce risk. This has already begun, but only in an incremental, haphazard way, from reading blogs like Henry Blodget's *Silicon Alley Insider* to get a veteran's view of the likely value of an acquisition, to stealthfully reading angry bulletin board postings by former customers to get a fix on service failures.

But this is too time-consuming, too inaccurate, and too anecdotal. Protean Corporations are going to need solid, verifiable answers to assess the true value of their own intangible assets, as well as those of their competitors, potential acquisitions, and strategic partners. They need to understand the true nature of their own Cloud, of their Family members, and of their Neighborhood. The Intellectual Capital community has until now failed to give the corporate world those answers—even though it has the greatest potential to discover them—because it has had no motivation to codify its processes and because IC remains largely an intellectual exercise in an endless quest for perfect answers.

But the perfect is the enemy of the good, and companies of the new global economy, desperate to understand the incoherent and ever-changing marketplaces in which they find themselves, will demand practical solutions, systematic processes, and standardized results. They will get those answers whatever it takes. And whoever provides those solutions will undoubtedly find a strong foundation in the world of Intellectual Capital.

It will be those answers, combined with existing financial tools, that will ultimately enable Protean Corporations to fulfill their first Objective, which is to maximize the value of *all* of their endeavors.

BEYOND BUSINESS

That word *all* may prove to have some interesting and unexpected implications.

As noted earlier, one of the most exciting characteristics of Intellectual Capital measurement is that it appears to work not only on commercial enterprises—for-profit companies—but for *non-profit* enterprises as well.

Within the Protean Corporation, the ability to measure intangibles would have the salutary effect of enabling the company to actually measure the contribution to the overall value of the company of traditional staff operations, such as finance and HR. It would also enable the company to measure the value of the Core, and incorporate that measurement into the overall valuation of the company.

Outside the company, the ability to measure the value of non-profits gets even more interesting. For example, it would enable a corporation to determine the efficiency of its charitable activities, foundations, and community involvement. It would also be able to scrutinize the recipients of its largesse to see if they are as worthy as others applying for the same attention.

But the most important application of the value measurement of non-profits is with another interesting global phenomenon that surfaced about the same time as Intellectual Capital and for many of the same reasons.

This is *Social Entrepreneurship*. The term has become quite popular in recent years, but few people who have heard it can actually give its precise definition. This isn't their fault: for reasons dealing mostly with fund-raising, a number of parties have found it advantageous to keep the phrase as nebulous as possible so that it can mean all things to all people.

Strictly speaking, *Social Entrepreneurship is the application of the entrepreneurial methodologies found in the for-profit world to enterprises targeted at creating systemic social change. Social Enterprises, unlike most traditional charities, are scalable, and innovative in their application of appropriate technologies, and their success or failure is measurable relative to other social enterprises.*

In a more nuanced view, social enterprises recapitulate the development cycle of for-profit entrepreneurial start-ups by mapping the same steps onto the non-profit world of foundations and charitable giving. They begin with a small team of like-minded individuals who share among them the full spectrum of skills needed to run a new enterprise. Seed funding usually comes from the founders themselves, or "angel" investors in the form of small charitable groups such as churches, local governments, or family members.

As the social enterprises become more successful, and reach the point in their development when they are ready to "franchise" their operations out to multiple locations, major foundations and government agencies step in to serve as venture capitalists, providing them with the capital they need to ramp up. The culminating event for social entrepreneurs—the equivalent to the IPO for commercial start-ups—is when the enterprise finally frees itself from dependence on one or two big foundations and takes its message "public." That is, the social enterprise has now reached a level of general awareness, has a sufficiently compelling story, and can present a strong enough story of financial/cultural success so that it can shift its fund-raising to the general public. This represents a quantum leap in the SE's ability to raise development capital, and at the same time frees the foundations to go back and incubate the next generation of social enterprises, all while showing a successful ROI to philanthropists in order to raise future funding.

That is how it is supposed to play out. It is a beautiful model. Unfortunately, *it has almost never worked.* We have a few historical examples of social entrepreneurs who have successfully run their non-profits through this development cycle—the Red Cross being perhaps the most famous example (and making Clara Barton one of the most successful entrepreneurs in history). Today, the most shining example is Mohammed Unis, the Bangladeshi banker who founded Grameen Bank to make micro-loans to the poor—and earned a well-deserved Nobel Peace Prize.

Even though he has largely retired, Unis is still held up as the epitome of the social entrepreneur. The shortage of comparable figures ten years after the rise of social entrepreneurship as an international movement should be telling. It's not that there aren't other important and compelling SEs around; it's just that almost none has managed to get past their dependence on big foundations. Even those hybrid social enterprises that mix for-profit operations with non-profit programs, such as the foot-powered water pump builder Approtech in Kenya and the low-cost Indian cataract surgery program, Aurolab, still depend heavily on international foundations to stay in business.

In other words, no matter what the nomenclature says, most social enterprises remain essentially traditional charities that, in the manner of smart charitable institutions everywhere, have found a canny way to redefine themselves in order to tap into huge new sources of charitable giving.

This is not the fault of those non-profits. On the contrary, their task is to stay alive and do their good works. The fact that they have so skillfully changed their messages to grab some of that targeted social entrepreneurship money from foundations such as the Skoll Foundation may be the single most entrepreneurial thing about them. Rather, the blame lies with the foundations themselves, which began with the goal of funding, training, and promoting social enterprises, then forcing them to stand on their own feet. Now they have retreated to their traditional role of funding attractive non-profits, most of them in the developing world, in perpetuity.

What began with a new generation of high-tech tycoons breaking with the past and creating a new, more muscular form of philanthropy—one that mapped the world of high-tech entrepreneurship, with its ruthless destruction of underachievers, its single-minded pursuit of value creation, and its long-term goal of financial independence, onto the world of non-profits—has now devolved into the same old system of hand-outs to those recipients with the best sob story, albeit with a New Age glitter.

There is certainly nothing bad about this kind of good work. But it does represent a lost opportunity to bring the kind of robust leadership, innovation, and value creation of for-profit entrepreneurship to the best-run institutions in the non-profit sphere.

So what went wrong?

Coincidentally to writing this book, I was also heavily involved in the genesis of the social entrepreneurship movement. I sat on the board of one of those major foundations, participated in the movement's first summits, and even coproduced the best-known television series on the subject, PBS's *The New Heroes*. So I had a unique vantage point on what went right at the beginning of the movement, and what is going wrong now.

There are a myriad of explanations why social entrepreneurship has not lived up to its initial promise, but in the end it comes down to one thing, the same thing that stalled the Intellectual Capital movement: *lack of accurate and universal metrics.*

Ten years later, it is still impossible to compare, say, Inderjit Khurana's train platform schools in India with the Delancey Street prisoner rehabilitation program in San Francisco with Sompop Jantraka's program in Thailand to rescue sex slaves, and determine which has more or less value vis-à-vis the others.[3]

Which one offers the greater return on investment, whether that investment is money, time, or emotion, or the return is financial or social? No one has the foggiest idea. And even if we assume that a sizable percentage of this value is so purely subjective that it can never be accurately measured, the sad fact is that we can't even measure 20 percent of the value of those operations, a tiny fraction, but still on par with what we know about most for-profit start-ups.

Over the years there have been a few attempts to come up with a way to audit and compare different types of social enterprises in different parts of the world. Most of these attempts have used Intellectual Capital measurement as their springboard. But all have come to naught, not least because the recipients themselves are highly motivated *not* to face this kind of scrutiny.

And why should they? Good storytellers get good funding, and those are rarely the kinds of people who care much about record-keeping. By the same token, standardizing the process of evaluating social enterprises would mean that some will be winners and others losers. Nobody wants to see an AIDS clinic or a day care center or a program to take poor children off the streets fail because it is badly run, which is why foundations, however pragmatic they are going in, inevitably end up carrying a growing army of charity recipients rather than let any one of them fail.

But real entrepreneurship is about failure: failure focuses, it disciplines, it eliminates mediocrities, it instructs, and most of all, it frees up resources and talent for the next opportunity. The social entrepreneurship movement talked tough; it wanted all the benefits of entrepreneurial thinking, but it couldn't face the reality of entrepreneurial Darwinism. That's one reason that Bill Drayton and his foundation, Ashoka, which created the social entrepreneurship movement, have quietly been abandoning the term "social entrepreneurship" and replacing it with the more benign "change makers."

This is not to say that the social entrepreneurship movement is dead; far from it, the field today enjoys unprecedented publicity, adherents, and funding. But philosophically it has stalled, and it cannot move on and fulfill its destiny until it finds a way around the problem of value measurement.

What would the solution to this problem look like? Four years ago, Sally Osberg, the head of the Skoll Foundation (the leading foundation in the field, created by eBay pioneer and movie producer Jeff Skoll), made a tantalizing suggestion: If social entrepreneurship needed metrics, why not force their creation from the other side? That is, why not make a market in which "equity" shares in social enterprises could be bought and sold? Not only would this serve as a true "Going Public" moment for social enterprises that listed themselves on the exchange, but the very existence of such a market, in which money could be made or lost, would lead investors to demand a more precise accounting of the true value of these enterprises. That in turn would lead to the rise of accounting standards for non-profits, audits, and regulations on reporting.

But what exactly would be traded on this exchange? There was the quandary. My contribution to the conversation was that we not only didn't know, but in fact, we didn't *need* to know. What was needed instead was to bring together the top minds in the financial world—from stock market legends like Muriel Siebert to financial geniuses such as Mike Milken to the Secretary of the Treasury, the Chancellor of the Exchequer, and the heads of major Exchanges—and provide them with an education on the nature of social enterprises, and trust *them* to come up with a financial instrument that would represent equity in these non-profits and that could be traded.

There seemed no doubt that such an instrument could be devised—why would it not with this group?—and when that happened it would set off a chain reaction. The financial instrument would quickly establish its own exchange, and that would in turn convince social enterprises of the benefit of determining their true value, which in turn would at last force common standards for the measurement of intangible assets. That would lead to the rise of new enterprises dedicated to measuring, monitoring, and enhancing these assets.

Social enterprises would then be integrated more efficiently in the world economy, the best of them suddenly awash in capital for development (freeing foundations to start the cycle again). Meanwhile, commercial enterprises, notably Protean Corporations, finally would now have the IC auditing tools to measure the true value of all of their operations.

But it never happened. The social entrepreneurship community got right to the brink, even to the point of MBA students at Oxford University's Said Business School volunteering to prepare the briefing documents for such a meeting of financial Legends, then retreated from taking such a fateful step. There have since been a few attempts in both Europe and the U.S. to create some sort of stock exchange for social enterprises, but lacking that crucial financial instrument, none has gained much traction.

It was an opportunity lost, but it won't be lost forever. As with Intellectual Capital measurement, the need to place a value on entrepreneurial non-profit enterprises—and thus allow them to compete for funding on merit rather than sob stories—is only going to increase. The sooner those breakthroughs take place the better. And if they don't occur in the industrialized world among the First Billion, they will certainly appear in the developing world among the Second and Third Billions, where charities and other non-profits influence far more of daily life.

LEAPING BOUNDARIES

Why have I just devoted two whole sections of this book to a discussion of such seemingly peripheral subjects as Intellectual Capital and Social Entrepreneurship?

Because I am setting the stage for what will be the Protean Corporation's most breathtaking leap of all.

When we describe this new type of organization as "Protean," or as a "shape-shifter," the implicit message is that the Protean Corporation will change markets and industries, and even leap back and forth between manufacturing and service, physical and virtual (i.e., Web-based).

None of this should be too surprising: we are already seeing companies do that today. As noted earlier, IBM, in one of the most extraordinary on-the-fly reorganizations in business history, managed to transform itself from a computer hardware—indeed, *the* computer hardware—company into a services company while hardly missing a beat. Apple is in the middle of a transformation from a personal computer company to an entertainment hardware/software/content company, and Sun Microsystems (however fitfully) went from a computer workstation company to a software vendor.

Therefore, to say that the Protean Corporation will make these jumps more quickly, and that it may undergo these transformations at multiple locations within the company, sometimes in opposite directions *at the same time*, is impressive, but hardly shocking. Even to say that the Protean Corporation will have a solid core of employees surrounded by growing numbers of contractors and "alternative" employees, while it may be radical, still is at the end of trend lines we can already identify in companies today.

But now we start to go off the map: if a Protean Corporation can quickly move back and forth between different businesses, even different economic sectors, in its endless pursuit of maximizing value, why should we stop there? Why not pursue value everywhere we can find it and measure it?

Hence the discussion of Intellectual Capital, and by extension Social Enterprises. Though we can still measure only a fraction of the "other," intangible assets of an enterprise using the new IC tools, that's about as good a job as traditional accounting tools accomplish in auditing the real value of a modern company. And if we can measure that value, then we can pursue it *wherever we find it*. Suddenly, we are no longer talking two distinct kingdoms of enterprise, but merely two different types of Protean Corporation, both measured with the same yardstick.

In other words, *why shouldn't a truly Protean Corporation also be able to move back and forth, in whole or part, between being a for-profit and being a non-profit organization?* If the goal is to maximize value, why shouldn't the company be able to, as the situation fits, abandon profits and instead pursue success through alternate forms of value creation? Assuming that an equities market exists to deal with intangible assets, why shouldn't a pharmaceutical company that develops a useful but low margin vaccine with particular application in poor nations decide that instead of burying the product or simply donating it (which inevitably leads to inefficiencies of distribution) they want to establish it as a non-profit operation *inside* the company with the goal of increasing the value of the firm's social entrepreneurship tax credits or whatever financial instrument is in play?

The reality is that companies already face this dilemma on a regular basis. With strictly traditional accounting as their only real value measurement tool, they regularly abandon or turn away from healthy markets, abandon useful new product ventures, and even shy away from corporate philanthropy, because of the perception (usually accurate) that the stock markets will look askance at these "distractions" from meeting their performance estimates.

Recognizing that they still want to contribute to the general welfare, but also rightly not wanting their stock to be punished for their own good works, companies often fall back on proven, but again largely inefficient, behavior: establishing company foundations, giving away obsolete or insufficiently profitable technologies to charitable organizations, sponsoring events and then taking the tax write-off. None of these strategies is designed to create value—at least not in any way that can be measured accurately—but instead they are mostly just a way to feel good, get positive PR, and not irritate investors. Unfortunately, few companies are ever lauded for these efforts to buck the system and help the needy; rather, they are more often vilified for being too money-obsessed and stingy. So much for doing good.

Surely there is a better way to do this—and Intellectual Capital measurement (and the resulting equity market it will create) offers the way out. Brokers, analysts, and investors are never going to be convinced to consciously add a surplus valuation (though they regularly do so unconsciously) to a company's stock price for what that company does in the non-profit sector, but they will rush to speculate on that same behavior if there is money to be made doing so.

Look again at Social Entrepreneurship. Were social enterprises capable of being audited, using standardized metrics, and their true value determined—and in turn that value could be monetized—we would see not only an explosion of such enterprises around the world, but more important, an exit strategy, a liquidation event, would emerge. And when that day arrives, the boundary between for-profit and non-profit will become more semantic than actual.

As for the Protean Corporation, if it is to truly be a shape-shifter pursuing value in all of its forms, there is every reason that non-profit social enterprises should be part of its portfolio, and that competence aggregators should have the creation of such organizations as an option.

This gives us an important new modification to our image of the Protean Corporation. We've already seen it as an amoebalike creation, changing its shape to best fit into the vacuums created by market opportunities whatever form they take. Now to this we add the ability of the Protean Corporation to also move into value-laden opportunities in the non-profit sector as well.

Can this actually happen? Is it practical? Is it even legal? Yes, not yet, and no.

Yes, there is every reason why a company could pursue opportunities in the non-profit world the way it currently does in the commercial world. And as competition among non-profits (and, in case you don't realize it, the competition there can be at least as ruthless, if also much more passive-aggressive, than in the for-profit sector) grows more like regular business competition, thanks to the rise of social entrepreneurs, it should actually become easier to enter that world. For example, while a corporation might find running a soup kitchen to be a difficult application of its resources, establishing a regionwide network of soup kitchens designed to provide the maximum nutrition at the lowest cost and the highest quality service is something that any company can understand.

But, as I've already explained, it is not yet practical because we have no way of valuing non-profits, of determining if one is more successful than another, and of monetizing that success in a secondary market. Until that happens, no corporation that is responsible to its shareholders should ever take the risk of pioneering this field.

Will that valuation process ever be devised and ratified by national governments and the companies themselves? Nothing is certain, but I believe that the combination of companies, investors, and markets realizing that they have no real handle on corporate value and are, in fact, nearly blind—and the growing pressure on non-profits to justify their existence and compete for limited charitable funds—will force the creation of Intellectual Capital, or some other form of intangible asset, measurement sooner rather than later.

If you want to become a billionaire, or perhaps win the Nobel Prize for Economics, come up with that financial instrument and ignite the creation of that stock exchange.

Finally, as you no doubt have already concluded, running a hybrid company that is part non-profit and part for-profit, or sometimes all of either, and that switches back and forth between them with lightning speed, is probably something the U.S. Justice Department and its counterparts around the world look upon with real concern—in particular because it seems like a perfect way for a company to escape the consequences of bad business decisions by seeking refuge as a self-declared non-profit. Conversely, one can imagine a clever scheme by which an enterprise could hold onto a non-profit status until the right moment—based on taxes, regulations, competition, etc.—when it suddenly announces that it is a for-profit business.

These are real concerns, but I think they are overrated. What's missing from these worst-case scenarios is that such jumps will be difficult in an environment in which there is sophisticated reporting of not only financial, but intellectual capital, data, and when smart money is on the table on both sides of the commercial/non-profit divide.

Today, investors make a lot of money on the gap between the financial balance sheet of the company and the value of that company's intangible assets. Once those "other" assets are more carefully tracked, that gap will greatly diminish. That will likely diminish the volatility of most stocks, even as it creates a whole new world of new, noncommercial investments. But that improved scrutiny will also mean that it will be very hard for a company to hide from its failure on the for-profit side by seeking sanctuary on the non-profit side, or vice versa. The "sides" themselves will increasingly disappear as both commercial and social enterprises become part of a continuum of entrepreneurial practices operating under the same set of rules and regulations.

This isn't to say that the Feds won't still oppose the breakdown of the historic legal wall between commercial businesses and charities. But the argument that it will increase business malpractice and white collar crime will simply not hold up in the face of real-life company behavior. And when government tax collectors realize that Protean Corporations are creating, with their internal social enterprises, a whole new source of taxable revenues, they'll probably come around pretty quickly. If they don't, reactionary governments will quickly find that their domestic companies, with their smaller and more mobile Core of employees, can quickly move—if only virtually—to progressive nations that are early adopters of this new corporate model.

ON AND OFF THE MARKET

For-profit/non-profit is only one of the ways a Protean Corporation might change its fundamental business model in order to pursue maximum value.

There is another way, even easier to achieve, because it requires no great breakthroughs in Intellectual Capital measurement or the creation of revolutionary new equities markets. However, this other model is even more likely to get a quick response from governments everywhere, in particular in the United States from the Securities and Exchange Commission.

This is the idea that a truly Protean Corporation should not only be a shape-shifter in terms of its employment, its new business operations, its markets, and even its balance sheet, but ultimately it should even be Protean in terms of its ownership.

In other words, a Protean Corporation should be able to switch back and forth, in all or in part, between *being publicly and privately owned.*

Here, at least, we have some precedent. Every year, especially in slow economic times, a few cash-rich companies will decide to buy back some of their outstanding stock. This reduction of shares has the advantage of driving up the stock price, reducing external ownership, and limiting per share price volatility by setting a baseline for what a company determines its own value to be. It also increases market confidence: rightly or wrongly, a company that invests in itself is a company that believes in its own future.

There are also companies that make the fateful choice to buy back *all* of their stock. That is, they "take themselves private." Far from being cases of corporate optimism, these total buy-backs typically are seen as symptomatic of a company in real trouble, trying to limit outside investor interference when its stock is in near collapse.

There are some giant companies that are still privately owned, that managed to bootstrap themselves to billions of dollars in annual sales without ever having to go to the equity markets for capital. Mars, the candy maker, is one of the biggest examples of a highly successful private company. Its ownership is entirely held by a single family.

Being public has some real advantages. For venture capitalists and other investors, Going Public Day creates a liquidation event for their investments, enabling them to pay back their own investors and move on to new investments. It is also payback time (usually after a lock-out period to protect the fragile new stock) for the founders and early employees of the company who are rewarded for the risk they took getting involved at the beginning. Going Public Day is also usually the source of the new capital the young company needs to grow to its next phase. Finally, public companies enjoy the growth in value that comes from the climbing prices of their stocks.

But there are advantages to being a private company as well. Less government scrutiny because there are no (non-insider) shareholders to be legally protected; reduced reporting requirements; greater privacy (private companies are under no obligation to speak to analysts or reporters); greater maneuverability because major corporate initiatives don't have to be approved by a board of directors or by shareholders; and none of the expense and misery of annual reports, annual meetings, shareholder suits, and single-share interest group activists. It's a nice life, if you can afford it and can live without the attention.

So we do have considerable precedent for private companies going public—every firm that has ever had an IPO—and even some precedent for public companies going private. But what we don't have are companies that regularly move back and forth between the two, or even make some of their operations private and some public.

Remarkably, given the revolutionary idea of companies going all or part for-profit/non-profit, it may be this public/private scenario that proves the most difficult to realize. So let's explore the two potential scenarios for public/private—all or part—in turn.

First, should it be possible for a company to easily and quickly move back and forth across the traditional boundary of a public and private company? As with for-profit/non-profit, the worry here with most regulators is that such a process will be abused: that every time a firm fears bad publicity (you can tell that I used to be an investigative business reporter) it will jump behind the security wall of becoming a private company. This is not a trivial problem, and one thing we don't want to do is either close off shareholder access to public corporations or deny private companies their privacy. No doubt others will have better ideas, but for now I think the solution is to maintain the status quo regarding the reporting requirements of both sides.

However, I would make one addition to the law: As long as a private company remains private, it enjoys all of the current levels of privacy available to it. But the moment it crosses over and even briefly becomes a publicly owned company, those protections disappear forever, and the company will henceforth have to accept some level of greater disclosure whichever side of the wall it is on.

Will a company have to maintain the same level of reporting when it is private as when it is public? Probably not, but some amount of sunlight will have be maintained on a company's operations when it is privately owned to ensure that the cross-over isn't taking place to hide information from shareholders. Meanwhile, the private company that *never* wants to go public will still be able to enjoy all of the privacy conferred on a traditional privately owned firm.

Next, what about the company that wants to take some of its operations public, but leave the rest privately owned. Now we're starting to go into very slippery territory. A benign view would hold that the company simply wants to take its hottest properties and obtain the maximum value for them, attracting capital for future expansion, all while protecting slower-moving company operations from the rigors of public scrutiny and stock speculation. A more malevolent view would see this as a great opportunity for company founders to pump up their shooting stars on the stock market, while filling their own pockets from the real lucrative businesses they keep private. And that doesn't even address the matter of where the newly raised capital from a new equity offering would go. Would it be barred from being invested in any private part of the company? And if so, how would that be monitored?

It all sounds like a huge regulatory mess. But then, a lot of modern business is just that. And we do have a kind of precedent for public/private divided companies: public companies with essentially private, wholly owned subsidiaries, and private companies that spin out and still hold majority ownership in new public companies. This is a long way from a company converting its internal operations back and forth between private and public ownership, but it does suggest that there exists an underlying desire for a solution coming from this direction. And the new requirement for added reporting and transparency by private enterprises that have lost their "public" virginity will make the decision behind any internal private/public moves more comprehensible.

One thing is certain: the ability of companies to move as a whole from public to private and back again will be allowed long before it will become legal (if ever) to do so in part.

The final question we need to ask is: Will this public/private conversion ever actually happen on a regular basis? Can it ever really be made that simple and easy? That's a good question, because today both "going public" and "going private" are hugely expensive, complicated, and time-consuming operations that no company ever enters into casually. Going

Public requires filing with the SEC, lining up underwriters, preparing a prospectus, dividing the company management in half (one half to run the company, the other half to tackle the public offering), taking the company into a publicity "quiet period," running a road show to drum up investors, Going Public Day, then an extended founding shareholder lock-out and vesting period that must be monitored to protect stock values. Going Private, by comparison, is much less complicated—you merely have to buy back the stock from the shareholders—but much more expensive. Either way, these are not operations anyone would describe with the words "quickly" or "easily."

So is the very idea of public/private Protean Corporations a moot point? I don't think so, because so far we have ignored a very potent distinction between then and now: the existence (one hopes) of intangible asset accounting, new financial instruments to capture the results of that accounting, and new exchanges to trade and speculate on the value of those instruments.

So far, we've only dealt with this other equities marketplace as a way of incorporating the non-profit sector into the larger economy, and only noted by way of passing that many social enterprises will to one degree or another, in fact, be for-profit (or at least break-even) operations. One of the pioneers in this new direction is Jeff Skoll, who as we've already noted is also one of the dominant figures in social entrepreneurship. Skoll has earned a lot of attention in the last few years for his creation of Participant Productions, a Hollywood movie production company. Participant, which has made such movies as *Syriana; North Country; Good Night, and Good Luck;* and *An Inconvenient Truth*, has been celebrated (and honored with a number of Oscars) for making socially relevant films that mainstream studios would never touch.[4]

Less noted is the fact that Participant pursues these ventures, which match its social enterprise goal of creating system social change, by using a very different accounting system from any other production company in the movie business. As Jeff explains it, his bottom line is composed not just of box office receipts and other merchandising revenues, but also total social impact, as measured by contributions to related non-profit groups, changes in laws, and media coverage. Participant reinforces this process by creating robust websites to accompany the movies, complete with extensive links to related non-profit groups.

Though it is hard to affix a precise monetary value to these more subjective results, Skoll and his team make rough estimates and come up with a crude intangible assets accounting. The resulting figure is then added to the actual revenues to come up with a hybrid bottom line that, compared with expenses on the movie, tells Skoll if his film is profitable *according to his terms.*

Strictly on financial accounting terms, Participant loses money on nearly all of its films. On the other hand, in terms of awards, publicity, and goodwill, Participant may be the single most successful Hollywood production company of the twenty-first century to date. Its success has enabled it to enlist the biggest Hollywood stars and attract the best screenplays. It makes movies that no one else can afford to make, while Jeff Skoll gets many times the bang for his buck as a philanthropist.

Participant is likely to be the harbinger of a growing number of profit/non-profit hybrids in the years to come, becoming a flood should Intellectual Capital or some other form of intangibles accounting be standardized, and the right instruments and markets emerge behind them. And with that in place, we suddenly have a very efficient and healthy system not just to enable social enterprises to monetize their assets, but also for *public and private companies to convert their assets as they transition from one side to the other.*

A public offering of stock is a complex process; so is raising the capital and buying back all of your company's outstanding shares. But converting stock from one form to another is a lot quicker and easier, as we see every day when companies convert preferred stock to common stock, series A to series B. When going public or private becomes a simple act of stock conversion by an established company (obviously an IPO would still be necessarily a complex process), it is certain to happen a lot more often. In the Protean Corporation, where it may require only a recommendation by the Inner Ring of the Cloud, ratification by the Core, and confirmation by the Board, it could happen often.

As for hybrid public-private companies, that still remains a quandary in my mind. However, it is hard to believe that in the new economy, where companies glide back and forth along a continuum from wholly non-profit to wholly for-profit, and from service to manufacturing to virtual communities, there won't also be some intermediate points between the publicly owned corporation at one pole and the privately owned company at the other. And, it should be noted once again that companies already offer several different types of stock to their shareholders, including Preferred and Common.

In the fuzzy reality that will be a global economy filled with Protean Corporations, it is also hard to believe that company-owned enterprises with a wholly different ownership structure will not be allowed to function inside the Cloud, or that shareholders won't demand and receive sufficient information to judge the value and role of those satellites, and buy or sell accordingly.

PLAYING FOR KEEPS

An ever-changing workforce, ever-changing businesses, moving back and forth between for-profit and non-profit business strategies, sometimes publicly owned and sometimes privately held, the new global enterprise of the twenty-first century now fully lives up to the title of *Protean Corporation.*

We've looked at the shape and form of the Protean Corporation, toured its Neighborhood and Community, and have seen how it is likely to behave.

Now we have one last task before we finish. That is to look at what happens to society itself when the traditional corporation is supplanted by this new type of organization. As we noted earlier, technology transforms business, and business in turn transforms society.

So let's take a look at the Protean Society to come.

PART
V

THE PROTEAN
SOCIETY

CHAPTER

THE WORLD'S FIRST ENTREPRENEURIAL SOCIETY

THROUGHOUT THIS BOOK I have tried to show again and again that for all of its unusual appearance and behavior, the Protean Corporation is in fact the natural outcome of trends already at work today.

As we have seen, over the three centuries of its existence, the corporation has undergone a radical transformation in design at least a half-dozen times: all of them driven by technological or organizational revolutions, all of them unexpected, and all of them leaving the organization looking

drawing budding tech entrepreneurs not just from around the country but around the world. Entrepreneurship creates most of the innovation in the United States, almost all of the new jobs, and most of the new wealth. And with the exception of that minority of people whom I've identified as potential Core Employees, almost no person in the United States, especially anyone educated as a professional, wants to surrender control of his or her career to anyone else, especially not a company.

This has been a quiet social revolution, all but unnoticed even by people who make it their business to follow social trends. But the data supporting the reality of this transformation are absolutely stunning.

For example, when Intel Corporation decided to survey its employees in 2005, it was stunned by the results. The company found that 75 percent of its professionals worked with someone on another continent on at least a weekly basis—and two-thirds worked on three or more teams in parallel.

That was surprising enough, but what was really shocking was the discovery that at Intel, *18 percent* of the professionals had *never* met their boss face-to-face, and half of them *never* expected to.

These were numbers no one had ever seen before, and that was just the beginning. Two years later, when Chuck House and his team at Stanford's Media X Institute sought comparative numbers from IBM, Sun, HP, Microsoft, and Cisco, the "average" was even *higher*—20 percent had never met their boss face-to-face, and all of the other numbers were similar to Intel's.[1]

(Tellingly, once the results were known, both HP and Intel issued "edicts" to curtail working from home, and from building geographically split teams, which not only missed the point, but led to the exodus of some of those companies' best talent.)

Statistics like this only confirm that not only is the workplace undergoing a massive evolutionary change, but that we are already well into the process. There is no going back, and any company that attempts to restore the status quo ante risks an exodus of its best people.

This same sense of independence and entrepreneurial self-sufficiency is also showing up in every other corner of modern American life. The single most memorable image of the War in Afghanistan is of a U.S.

Special Forces soldier, equipped with high-powered wireless communications and GPS, and heavily armed with the latest combat weaponry, riding into battle against al Qaeda on a *horse*. In Iraq, the militant jihadists and Baathist terrorists were largely defeated not by mass operations, but by clever and adaptive small unit tactics, neighborhood watches, and on-the-spot solutions to potentially lethal challenges (like welding extra plating to Humvees).

In the presidential primaries in early 2008, the media faced unprecedented difficulty in predicting caucus results in various states, both because of the growing number of "independent" voters who refused to affiliate themselves with either major party, and because of the growing willingness of average people to simply lie to pollsters to maintain their privacy. In several key primaries, one party's winner was determined by voters registered with another party who crossed over to vote.

Meanwhile, the candidates found themselves walking through an unprecedented minefield on the campaign trail: every misstatement or faux pas on their part was picked up on a cell phone or digital camera and posted onto YouTube or parsed and dissected in a thousand blogs. No longer could they claim to have been misquoted or the subject of lies and false claims.

Even higher education, that bastion of the enduring status quo, has found itself under assault by the combination of technology and entrepreneurship. The largest college in America today is the University of Phoenix, an online degree program (the same is true with the India Institute of Technology in Bangalore, which teaches most of its courses over several hundred cable television channels). Millions of Americans are now eschewing the ivy-covered walls of academe for a laptop in the living room—and creating their own custom degrees. So powerful has been this wave of online education that even some of the nation's most distinguished schools, including Stanford and Harvard, have been forced to offer classes online.

Every evening, several million young people in the U.S. (and more than one hundred million more around the world) forgo the passive experience of watching television and head online to form up into teams and participate in games such as World of Warcraft or CounterStrike, where they battle each other in alien or foreboding landscapes, and live or die by their wits and skill. So attractive are these games that they have sunk the Nielsen television ratings for this age cohort, one of television's most lucrative, and cut into network profits. And, of course, as already noted, there is South Korea's Cyworld, which is now arguably more important in the lives of its younger citizens than school, sports, and television *combined*.

And that is just the gamers. One quarter of a billion people around the world now regularly visit and call MySpace, Facebook, and the avatar-based alternative reality of Second Life their "other" home. These sites are specifically designed to appeal to the entrepreneurial personality, enabling users to create their own pages and populate them with images, Web applications, and text that best capture how they see themselves—creating a little start-up enterprise out of their own lives or, in the case of Second Life, establishing whole new personas that can interact with others, and actually speculate on real estate and other commodities.

There are an estimated one hundred-million-plus bloggers in the world, most of them hoping to sell enough advertising to turn this work into a full-time job. Meanwhile, another seven hundred and fifty thousand eBay sellers in the United State now consider their work on that website to be their primary or secondary source of revenue.[2] Add to that several million online stock traders and the millions of members of a score of other new Web-created professions and you can see the emerging outlines of that vast army of self-employed contractors and freelancers we've been talking about. Meanwhile, unions, once the heart of American labor, are suffering their lowest levels of membership as a percentage of the workforce since the days of Samuel Gompers before WWI—reduced to little more than government workers, teachers, auto workers, and teamsters. And in many elections these days, a large minority (and perhaps sometimes even a majority) of union members vote for the candidate *not* backed by the union, ending the voting bloc solidarity that was once the heart of union power and influence.

Even Apple, which perhaps enjoys the most fiercely loyal customers in all of high technology, found to its surprise that as much as 40 percent of the purchasers of its popular iPhone never signed up, as required, with AT&T for service. These thousands of customers weren't forgetting to use their phones; rather, they appeared to have hacked them to be usable with a different wireless service. They join the millions more who have grown accustomed to illegally downloading music, television shows, and movies.

I haven't even touched on home schooling, in which nearly three million families have, for various reasons ranging from religion to frustration with the quality of the curriculum, pulled their kids out of public schools and tackled the challenge of teaching their children themselves, relying heavily on Web-based texts and tools to do so.

Add to that the massive shift among Protestant worshippers away from traditional churches and faiths to more individual-oriented evangelical faiths and vast, technologically sophisticated suburban megachurches. According to a 2007 Pew Forum Study, nearly 45 percent of Americans have switched their religious affiliation, moved from being unaffiliated with any faith to being affiliated with a particular religion, or dropped any connection to a specific religious tradition altogether—an astounding degree of cultural mobility on something as deep as spiritual faith.

Meanwhile, more than half of all U.S. Protestants now consider themselves Evangelical (26 percent of all Americans) and 16.1 percent classify themselves as "unaffiliated," with almost half of that latter group still claiming to be "religious." This last group is also characterized by comparative youth (31 percent are under thirty years old).

In other words, nearly half of all Americans either now are not affiliated with a religion or belong to a sect that emphasizes spiritual individualism—and the younger you are the more likely this is to be the case.[3]

I could come up with a hundred other examples showing how everyday Americans (and many of their counterparts around the world) have abandoned—even actively resisted—structured organizations, institutional rules, and mass movements and embraced the kind of individualism, independence, self-management, self-employment, and higher-risk lifestyle that we typically equate with the entrepreneur. I bet you could too.

All of this too has happened without the presence of Protean Corporations.

IN THE MIX

In other words, our society does not need to introduce a new type of corporate organization in its midst to become an Entrepreneurial Society—a culture defined more by entrepreneurship and the entrepreneurial personality and mind-set than by another type of profession or character. We are already there, and the rest of the world is following along a few steps behind us.

But when you add Protean Corporations to this mix these traits become amplified. Place several thousand Protean Corporations at the center of a Web-based economy, and the changes will be far-reaching and profound.

For example, the growing population of "free agent" workers and professionals makes possible the rise of Protean Corporations, but once they exist, those same enterprises will turn around and, in effect, subsidize the liberation of many, many more.

And, once those millions of freelancers and loosely bound employees become tens of millions, the entrepreneurial shift we are already experiencing will become both more defining in areas where it is now being felt, and more pervasive where it currently is not. It will, I believe, eventually threaten every traditional institution in modern society, challenging each in turn to either adapt or fade away. I also believe that adaptation will be toward a Protean model as it is the only one that allows this sort of flexibility and adaptability while at the same time preserving the internal integrity of the organization. But even if it is not, *any* solution will have to answer the need for members to retain their independence, their freedom of motion, and the management of their own lives.

Once you imagine a society filled with these types of organizations in every part of daily life, from industry to government to schools to churches, from work to play—and then you apply Davidow's dictum about the secondary consequences of such revolutions—the world of the future looks like a very different place, for good and ill.

At the beginning of this book I said that I am not an absolutist and this book is not a utopian fantasy. As already noted, entrepreneurship, self-employment, and freedom of movement (at the possible cost to job security) do not appeal to everyone. For those who find this lifestyle anathema, life in the Core of a Protean Corporation (or other "Protean" institution) will look like prayers answered. But not everyone who wants such a life will qualify—and those who don't will find a career in the Inner Ring a poor substitute for the comparatively more predictable life in the traditional corporation. Ironically, this could even lead to *more* union organizing or collective bargaining at this level of employment, and perhaps a different kind of frustration at unions that are themselves becoming more Protean.

At the same time, even as the Core and Cloud find themselves in a mutually beneficial and symbiotic relationship (the Core establishes the most appealing work environment for the Cloud; the Cloud does the work to underwrite the Core), tensions could increase between the Inner Ring—whose members may enjoy nearly lifelong employment and may resent the influence and security of the Core—and the members of the Core, who may covet the salaries and power of the Inner Ring. These tensions are no more serious than the jealousies and power struggles of the traditional, vertical corporation, but to deny their existence is to indulge in fantasy.

Even more interesting sociologically is the possibility that society itself will begin to stratify along the fault lines found in the Protean Corporation. Until now, the nature of corporate, civil service, and non-profit life has been a general mixing of the these different personality types: the wildcatting, maverick salesperson working alongside (or at least in the same company with) the finance professional dreaming of a gold watch, next to the hired gun manufacturing engineer who is more loyal to his profession than to his employer.

These distinct groups are already beginning to pull apart as artificial aggregators—office buildings, vertical organizations, factories, and other organizing and centralizing schemes—become obsolete. The Protean Corporation is an attempt to hold these diverse constituencies together in a new, more viable format for the demands of a new century, and in the process to stave off the chaos of a purely virtual organization. But it will come at the cost, to one degree or another, of creating mutually exclusive organizations *within* the enterprise. The hope is that the combination of greater rewards for all and a system of checks and balances will hold these groups together.

The same forces are going to be at work in the larger society. It too will increasingly feature small groups of individuals at the heart of almost every organization whose task it will be to keep those organizations healthy. And a large part of that health will come from recruiting active participants/employees/volunteers from the majority: the increasingly mobile, untethered, and independent millions that will make up most of the larger society.

My guess is that, faced with the same challenges as corporations, most of society's institutions will find their way to a new organizational scheme that resembles the Protean Corporation. They will feature a Core of dedicated "true believers," surrounded by a ring of committed workers, devoting most of their time to establishing and nourishing an organizational philosophy and rules of behavior, and creating an environment designed to attract the best (or the most) like-minded individuals.

We are already seeing this kind of reorganization taking place in our most culturally sensitive institutions. The United States military, for example, has grown more versatile and adaptive, even as it has become smaller. The modern military is essentially a core cadre of career officers and NCOs that maintains standards, updates strategy, and distributes resources. This Core/Corps is surrounded by a larger ring of officers and enlistees who are committed for a period of time to the military, conduct its smaller operations, and serve as the loci for rapid expansion during times of national emergency. Surrounding this Ring is a larger cloud of consultants, contractors, and part-timers (the ready Reserves, the National Guard) ready to be put to work, ramp up production, or be sent into the fight, as needed.

The two major political parties have also evolved over the course of the last quarter-century as the number of hard-line GOP voters and Yellow Dog Democrats—party members who could be counted on to vote the straight ticket in every election—has dwindled and the number of Independents; Third Party members; and registered, but loosely affiliated party members has grown. The era when you voted the party of your father and grandfather ended some time in the twenty years between the elections of John Kennedy and Ronald Reagan, and it will never come back, at least not in our lifetimes.

As a result, the two parties have themselves become Protean, without having been identified as such. They too consist of a solid core of full-time and largely permanent professionals who manage the party, direct fund-raising, organize the conventions, and dole out money to campaigns. And these cores—the Democratic and Republican Party Committees—are surrounded by a ring of semipermanent Party members, in particular the thousand of elected representatives and officials around the country who bear a party affiliation, and their full-time staffs.

In all, this is a comparatively small group of people. But it has enormous reach, which is exercised every two years during elections, when the respective Parties reach out to their respective Clouds of volunteers, precinct workers, consultants, marketers, and thousands of other individuals who have a stake in one or more election campaigns or their outcomes.

Ultimately, and especially during the quadrennial presidential election, this Cloud expands outward to embrace millions of individual voters, who are called upon to make donations to the party's candidate, volunteer time to convince others to vote, or just to vote. The 2008 Obama campaign is a textbook example of this "Cloud" behavior.

Here in the twenty-first century, in an increasingly entrepreneurial society, it is no longer enough simply to announce a slate of candidates, assume party members will vote that slate, and focus your resources on getting those members out to vote. As much as 40 percent of the population still considers itself "undecided" just weeks before a major election. Even solid, traditional Party members themselves can no longer be trusted to vote the Party line; consider how many of those union members, even when part of their dues are committed to one candidate, will still quietly vote for his or her opponent.

Thus, much of the energy and money of the modern American political party is spent on "recruiting" and "educating" voters in much the way that the Core of a Protean Corporation will devote its time to recruiting and training "alternative" employees. Hence, the vast sums spent these days on advertising a candidate, even to his or her own voter base. The political conventions, for nearly two centuries a kind of quadrennial gathering of the Tribe and family reunion, have now become largely marketing and promotional events targeted at the hooking wavering independents.

THE BIGGEST LAGGARD

It's interesting to note that even as this Core/Cloud organizational philosophy seems to be sweeping across all of society, the one place where it has largely failed to take hold is government itself (and those industries heavily under its influence). Though it does have legions of contractors, the federal government in the United States (and in most countries) continues to grow and does so along traditional lines by hiring full-time, heavily benefited workers and offering them almost perfect job security.

It shouldn't be surprising, then, that the sheer mass of government continues to increase, placing an ever-greater burden on taxpayers and gobbling up an ever-greater share of the economy in both bad economic times and good. The government doesn't have any other way to grow; and because, in a traditional vertical organizational structure, more people at the bottom means more power at the top, there is every motivation for government leaders, Republican and Democrat, to just keep hiring.

This philosophy extends outward into any sector of the society in which government (not just federal, but state) has sufficient control, such as education and, increasingly, health care. Only the military, with its separate chain of command and obvious and measurable success or failure, has escaped. We all call this the "bureaucracy" and have become so accustomed to its sluggishness, turf defense, and incompetence that we cheer even the slightest improvement—like shorter lines at the DMV— because we have long grown inured to it as a portion of our lives that just doesn't work as well as the rest. And were it not for the power of technological innovation coming from the far quicker and more innovative commercial side—inventing (or at least making practical) data processing, the Web, and other productivity tools—it would still be 1940 at the Passport Office.[4]

But technology can take government only so far; beyond that requires a change of organization and operating philosophy. And the pressure is growing on government from almost every direction to make those changes. With millions of parents pulling their children out of public schools, Libertarian-oriented third parties regularly attracting numbers almost unparalleled in U.S. history outside of great national crises, and even the military, once the most hidebound of bureaucracies, throwing out the rule book, the federal government (and most state governments) is going to have to change. It's either that or lose even more of the influence and sovereignty it has already surrendered to the global economy, the increasing fungibility of labor, and the Internet.

This will not go down easily. Liberals will hate the idea of shrinking government down to a smaller Core and detaching all of those civil service (i.e., union) employees to the Ring or, worse, to compete as freelancers out in the Cloud. The fact that government could, at times, be even bigger than it is now will be a poor consolation. Conservatives, by comparison, will likely love the idea of getting all of those millions of government employees off the payroll, but will fight both the idea of government having the potential to get even bigger, and even more the notion of a solid core of essentially permanent bureaucrats (though that is close to what we have now).

I'm not here to make a political point, only to note that these outside pressures only grow stronger by the year, and if government is to stay relevant beyond mere coercion, if it is to keep up with and respond to the desires of the public, if it is going to show levels of efficiency and productivity anywhere close to the commercial world, and if it is to stop being a growing burden on the rest of the economy, it is going to have to adopt some of the changes taking place in the business and non-profit worlds. Like it or not, government too is going to have to become more Protean.

NO GOING BACK

A society that becomes Protean is much more innovative, adaptive, responsive to change, and flexible. It is also more audacious, which can get it into trouble, and more impetuous, which can send it hurtling down the wrong path.

It is a society that is much more efficient with its resources, both physical and intellectual. But it is also a fitful society, losing interest in one activity to suddenly turn and race off in pursuit of another. And while it is good at husbanding its resources, it is also profligate with the creations constructed from those resources, accepting high levels of failure in pursuit of the one or two winners.

Time in a Protean Society will seem to accelerate, distances further shrink, anomie and a sense of isolation will increase—but so will excitement. History will dim, and the future will be forever more interesting than the present.

In other words, it will be a truly entrepreneurial society, albeit with a sanctuary where those who don't wish to partake in the race will still have a way to be productive, even vital. It is the presence of this group, at the very center of the Protean Society, rather than marginalized or forgotten as they would be otherwise, that is the crucial difference to a purely Virtual Society. And I believe it is precisely this difference that will keep the Protean Society (like the Protean Corporation) from spinning apart. The Core—more accurately the many Cores that will inhabit not only government but hundreds of thousands of organizations—gives the Protean Society a stability, a continuity, and a purpose it might not have otherwise.

But this small minority will not be enough to keep the world of the future from being much more chaotic and subject to rapid swings as the population swarms around one fad or idea after another, or pursues the latest money-making trend or career opportunity. Protean or not, that is our society's near-term (and probably long-term) fate. Even if Moore's Law were to stop tomorrow, it would still take us a generation or more to spin out all of the implications of the technology innovations we have right now. And the latest studies suggest that Moore's Law is likely to tick on for at least another twenty years. Even without it, Metcalfe's Law is going to keep rewarding the expansion of the Internet and wireless to even the tiniest corner of the planet, creating a truly global economy.

What's more, the Second Billion is already here, and the Third Billion, like it or not, is coming as well. They will not be stopped: it is their ticket out of generations of poverty. Their very presence will make the world and its economy more volatile. More inventions, more fads, more ideas, more wealth, more crime, more terrorism, more opportunity, and more competition—these billions bring it all in their wake.

And, so far, we haven't even discussed cumulative and cross-pollinating effects. The incredible advances in computer hardware and software technology over the last thirty years made it possible to map the human genome at a speed no one thought possible. Now, that same technology, even more improved, is tackling human proteins, offering the potential for unprecedented control over the operations of the human body at the cellular level. Similarly, computer-powered accelerations are taking place in everything from nanotechnology to solar power. The same process is making microprocessors so powerful and so cheap that they can be embedded almost everywhere, even tossed into the air to follow weather patterns. And these billions of chips can also be added to the global network with an impact we can't even yet imagine.

Those who study these movements are more apocalyptic than the rest of us. Tom Hayes, the marketing veteran I mentioned before, has predicted, in *The Jump Point*, that around the year 2012 the collision of these three billions with broadband wireless and Web 3.0 or Web 4.0 is going to create a historical discontinuity the likes of which we haven't seen in generations, reconfiguring the entire global market and creating a whole new set of winners and losers.[5]

Ray Kurzweil, the famous computer genius, has gone even further, predicting in books and articles something he calls, drawing on the moment when the universe began, the *"Singularity,"* which he predicts to occur sometime around 2030.[6] It is Kurzweil's belief that as the curve of Moore's Law goes vertical around that date, computers—or even microprocessors—will enjoy complexity and data density equivalent to the human brain. Combine that with biomedical tools of sufficient precision, and Kurzweil believes it will be possible to map the location of every neuron in a human brain, as well as its state, and port that information over to computers, personal memories and all. At that point, says Kurzweil, the boundaries between flesh and silicon will disappear, and human minds—wherever they are located—will themselves climb aboard Moore's Law, tapping into vast databases and enjoying telepresence all over the Web.

You don't have to buy entirely into either Hayes's or Kurzweil's arguments to accept that life is going to get a whole lot faster, richer, and more complicated, powered by asymptotic growth in both information processing and communications networks, and enriched by a host of new applications—from 3-D modeling to biometrics to global libraries.

Sometimes, this is going to look like the greatest opportunity in history, a banquet of experiences and the final fulfillment of the democratic dream for mankind; other times it will appear unpredictable, anarchistic, and very dangerous. And because daily life will also grow very fast, all of those emotions may race through our minds in the course of a single day. Every minute, some new idea, meme, fad, or threat will pop up somewhere in the world, and then proliferate in a matter of days, even hours, around the world via blogs, YouTube, and social networks. Some will stick and enter mankind's collective global culture; most will prove evanescent, disappearing as quickly as they appeared. But even the most short-lived will probably make someone, somewhere, a fortune.

So, whether we like it or not, there is no going back. The world is going to speed up radically. Business opportunities and even entire markets are going to appear and disappear at lightning speeds, giving only those astute enough and quick enough a chance to exploit them. In one developed nation after another, beginning with the United States, and ultimately including large swathes of even undeveloped countries, citizens are going to become even more entrepreneurial in their careers and even in their lives.

With these changes will come a host of challenges: for the individual both at work and at home, for businesses both internally and in the global marketplace, for nations both domestically and in the international arena. These challenges will become either devastating problems or un-precedented opportunities, depending upon how we meet them.

THE RIGHT BALANCE

Throughout the course of this book, I have accepted the inevitability of this future and its challenges, and tried to come up with a strategy for businesses and other institutions to meet that future and succeed. I've looked closely at the two opposite approaches to this challenge: the tra-ditional organizational model (itself the product of considerable evolu-tion) and the perfectly decentralized "virtual" corporation (a model, in part, of my own making).

I found both to be wanting: the former because it cannot adapt to the rapid changes already taking place, much less the ones coming in the near future, and the latter because in its quest for perfect flexibility and adapt-ability, it loses its own identity and purpose.

I've also searched for a new organizational model that is not so radical in its design or that requires such a complete restructuring of current models that no company or other institution could justify risking the attempt.

What I have come up with and presented in this book is the Protean Corporation and, by extension as these enterprises come to dominate the economy of the future, the Protean Society.

I believe the Protean Corporation offers the best scenario for com-panies to be able to move more quickly, adapt to rapidly changing marketplaces, and, perhaps most important, attract the talents of an in-creasingly entrepreneurial workforce.

Yet, through all of this, the Protean Corporation still remains a *real* (as opposed to virtual) organization, with an identity, a history, a purpose, and (perhaps even more than in most contemporary organizations) an actual culture that is demonstrable, enduring, and measurable for the first time. It will do much of this through powerful, new, intellectual capital audit tools just now being created. Further, thanks to these new types of audits, Protean Corporations will even be able to value and monetize those assets that until now were considered merely enhancements and costly additions to overhead.

In the near term, just as important to senior managers and boards of directors as the improved functionality of the Protean Corporation, is the fact that there is a clear path to get from here to there. In practice, a modern corporation transitioning to a Protean Corporation will essentially pull in two directions: the center of the company will retract and condense into the Core and Inner Ring, while the already less permanent positions in the company will move outward into the Cloud.

This is not an easy transition and it will likely lead to some hard feelings, but it will be a whole lot less jarring than massive lay-offs, and the resultant hard feelings of ex-employees and the reluctance of new talent to apply for jobs, or even the death of the company when it falls behind its more nimble competitors. Just as valuable is the internal analysis that will be used to identify key employees, and the long-term usefulness to the company of inviting them into the sanctuary location of the Core.

Creating and populating that Core, setting its members to work codifying the corporate culture, and establishing the right environment to attract the best Competence Aggregators are the most important tasks of a newly Protean Corporation. Everything follows from there. With the right setting in place, and the right talent in position around which to gather teams and chase emerging opportunities, the Protean Corporation can suddenly exhibit enormous speed and flexibility. It will begin changing shape almost from the first day, adapting to markets that are themselves rapidly morphing to other forms. No other organization can match this performance and still remain an organization.

The same is true for the larger society. The key to retaining what is best about our enduring institutions and traditions lies in identifying the key individuals at the heart of them and holding onto them during this time of great transformation. One of the best features of the Protean model is that it finds a home for these individuals—indeed, a place of honor and authority—where otherwise they would be marginalized, even driven out to an uncertain fate in most other schemes.

But even as you build your Core and fill it with your Core Employees, it is absolutely vital to circumscribe their powers. They are, in the end, people of the past, not the future; they represent stasis, not change. It is the rest of us who represent the future, who embody that change. And by giving those few others the task of preserving what is defining and enduring, they in turn free the rest of us to pursue our ever-changing, ever-shifting dreams.

The Protean Society belongs to protean imaginations.

APPENDIX

Core Size

How big should the Core be? The obvious answer is that it should be big enough to get the job done, but not so big that it is a drain on the company.

Because its members are not directly aiding the bottom line, the Core is, by definition, a drag on the company's budget. Just as important, having too large a Core runs the risk of creating a debating society in which nothing gets done.

Only with experience will we really be able to determine the optimum size for a Core of a company in a given industry and of a given size. My sense is that the absolute number of Core Employees in a company should grow slower than the rest of the company, and probably do so as a series of incremental jumps, trailing along so as not to put too much drag on the company's profits.

Here is one possible scenario for a company growing from ten employees to one million over the course of a several decades—a not unlikely possibility in the global marketplace of the twenty-first century.

◄ 10 EMPLOYEES/10 CORE EMPLOYEES ►

It is important to recognize the qualitative differences between a start-up company and an established one. One reason that many entrepreneurs are attracted again and again to the process of creating a new company is not just the potential for great wealth, but the excitement of being part of a team—of wearing every hat in the company, from CEO to janitor, as the situation demands it. In that sense, *every* member of a company in its earliest days is involved in the task of creating and nurturing a corporate culture. And it is only during this period that the Core and the Cloud are all but synonymous. But for the same reason, the job of being a Core Employee in a start-up company is not a full-time profession, but just another part of the workday job requirement.

It is important to distinguish between a start-up company designed to grow much larger, and simply a small business—say a hardware store—that will always remain about this size. In the latter case, the Core may always remain the owner and perhaps another employee (a son or daughter). But should that small business suddenly shift toward a large-scale business model, i.e., the McDonald's transformation under Ray Kroc from a single restaurant to a national, then international, franchise—it too will have to form a Core and a Cloud.

◄ 100 EMPLOYEES/20 CORE EMPLOYEES ►

We've now gone from 100 percent of the staff as part of the Core to just 20 percent, a sizable percentage but still not a direct line cost, as these individuals would still maintain their regular jobs and yet also be involved in the maintenance of the now established corporate culture. Immortality would still be a part-time job in a busy day.

When you talk with serial entrepreneurs, this time in a young company's history is often the saddest: some of the early excitement is still there, and even most of the sense of a team with a common cause. But jobs and responsibilities are now more distributed and fixed, and for the first time, there are employees (often executives) who join the company not to be part of a crusade but for their own career development. This is also the time—which every entrepreneur dreads—when an employee steals from the company for the first time, a painful sign that the days of a common cause and mutual respect and support are over.

Thus, it is during this second phase when a company typically bifurcates between those individuals who are deeply committed to the long-term success of the company and who identify with its culture and business philosophy, and those individuals, many of them quite talented and competent, who see the company as simply their latest jobs. The former will ultimately form the Core; the latter will stake out different orbits in the Cloud.

◄ 1,000 EMPLOYEES/20 CORE EMPLOYEES ►

Notice the sudden change. The company's employment has grown tenfold since the last milestone, yet the number of Core Employees has not changed.

A lot has happened during this interval. A typical company of this size is five years old or more. And fully a quarter of those "employees" are now connected to the company in some manner different from the classic full-time/at the office relationship. The company is also likely by this point to have entered into a number of international strategic partnerships and perhaps even established some sales offices in other parts of the world.

If the company has not already done so, it is now crucial that it develop a dynamic and living Mission Statement, a list of corporate objectives, and begin the process of enshrining cultural events (company picnics and parties, offsites, coffee breaks, profit sharing, archives, etc.) that until now have been mostly ad hoc. This is serious duty, and when one includes not only creating these edifices but educating employees about them and enforcing their adherence, what had once been a small part of the day now becomes a full-time job. In other words, the moment has come to shift the Core Employees from part-time to full-time.

It is quite probable that many of the Core Employees from the previous era will choose not to make such a commitment, but take their chances with careers in the Cloud, or even at another company (the latter of which would suggest either a failure in the selection process or deep structural problems within the company). But it is just as likely that there will be employees who were not part of the founding, but who have developed a deep commitment to the company and want to make it their lives—and they would be the perfect candidates to fill those open slots.

This is also the time when many entrepreneur/founders find themselves out of their league as managers and executives and, having no other recourse, hang on to senior positions such as CEO, though neither they nor the company are happy with the arrangement.

The result, as we have seen over and over in Silicon Valley, is the founder of a great company who stumbles and is fired from the company he or she loves, and who is in turn beloved by the employees. The classic example is Al Shugart, who founded the highly successful disk drive company that bore his name, was fired by the board, then went off and founded an even more successful disk drive company, Seagate, and was ultimately fired from there. How different the story would have been had Shugart been able to gracefully step down at either company, yet remain in a vital role nurturing the corporate cultures he had helped to create.

One might object that taking 2 percent of the employees, many of them key players, and shifting them away from line jobs and productive work that contributes to the company's bottom line is an extravagant expense. Here are three reasons I don't believe that is the case:

1 > This work to establish the company's purpose and rules of behavior has to be done, especially in the modern global economy, when even during its earliest years, a firm is likely to have large numbers of contractors and part-timers and to have employees scattered around the globe in other societies (thus increasing the odds of dysfunctional behavior).

2 > Because this work has to be done, it will be done by *somebody*. If there isn't a Core to do the job, then it will be assigned to employee committees, many of them composed of employees with little experience or commitment to the company, to senior management, which will have a skewed perspective on daily life at the company, or to Human Resources, which has its own agenda as well as limited perspective on "line" work in the company.

3 > No matter who is chosen to do this work, when you add up the lost manpower devoted to meetings, drafting these documents, educating

the company on its contents, and enforcing these rules, you are still looking at about a 2 percent annual operating expense. (And should you choose not to do this work to formalize a company culture, your long-term costs from misdirected product efforts, misread markets, lost employees, and litigation will be far greater than that.)

What that means is if you are going to build and maintain a corporate culture that will make your company robust and healthy enough to compete in the emerging tech-driven global economy, you are going to have to systematically codify that culture, teach it to every new employee or contractor no matter how tenuous their connection to the company, and then enforce those rules consistently and conscientiously.

In effect, you are going to have to develop some kind of Core, whether you want to or not. And to populate that Core with experienced and dedicated employees willing to commit themselves fully to the long-term success of the enterprise, your best strategy is not to turn it over to some company department or to informal employee committees, but to assemble veteran employees from across the company who have *already* shown their commitment to the company's long-term success and a deep understanding of its culture and values.

The best strategy for filling the Core you need is to fill it with the Core Employees you identify and recruit.

‹ 10,000 EMPLOYEES/100 CORE EMPLOYEES ›

The company has now jumped in employment by another order of ten, while the Core (at least the Core Employees, we'll deal with staff later) increases by a factor of five. The Core Employees now represent 1 percent of the company.

Why the jump? The biggest reason is that a company with 10,000 employees undoubtedly has not only international offices, but international divisions. It is also likely to be a publicly traded corporation, which means all sorts of new issues regarding financial reporting, shareholders, employee stock options, and foundations. This will place additional pressure on the Core, and will eventually force it to become less monolithic and more divided into committees, teams, and task forces.

Of course, this expansion creates its own problems. While it is easy to imagine twenty Core Employees sitting around a table drafting texts or discussing a particular employee ethics violation, it is hard to picture the same thing happening with one hundred participants. As a result, the Core Employees will have to develop some sort of organization structure, perhaps with its own chairperson, recording secretary, task force leader, and parliamentarian. The precise nature of this structure is not self-evident either from the nature of the group or its charter, and therefore it probably ought to be developed over time by the participants themselves and probably should remain informal. The Core Employees are supposed to be equals, no matter what their history, wealth, or shareholdings; therefore, any kind of rigid hierarchy would be anathema. However, only experience will tell.

◄ 100,000 EMPLOYEES/500 CORE EMPLOYEES ►

Once again, an order of magnitude increase in total employees, and a five times increase in the number of Core Employees, which now represent .5 percent of the company.

Why this increase? Because a corporation of this size—which today would be one of the world's largest companies—is almost certain to have multiple subsidiaries based throughout the world. It also very likely to have established a sophisticated and busy mergers and acquisitions program. And it will have several million shareholders.

All of this presents major new challenges to the task of maintaining and spreading the corporate culture. We have seen in recent years just how difficult it is for one large company with a strong culture to absorb another large company with an equally strong culture—HP's acquisition of Compaq being a classic example—without nearly dying from the shock. With two billion new customers coming online around the world in the next generation, these kinds of mergers are going to be commonplace, and often between firms separated not just by continents but by incompatible attitudes toward doing business.

At the same time, given the radical expansion of the market, many companies of this size will also still be in the growth mode that currently characterizes much younger companies. These fast-moving giants may find themselves adding 1,000 new "alternative" part-time employees— about the size of a typical manufacturing division today—*per day*.

If nothing else, this is going to require a training and acculturation apparatus that has little precedent short of a nation going to war. And the only way to deal with this potentially lethal challenge will be to expand the Core to the size of a medium-sized company today, and reorganize it into a much more complex structure.

How complex? That's not an easy question to answer. On the one hand, the whole point of the Core Employees is to create a body of equals collaborating in the care and cultivation of the company's structural health. On the other hand, the notion of pure equality goes against what we know about human nature. The first twenty will certainly be able to operate in a largely collegial way, but even then there are apt to be disagreements that split the group into opposing camps, as well as subgroups that form around natural affinities of interests and personalities. It is also almost inevitable that some Immortal or another will rise to dominance and leadership even in this small group. However, most of these distortions can be limited by rules on voting, and what hierarchy remains is probably both salutary and the precursor of what is to come.

When the Core grows larger in the next phase of the company's development, there will undoubtedly be a management structure, a leader, and committee heads. But once a company achieves a Cloud of 100,000 employees, the Core is going to have to take on a real structure, part mid-sized company (or more accurately, consulting firm) and part legislature (with a combination of plenary sessions, committees and subcommittees, and a multilayered leadership). The Core might also begin to locate semiautonomous satellite operations in key geographic regions to represent those regions to the company (like a Senate) or assign Core Employees to serve as representatives for several thousand employees each (like an Assembly or House of Representatives).

All of this is preparation as well for the next step:

‹ 1 MILLION EMPLOYEES/1,000 CORE EMPLOYEES ›

One last time, we increase employment by an order of magnitude, while we again double the number of Core Employees.

The idea of numerous companies with a million or more employees is pretty fantastic. After all, leaving aside the Catholic Church and a few other noncorporate organizations, there really aren't any million-employee corporations in the world—yet.

But they are coming, and many of them from the most unlikely places. For example, Bangladesh's Grameen Bank, that celebrated micro-lender created by Nobel Peace Laureate Muhamed Unis, has about five hundred thousand full- and part-time employees (at that level of poverty, the two terms are not particularly descriptive). Federal Express has more than a quarter-million employees; McDonald's has about a half-million employees working out of thirty-one thousand locations in one hundred and twenty countries. And Wal-Mart, the world's largest company, already has passed the 1-million employee mark and is now approaching 2 million. Its revenues, $351 billion in 2007, suggest that not only is the $1 trillion valuation for a company now well within reach, but so is the company with $1 trillion in annual revenues.

A company of this size is no longer simply a business, but a social force. It cannot maneuver in any direction without its giant footprint profoundly affecting the fortunes of surrounding communities. The economies of entire nations are directly linked to its financial health, and a good or bad turn in its financials can set off an equivalent turn in global stock markets.

Very few companies can ever reach this size without a strong sense of self: an established corporate culture, a body of myths and legends, a carefully defined corporate mission, and well-established rules of engagement. Most, perhaps all, also have some sort of proto-Core—not as sophisticated as the one being described here, but a de facto body of trusted veteran employees who are regularly assigned the task of creating formal corporate objectives, writing employee guidelines, and heading up new employee initiatives. These proto-Cores are typically compromised in some important way; they are biased toward senior managers, they require participants to keep their existing jobs *and* take on these new responsibilities, or they are created in *response* to a crisis rather than in *anticipation* of one, but they work well enough, and the company muddles through.

But at this immense size, when the company begins to impact the surrounding society as much as it is impacted by it, companies can find themselves in huge crises for which they are wholly unprepared. These come in all sorts of bizarre forms, none of which the CEO or chairman of a smaller company ever needs to think about, and thus has little experience in dealing with:

Antitrust

The company by its very size and success is seen as threatening to the economy. This can often become a political matter, as with the European Union's attacks on Microsoft (and more recently, Google) to preserve its sovereignty and protect its domestic industries.

International Scandal

Any group of one million human beings is going to experience a sizable crime rate—murder, vice, fraud, mass shootings, etc.—for which the employer will in some way be held accountable.

Terrorism

A very large company can come to represent the country of its origin, and thus become a surrogate for that nation. Thus, the burning of McDonald's in protest of U.S. foreign policy. In the future, attacking a key facility of a trillion-dollar company in order to cripple the firm can be an effective way of attacking an entire economy.

Backlash

A huge company, by definition, dominates its market. And that dominance can in itself be a cause for anger, resentment, and backlash in the form of boycotts, class action suits, and passive resistance. Companies, especially those that believe they have behaved in a responsible, enlightened manner, can be stunned when they find themselves demonized and scapegoated merely for their success.

Politics

Hauling a corporate CEO in front of a Congressional or Parliamentary committee is a powerfully symbolic way for governments to reassert their control over industry. As companies grow bigger and more international—and thus less controllable—this will increasingly be seen as a useful tool for keeping them in check.

Unionism

Organized labor has every motivation to target very large companies: they can double their membership in one fell swoop, they need target only a single set of perceived abuses and grievances rather than a wide range of them across an industry, they need only one vote to win big, and when a super-giant company falls, the concussion not only touches multiple industries but can be heard around the world.

THIS IS WHY BIG, experienced, and established companies often suddenly find themselves in serious trouble when they reach this size. Until now, they have been able to muddle through in a responsive mode, quickly assembling teams and committees to address problems as they emerge. But these new challenges are very different from the ones that came before: they involve constituencies over which the company has almost no influence; have consequences that are determined outside the balance sheet; and create deep, and sometimes explosive, emotions that can affect the company's operating environment and morale for years, even generations.

This, I believe, is yet another strong argument for an established, rather than ad hoc, Core dating back to the earliest days of the company. Such a Core can begin addressing these potential crises even when the company is a fraction of this size. It can establish task forces of Core Employees to deal specifically with these larger social and cultural issues long before they become a risk, and thus have individuals and procedures (not to mention outside resources such as labor attorneys, security specialists, lobbyists, and publicists) in place to check these challenges at the moment they first appear.

I am convinced that this is only possible when the company has a body of individuals who understand the company's personality and behavior, who have worked together for years and thus can move quickly and smoothly in concert, and who have the time to study the problem in advance and prepare solutions for multiple scenarios. And it is precisely because these new pressures on the company will be in addition to the existing task of maintaining the company's culture that the number of Core Employees will double this final time. Beyond this, I suspect that the Core will no longer grow, no matter how large the company becomes.

(Having said that, I immediately want to add one caveat: Some business theorists have speculated that as some businesses grow to supercorporation size, with employee rolls exceeding the population of some small countries and their capital valuation exceeding that of many midsized countries, they may choose to take on additional operations until now reserved only by sovereign nations.

In the United States, we've already seen Wal-Mart move to fill the gap between popular expectations for affordable prescription drugs and the federal government's ability to deliver them. Other large companies, especially those operating in dangerous parts of the world, are creating their own sophisticated security forces; while still others are responding to weak local public schools by essentially setting up in-house GED programs for new employees that recapitulate four years of high school education in a matter of months. All of this suggests that the possibility of companies one day creating militias to defend their facilities, in-house universities, and most incredibly, establishing and managing their own currency, is not entirely science fiction.

Should some of these predictions come true—and for now, the legal and social obstacles to the more radical propositions seem insurmountable—very large companies may find they have to increase the size of the Core one more time to deal with the challenges of overseeing a university, a constabulary, or treasury and mint.)

NOTES

1 > A NEW BUSINESS MODEL FOR A NEW WORLD

[1] "The New Me Generation," by Jake Halpern, *Boston Globe Magazine*, September 30, 2007.

[2] Ibid.

[3] "Joseph M. Juran" entry, www.wikipedia.com. See also F. John Reh, "Pareto's Principle—The 80-20 Rule," www.about.com, http://management.about.com/cs/generalmanagement/a/Pareto081202.htm.

2 > THE SHAPE-SHIFTER: THE PARADOX OF PERMANENCE AND CHANGE

[1] *The Virtual Corporation*, introduction.

[2] "Proteus" definition, www.wikipedia.com.

[3] Ibid.

[4] "Proteus" biography, www.theoi.com/Pontios/Proteus.html.

3 > THE RISE OF THE CORPORATION

[1] "East India Company," Dutch East India Company section, MSN Encarta.

[2] It may also have been the most successful company of all time, not only establishing colonies for the Netherlands in Indonesia, South America, and what is today New York City, but also paying an incredible 18 percent annual dividend every year for *two centuries.*

[3] "From filing and fitting to flexible manufacturing: a study in the evolution of process control" by Ramchadran Jaikumar, monograph Harvard Business School, 1988.

[4] Ibid.

5   Ibid., section 3.

6   Ibid., section 4.

7   http://park.org/Pavilions/WorldExpositions/philadelphia.text.html.

8   http://www.pbs.org/wgbh/amex/carnegie/sfeature/mh_horror.html.

9   "Louisiana Purchase Exhibition" entry, www.wikipedia.com.

10 *The Visible Hand*, pp. 275–282.

11 "The Principles of Scientific Management" by Frederick Winslow Taylor (1911):
    http://www.marxists.org/reference/subject/economics/taylor/principles/ch02.htm.

12 Robert Kanigel, *The One Best Way: Frederick Winslow Taylor and the Enigma of Efficiency*
    (New York: Viking, 1997).

13 John dos Passos, *The Big Money/USA Trilogy*, "The American Way."

14 "Progressive Era" entry, www.wikipedia.com.

15 "May Day Riots of 1919" entry, www.wikipedia.com.

16 http://www.theinstitute.ieee.org/portal/site/tionline/menuitem.130a3558587
    d56e8fb2275875bac26c8/index.jsp?&pName=institute_level1_article&TheCat=1008
    &article=tionline/legacy/INST2001/dec01/history.xml&.

17 http://plato.stanford.edu/entries/vienna-circle/.

18 An excellent narrative on the story of Durant and Sloan can be found in David
    Farber's *Sloan Rules*, Chicago: University of Chicago Press, pp. 28–45.

19 Allyn Freeman, *The Leadership Genius of Alfred P. Sloan* (New York: McGraw-Hill, 2005),
    p. 6.

20 Ibid., p. 7.

21 Ibid., p. 18

22 Ibid., p. 23.

4 > PACKARD'S WAY: THE TECHNOLOGY ERA

1   David Packard, *The HP Way* (New York: Harper Business, 1995), pp. 165–166.

2   Michael S. Malone, *The Microprocessor: A Biography* (New York: Springer-Verlag, 1995),
    pp. 165–168.

3   Michael S. Malone, *Bill & Dave* (New York: Portfolio, 2007) pp. 147–150.

4   Ibid., pp. 249–252.

5   Ibid., pp. 186–195.

5 ▸ THE CENTER CANNOT HOLD: THE VIRTUAL ERA AND ITS FADING RELEVANCE

[1] Tom Hayes, *Jump Point* (New York: McGraw-Hill, 2008), p. 51.

[2] "If you can't master English, try Globish" by Mary Blume, *International Herald Tribune,* April 22, 2005.

6 ▸ THE CLOUD, THE CORE, AND THE BOSS

[1] "Google and the Wisdom of Clouds" by Stephen Baker, *BusinessWeek,* December 13, 2007.

[2] Ibid.

[3] Dee W. Hock, *Birth of the Chaordic Age* (San Francisco: Berrett-Kohler, 2000).

[4] "Understanding the Personal Info Cloud" by Thomas Van der Wal, presentation at the University of Maryland, June 8, 2004. http://www.vanderwal.net/essays/moa/040608/040608.pdf.

[5] Much of this work is being done by IBM's CUE (Collaborative User Experience) Visual Communication Lab; see http://services.alphaworks.ibm.com/manyeyes/page/About_Many_Eyes.html.

[6] "Facebook CEO Admits Missteps" by Spencer E. Ante and Catherine Holahan, *BusinessWeek,* March 10, 2008. http://www.businessweek.com/technology/content/mar2008/tc2008037_151923.htm?&chan=technology_technology+index+page_internet.

[7] http://en.wikipedia.org/wiki/Brouwer_fixed_point_theorem.

[8] Chris Wilson, "The Wisdom of Chaperones," Slate.com, February 22, 2008. http://www.slate.com/id/2184487.

7 ▸ DENIZENS OF THE CORE

[1] Thanks to Tom Hayes for this idea.

8 ▸ RETHINKING THE CEO

[1] "Silicon Valley CEO Failure: Seven CEO Lessons for 2006" by Steve Martin, *Sterling Hoffman Newsletter,* http://www.sterlinghoffman.com/newsletter/articles/article223.html.

[2] Eric Schmidt interview for *Red Herring,* February 2003.

9 > WHERE THE REAL ACTION IS: THE CLOUD

[1] Leander Kahney, "Straight Dope on the iPod's Birth," *Wired*, October 17, 2006. http://www.wired.com/gadgets/mac/commentary/cultofmac/2006/10/71956.

10 > BRINGING IN TALENT: COMPETENCE AGGREGATORS

[1] The term is from Glenn Reynolds, author of the Instapundit blog. See also his book, *An Army of Davids* (Nashville: Nelson Current, 2006).

13 > REDEFINING SUCCESS: WHAT A PROTEAN CORPORATION ACTUALLY DOES

[1] Karl-Erik Sveiby, "Methods for Measuring Intangible Assets," April 2007. http://www.sveiby.com/Portals/0/articles/IntangibleMethods.htm.

[2] Ibid.

[3] For more information on these social entrepreneurs, see the PBS *The New Heroes* website, http://www.pbs.org/opb/thenewheroes/.

[4] For further information on Skoll's work, see www.ParticipantProductions.com.

14 > THE WORLD'S FIRST ENTREPRENEURIAL SOCIETY

[1] Source: Charles House, Media X Executive Director, "Building Effective Virtual Teams," Wallenberg Summer Institute at Stanford University, August 1, 2007. House notes: "In fairness, Intel's numbers and Sun's were based on reliable survey data; I think the others except for IBM were mostly anecdotal."

[2] http://pics.ebaystatic.com/aw/pics/au/new/eBayFactSheetApr06.pdf.

[3] http://religions.pewforum.org/reports.

[4] The irony, of course, is that the government invented or underwrote most of these inventions first, but never made them practical.

[5] *Jump Point*, p. 3.

[6] Ray Kurzweil, *The Singularity Is Near*, (New York: Viking, 2005).

INDEX

ABOUT THE AUTHOR

MICHAEL S. MALONE is one of Silicon Valley's most influential commentators on the nexus of technology and business. Currently a columnist for ABCNews.com, he is the author of *Bill & Dave*, the coauthor of *The Virtual Corporation*, and a regular contributor to the *Wall Street Journal* editorial page.